UNDERSTANDING STUPIDITY

by James F. Welles, Ph.D.

An Analysis of the Unnatural Selection of Ideas,
Beliefs and Behavior in Institutions and Organizations

First Edition: First Printing Nov. 1986
           Second Printing Apr. 1987
(Revised) Third Printing May 1990
           Fourth Printing Nov. 1990
           Fifth Printing June 1993
           Sixth Printing May 1995
           Seventh Printing Aug. 1997

Mount Pleasant Press
P. O. Box 212
Orient, NY
11957-0212

JWELLES103@AOL.COM

Table of Contents

Preface

Whenever I had occasion to tell someone I was writing a book on stupidity, the reaction was invariably the same—a delayed smile topped off by a slightly nervous laugh. This provided nearly daily confirmation that I was dealing with a taboo topic. There is something shameful about stupidity, and mentioning it in polite company in an inoffensive way was commonly regarded as an awkward form of comic relief. Beyond that, there was often an expression of amused interest that such an off-color topic would merit serious attention.

Originally, the attention wasn't supposed to be so serious. The book was to be light and jocular. It took on more of a serious tone as I came to realize how incredibly important stupidity is. It can be amusing; it certainly is interesting; but whether or not we can afford to continue indulging in our traditional blundering ways is very much in doubt. Stupidity is simply too important to be dismissed as some tragicomic source of humor. Above all, this is a book about people, and it presumes to say something profound about what being human means.

Almost everyone who knows me was implicitly if not too diplomatically appreciative of the fact that I was undertaking the task of explaining stupidity to the literate world. Who better qualified than I—an experienced expert on the topic. In personal, academic and business matters, stupidity has bedeviled my best efforts for years. There is no point denying the obvious: I have a deep, abiding interest in the topic.

Haunting me almost daily during the writing of this book have been vivid memories of my most stupid failures. Again and again I have replayed my most grievous mistakes. Why did I trust her? Why did I believe him? Why didn't I speak up? Why didn't I shut up? None of these personal experiences appears on the following pages even in an indirect sense. All examples presented are drawn from the impersonal public record. However, my motivation was intensely personal. If this book can help save anyone the bewildering confusion I have suffered while trying to make some kind of sense out of what people say and do, then the effort to write it will not have been wasted. My conclusions that not only do things not make sense but that they really should not be expected to may be incorrect, but I do feel compelled to offer these comments in the hope that they will at least generate some serious interest in bridging the sciences and the humanities.

Please bear in mind that the focus of the book is not on the individual elements discussed—the schema, neurotic paradox, positive feedback system, etc—but on the way they work to produce a dysfunctional whole. In this respect, I presume to have unified psychology by showing how the various fields of perception, cognition, learning, etc. relate to each other.

As for the structure of the book, only a few passing remarks are needed. Chapter I is a general overview, with the basic dimensions laid out and basic contentions, which are developed in following chapters, presented for initial consideration. If Chapter I skips a bit from one point to the next, Chapter II is loaded with filler material which should help clarify my case. Perhaps it should have been called "Definitions and Qualifications", as it really is a collection of many ideas and observations which simply must be presented as a matter of laying the groundwork for the arguments that follow.

Chapter III has very little to do directly with stupidity: It is a presentation of the "Schema" as a functional psychic mechanism. This material is presented because one must understand how the schema helps us adapt in order to appreciate how it contributes to maladaptation, which is the subject matter of Chapter IV. Chapter V is a consideration of stupidity in a cultural context. Chapters VI, VII, and VIII deal with stupidity past, present and future respectively.

Although the comments and conclusions presented herein are all very much my own, debts of gratitude are owed to several people who helped along the way. Special thanks go to C. O. Ingamells, a Peace Corps Volunteer in Jamaica, for his faithful and impassioned correspondence on stupidity during the early stages of this book's development. He provided an outline which, while superseded, helped me attain an appreciation for the multifaceted approach needed to make a book. Gratitude is also extended to Mr. William H. McNeil, historian and author. He is one of those rare breeds in the establishment who is self-assured enough to appreciate offbeat ideas. His suggestions that I generally shape up were not always heeded, but they did sober my attitude toward the task at hand.

Finally, respectful gratitude is offered to the resource librarians in Greenport, New York and at Holiday Park in Fort Lauderdale, Florida. Over an extended period of time, we played a real life version of "Trivial Pursuit". I was trivial; they pursued, invariably with thorough and satisfying results. There is too little good said in the world, so let it be said of them: They were helpful, they were professional, and they cared.

JFW
Orient, NY
Oct. 1986.

Preface Updated

It seems that almost overnight stupidity has switched from being taboo to being a fad. Nearly every week some commentator in the media holds forth on the topic. I wish I could claim some credit for this phenomenon, but I have to admit it is more due to **Forrest Gump** and **Beevis and Butt-head** than to me and my efforts. Still, stupidity is in—for how long, I do not know, but as I write this in April, 1995, it is all the rage.

Perhaps my influence would have been greater if I had done a better job of planning this book out. Unfortunately, it was not the kind of book which was laid out first with the results clearly in mind before the first word was written. Rather, it was a product of induction, with some fore-thought and organization but with inferential conclusions which surprised even me when I finally read it.

Not until I reached the last chapter did I realize I was really dealing with the limitations of science—the ethical dimensions of behavior which are beyond the range of science proper. A full understanding of human behavior will begin with psychology but must go beyond it and deal with metaphysics and morality.

Almost as an aside, I developed a model for how the human mind works. I did not set out to do this: the pieces of the puzzle sort of fell into place as I went along, so it was not until the end of the book that I realized I should make a statement which pulled it all together as I did in the epilogue. Since a reviewer—Dr. Thomas O. Blank of U. of Connecticut, Storrs—had such difficulty understanding the book, I have now decided to make a summary statement of the mechanism on page two. (Likewise, the reader can also thank Dr. Blank for the headers which now adorn the top of each page: he found the text by itself unfathomable and intimated headings would be helpful guideposts, so they have been added.)

The final realization for me as a reader was that I had taken Charles Darwin to task. Darwinian thought assumes that anything normal in life is adaptive—be it anatomy, physiology, coloration, behavior, etc., etc. Not until I finished the book did I realize I have challenged this idea by alleging that normal human behavior can be maladaptive. We all know that **ab**normal behavior can be maladaptive, but I am proposing that human behavior is a major qualification to Darwinian thinking because, by their very nature, behavioral trends tend to excesses unless limited by counter-trends. It may be that both Darwin and I are right—that normal behavior is immediately adaptive but at the price of adaptability. Perhaps if enough people take this book to heart, we will find a way to overcome ourselves and adopt a behavioral program set for long-term survival.

Against stupidity the very gods
Themselves contend in vain.

Schiller, **The Maid of Orleans**, III, 6.

I. Introduction

Who are we? What are we? Why are we? When seeking answers to these eternal questions, we tend to flatter ourselves by being accurate when it suits us and partial when it pleases us. In terms of our technological ability to use tools to make tools, we are truly awesome. In more general cognitive terms, our intellectual capacity to solve complex problems justifies the gratifying conclusion that we are intelligent. However, if this is true, it is only part of the truth.

It is also true that young people are turning to drugs and suicide for the escape they bring from a world in which adults hypocritically preach peace while preparing for and pursuing violence.[1] Basic social problems appear and reappear generation after generation in culture after culture. Not only have we failed to match our ability in mechanics and engineering with a comparable level of expertise in political and social relations, but our vaunted technological and intellectual genius is readily bent to destructive purposes which harm rather than help people. Thus, all things considered, we look pretty stupid.

Although students of human behavior have pointedly ignored our rampant stupidity, many have made careers by pounding intelligence into the ground. Rooms could be filled with the books written on the topic. No one could even keep up with the scientific literature produced in the field. Yet, as vast as this literature is, it leads to but one overwhelming conclusion—and nobody knows what it is. The only thing we know for certain is that whatever intelligence is,[2] it has never been tested on intelligence tests. So even if we are intelligent, we are not intelligent enough to know what intelligence is, so we do not know who and what we are.

If it is understandable that so much energy and effort should be devoted to the scientific study of intelligence, it is somewhat bewildering to find the much more common, actually dangerous and potentially devastating phenomenon of stupidity totally neglected. One could read the entire literature in the social sciences without finding so much as a single reference to it. At best, it is dismissed as the opposite of intelligence, but this just sheds more shade on the topic. Certainly, a matter of this importance deserves a hearing in its own right.

1

The Mechanism

In this work, we will use a mixture of two approaches to answer the question "What is stupidity?" One is to consider the conditions Barbara Tuchman, in **The March of Folly**, deemed necessary for an act to qualify as a folly: 1.) ample, relevant information must be available to the performer, who is in a knowledgeable state about the given situation; 2.) the act must be maladaptive for the performer; and 3.) there must be other possible ways of reacting available. An additional factor in the analysis of folly was "Best interest", with folly being the studied achievement of "Worst interest". Although we will eventually discard all of these considerations as inadequate for the purpose of defining stupidity scientifically, as we first examine and then dismiss them, we will learn much about the limitations of science[3] and the non-Darwinian essence of human nature.

The other approach is to answer that **stupidity is a normal, dysfunctional learning process which occurs when a schema formed by linguistic biases and social norms acts via the neurotic paradox to establish a positive feedback system which carries behavior to maladaptive excesses.** This book is really devoted to elucidating the interactions of the enumerated specifics of this commonplace process by which learning corrupts learning. By way of introduction, let us note that stupidity usually manifests itself in two interacting functions of the human psyche —the self-deceptive inability to gather and process information accurately[4] and the neurotic[a] inability to match behavior to environmental contingencies. Further, it has epistemological, social and moral dimensions.

*

In an epistemological context, stupidity is the failure to gather and use information efficiently. Traditionally, self-deception has been considered only in terms of the use or abuse of information present within a cognitive system—that is, a person would have to "Know" something in order to deceive himself about it. However, we must acknowledge it is also self-deceptive (i.e., misleading) and usually stupid for one to refuse to gather new, relevant information about matters of importance.[5]

Thus, when considering stupidity in relation to knowledge and data processing, it is imperative to distinguish between the related phenomena of "Agnosticism" and "Ignorance". Both words may be used to indicate the condition of "Not knowing", but they describe different ways of maintaining that condition. Pure, innocent agnosticism is not really stupid, in that it does not indicate an inability or unwillingness to learn. Agnosti-

---

a The definition of "Neurosis" as a "Functional disorder" is aptly ambiguous. **Webster's** probably meant a disorder of function, although the phrase might mean a disorder which is functional.

2

Information: Compromise

cism is the cognitive state when information is physically inaccessible (unavailable) to an individual or organization. Relevant data are simply not present in the environment in a form discernable to the sensory apparatus of the living system (person, group, etc.).

Ignorance, on the other hand, usually indicates stupidity in that important data are present and gatherable but unheeded. The reason that ignorance does not always indicate stupidity is that some information could seriously disrupt existing psycho/social systems were it to penetrate the cognitive defenses, so exclusion may sometimes be somewhat adaptive. This is really a rather complex process, as stimuli must be at least superficially perceived before being rejected by the system as being threatening to the existing belief structure or "Schema". Thus, motivation can play a role in ignorance if some relevant, available information is prevented from getting "Into the system" (i.e., accepted and incorporated into the cognitive program). This is likely to occur when a person senses that learning more about a particular matter might force him to undergo the most traumatic, terrifying experience one can be called upon to endure—he might have to change his mind.

It might be assumed that "Knowing is good", that there could not possibly be too much knowledge and that an excess of information could not possibly be unhealthy. However, people must compromise on both the quantity and quality of their information. In terms of quantity, people limit themselves by specializing—sacrificing breadth for depth, with each doing well if he knows something about anything. In terms of quality of information, people debase themselves by qualifying their standards—sacrificing validity for appeal, with each accepting whatever is suitable.

Unfortunately, these compromises not only fail to protect people from an overload of trivia but can keep them from knowing what is going on in their world. A given system can process only so much information so fast, and that should (theoretically) be important material, not insignificant detail. However, important material is not always brought to conscious light. At all levels, there is a secret aspect to human life—things which people do, although most of us should not know.

At the national level, every government has its covert band of operatives who skulk around doing whatever is necessary and improper. The general population and even most government employees are better off not knowing what is going on because the CIA, KGB and James Bonds are set up to betray the ideals which hold civilization together, so such important matters may be hidden from us.

At the individual level, too much candor can also be disastrous, as many doctors well know. There was a case of a terminal cancer patient who was given a useless drug (Krebiozen) and recovered. Upon learning the drug was useless, he had a relapse. Given a superstrength placebo, he again recovered, only to have a final and fatal relapse when learning that drug was useless.[6] This was a case in which belief itself worked a miracle cure; it was knowledge that killed.

As important as the quantity or quality of knowledge present in a system is the attitude toward gathering more. Often, people are hampered by their reluctance to learn more, although usually learning is helpful—particularly if it leads to a stronger, more inclusive belief structure.

Nevertheless, the desire to know is often tempered by a sense that learning more would be emotionally disturbing. This complicates any consideration of stupidity, when "Knowing" is one of the defining criteria for the condition. If a person does not know what is going on, he might do something maladaptive, but it is not stupid as such. However, if a person is making a point not to find out relevant information in his environment, is that not even stupider? If it would seem so, bear in mind we all have defense mechanisms to protect us from awareness of embarrassing cognitions and psycho/cultural mechanisms to help us cope with the unsettling cognizance of our inevitable death.[7] Thus, the condition of "Knowing" appears to be of little value when one attempts to determine if an act was stupid or not.

Once people gather information, they treat it in one of two ways, depending on whether they like it or not. The double standard is quite simple: that which is acceptable is accepted; that which is unpleasant is suspect. It might be ideal if all data were treated equally, but personal biases predispose people to be selectively ignorant.

In most situations, ignorance promotes a common characteristic of stupid decisions—irrelevance. When stupidity is in full glory, the most discrepant cognitions are somehow matched up in the most implausible ways. Further, obvious relevancies are ignored, so the behavioral world takes on the bizarre, chaotic quality of a Wonderland gone berserk. Cause /effect and means/ends relationships are coined at random. The monumental is trivialized and the crucial disdained as an afflicted mind locks in on and pursues its own worst interest with unrestrained abandon.

Unfortunately, the determination of "Relevance" is quite judgmental, so stupidity is an arbitrary/subjective phenomenon. Deeds once considered stupid may turn out to be brilliant. On the other hand, achievements initially hailed as works of genius may later be exposed as moronic[8] (as happened with the Maginot Line and the Edsel).

While much is made of the human brain's ability to associate various cognitions (ideas) in relevant cause/effect relationships, the amount of stupidity in the world suggests that the brain might also prevent or inhibit such functional associations while it promotes irrelevant connections. The

4

child's brain begins by treating all possibilities as being equally probable. Learning couples certain stimuli with certain reactions. No Behaviorist's model of functional rewards, however, could possibly account for the diversity of the world's religions nor the battle science has had to wage against both ignorance and agnosticism.

In this cognitive context, it appears that stupidity is a very normal way for the human mind to compromise with its own emotionally based inability to deal directly with information coming from the physical environment and rewards from the social environment. This is a schizophrenic reaction which permits us to cope with distinct but interacting features of the human condition. For each of us, the invention and development of our special strategies are functions of a commitment to a particular lifestyle defined by our culture and shaped by our experiences.

In terms of intellectual development, stupidity may justly be viewed as both adaptive and maladaptive. In the short run, it is adaptive in that it helps an individual adjust to his cultural group's values by permitting him to accept any obvious contradictions between the real and ideal. As a means to short-term adaptation, stupidity is a classic example of the "Neurotic Paradox" in action. The neurotic[b] paradox promotes behavioral patterns which are subject to immediate short-term reinforcement although the long-term results will be clearly negative.[9] (A drug addiction would be a commonplace example of this basic psycho/physiological principle of learning and life.)

If stupidity is adaptive, in that it helps one fit into his immediate surroundings, it is maladaptive over the long run, as it inhibits innovations and constructive criticism of the social environment. Individuals adjust to the group, but the group loses its capacity to adjust to its surroundings as members sacrifice their individual integrity, insight and ideas and conform for the reward of social acceptance.

Of course, the bottom line, net effect of stupidity is negative, but its universal presence cannot be understood without recognition of its role in helping people adapt to their immediate situation. Thus, it becomes clear how there can be so much stupidity around although it is, in the long run, maladaptive. Survival within the system is promoted if one is so stupid as to accept the system's stupidities. Also, short-term survival of the system (institution, group, whatever) is promoted through enhanced social cohesion and cooperation. However, these immediate gains are countered by

---

b The Psychotic Paradox, on the other hand, blocks short-term, immediate advantages for the sake of possible rewards to be gained later—as when a worker goes on strike, thus sacrificing the next paycheck for the sake of a potentially improved future.

Information: Positive Feedback

the long-term loss of induced inefficiency of information processing. Our cultural life is really a very human trade-off between these two dependent features: 1.) objective, rational, logical processing of information, and 2.) group cooperation and cohesion.

With the qualification of arbitrariness in mind, it should be noted that most people who find stupidity in others judge efficiency of processing information and usually do not even consider the social dimension of decisions affecting institutional life. Accordingly, what might be regarded as stupidity may in fact be a healthy, short-term compromise with group cohesion. Real stupidity comes when either factor (logical information processing or social cohesion) predominates to the disruption of the other.

One of the reasons a student of human behavior has difficulty generalizing about stupidity is that both opposite extremes can lead to stupid behavior. In a given situation, it may be stupid to do too much too soon or too little too late. Both overreaction and underreaction may be counterproductive. Hypersensitivity and insensitivity can both have negative effects. The Golden Mean may indeed be the best policy in most situations, but that leaves contradictory opposites having equally stupid results. Ergo, the student of stupidity, when citing a cause for the condition, must automatically ask himself if the opposite extreme might not also have produced a similar effect.

As long as a functional balance between polar extremes is maintained, stupidity can be viewed as a normal part of the human experience. It is a mechanism of cultural selection which will be found wherever people speak, organize and act. Static human systems usually cannot cope with themselves nor the conditions they create. An organization evolves to deal with a set of given circumstances and, in attempting to solve perceived problems, creates new problems. It then either adapts or stupidly tries to maintain itself until it is replaced by the next institution in the cycle of human organization.

It is important to bear in mind that such stupidity in moderation may be an effective defense mechanism which promotes self-confidence in an individual and cooperation within a group. It is only when it goes to excess that it tends to become stupidly maladaptive, but it is precisely this which is made probable when a behavioral or cultural trend develops into a self-rewarding, positive feedback system. When this occurs, a pattern of activity becomes rewarding in and of itself regardless of its extrinsic consequences. Behavior may then go to extremes because it is reinforced by the schema, which functions as an intrinsically gratifying, internal reward system for such conduct. In the absence of critical self-examination, individuals or groups may become victims of their own excesses as inner directed behavior becomes imbalanced and disruptively self-defeating.[10] Such

6

a disruptive imbalance develops when, through internally induced, sustaining, self-reinforcement, a system becomes removed from moderating influences of the external environment. This is exactly what stupidity is —a schematically generated, self-deceptive breakdown of the feedback mechanism between behavior and the environment.

This breakdown necessarily follows from stupidity's success in creating an arbitrary world that will maximize cooperation of group members. This can be done by blocking disruptive input as well as by inventing pleasing images and ideas. Such tactics may prove to be maladaptive, but this is the price for the immediate reward of enhanced social cohesion.

As effective as stupidity may be in promoting cooperation, it disrupts a system's capacity for effective learning. Understanding is sacrificed for the sake of social cohesion and cultural stability. The drawback of this intellectually limiting, contrived complacence is that it all but guarantees frictional competition and conflict with other equally maladapted groups.

One might reasonably expect that such competition and conflict would weed out stupidity so that the more intelligent systems would eventually prevail. However, it appears that there is at least as much stupidity now as ever before, so it seems that competition merely replaces one stupid system with another. If this leaves people with the option of being ruled by a bunch of idiots or a pack of fools, they can be excused from being too concerned about the difference. On the other hand, anyone who wants to understand what makes everyone else so stupid would do well to consider the factors which contribute to this most common mental state.

If it is human to err, it is even more human to speak, and it is in language systems that we find a major source of human stupidity. Language has two basic functions in society: it permits people to exchange information as it promotes cooperation. Stupidity necessarily follows from the compromise reached by people as they balance these two factors. When people speak, they usually both impart information and convey their group identity. This social aspect of language expresses common values and presumes common assumptions. It also means that critical information is often couched in terms and tones acceptable to all—which in turn means a lot of criticism is muted and stupidity glossed over, if not induced.

Much is made of the brain as a system for processing information, but there is relatively little interest in how information is not used or is misused. One common assumption is that if knowledge is misused, there was some breakdown in the rational system of the mind. In fact, much of the mishandling of data is systematic and based on social values implicit in language as a cultural rather than computerized processing medium.

While it is difficult to study how people don't do something, we must consider how and why people do not use certain information readily available to them. The answer has to be that some facts are emotionally disturbing and would be emotionally/socially disruptive if permitted to pass through the cerebral word processor. This emotional element throws off judgment—or provides a shifting basis for analysis. It is also the source of the "Motivated ignorance" which characterizes the human propensity to be not just uninformed about ego-defining issues but biased by the values implicit in the linguistic system used to process data.

Language is basically a coding system people use to accomplish two interrelated ends: information is conveyed and group cohesion is maintained or increased. Language categorizes experience so that generalizations about the environment are possible, but the labels (words) used for these categories often pick up emotional connotations which distort the processing procedure.[11] The evaluation of the informational component of language then becomes inextricably bound up with the emotional life of the individual or group.

It is this emotional factor which precludes objectivity within any linguistic system. Hence, stupidity is best construed as a social defense mechanism parallel to the Freudian defense systems which protect individuals from an overload of awareness. Just as many Freudian defense mechanisms are generated within individuals who fear self-knowledge,[12] stupidity develops within a society to inhibit unacceptably accurate cognitions of both personal and institutional ineptitude. Along with idiosyncratic forms of individual stupidity, members of a society exhibit collective forms of idiocy within the context of—or reaction against—social values.

The induced subjectivity underlines the essential social nature of stupidity. Society defines awareness of reality as it funnels fictions into our consciousness. The mind is really a socially conditioned filter which a given experience may or may not penetrate, depending on the value structure of a particular society.

In virtually all cases, stupidity is perpetrated subconsciously, in that the agent cannot sense, with his value system, that his actions are counter-productive in terms of that set of values. What he does sense is an emotional satisfaction that precludes any objective analysis on his part (and which is incomprehensible to any outside observer) because one does not consciously engage in self-analysis when cognitions are successfully shunted into emotionally acceptable if irrelevant categories.

In the rational/intelligent model of behavior, discriminative stimuli guide actions so that behavior is "Appropriate" and likely to lead to positive results: behavior is considered to be under "Stimulus control",[13] and this model is actually fairly descriptive of how the mind routinely handles unimportant matters. However, the more important a matter is as an ego-defining issue, the greater the role of the schema vis-a-vis immediate stimuli in shaping attendant behavior, with the result that actions become increasingly inappropriate and even counter-productive. To put it the other way, stupid behavior becomes increasingly common as a schema blocks the perception of impinging stimuli and an understanding of issues and/or creates substitute stimuli and idiotic ideas through fantasies.

The basic problem with the rational/intellectual model of the brain as a computer is that of the self-generation of bugs. Computers invariably have bugs,[c] but the brain has built-in emotional biases which fade in and out depending on the nature of the "Input". The appropriate computer model in this vein would be an electronically unstable machine with a defective program which functions to keep the hard drive steady by preventing major alterations of its programs. In human terms, correcting a program (i.e., changing one's mind) is necessarily emotionally involving and therefore done only reluctantly. In computer terms, any program is inherently maladaptive because of its necessary and inevitable impact on perception (i.e., the process of data input).

The act of perception can be broken down into two separate steps. First, information gets into the system as a result of selective attentional processes. The brain does not treat all external stimuli equally. Perception is a process of discrimination, with stimuli deemed "Important" getting attention denied the trivial. However, what is deemed important is in no way a function of objectivity, since the emotional component of information interferes with the accuracy of its handling. Some stimuli get favored treatment and are emphasized while others are ignored. The paranoid may perceive something trivial as threatening so as to justify his fear. Alternatively, someone else might pass over potentially upsetting stimuli as too disturbing to contemplate.

After stimuli enter the system, they are then organized into "Meaningful" units, with the meaning of "Meaningful" being about as arbitrary as anything can be. This process of organizing is linguistic categorizing, which commonly results in illusions and misperceptions. The net result is that selected data are arbitrarily construed to conform to and confirm the existing cognitive program—the Schema.[14]

The schema is the basic belief structure of the individual.[15] It is the frame of reference for the perception of stimuli, and it defines the behavioral repertoire available for response to them. The schema provides both general and specific expectations about their relations and may fill in in-

---

c The original bug was a moth which is now mounted on a wall in the library at the Aberdeen Maryland Proving Grounds. The term "Bug" has since been inflated to generic status to cover any form of electronic snafu.

formation, should experience with an object/event be limited. It is modifiable by experience as the individual interacts with the environment,[16] and minor adjustments are quite common and usually occur with little or no emotional reaction.

The schema is a verbal/behavioral construct through which situations are perceived in a linguistic context which systematically distorts incoming information so as to reinforce itself at the expense of contradictory, disturbing data. This is the basic mechanism of stupidity, as it necessarily causes people to be out of sync with their environment. The schema is a self-sustaining cognitive paradigm which maintains its emotional base by misperceiving the environment through verbal labeling of stimuli. It has something of a hypnotic effect, focusing attention on schema-confirming percepts so that these data can be processed while reality testing on the rest of the perceptual field is suspended. The garnered data then serve to strengthen further the schema as they are incorporated into it.

As a function of experience, the schema can both help and hinder the individual as he attempts to deal with problems in his environment. The schema is an advantage when the person confronts a problem similar to one already solved, as each time it gets easier to deal successfully with such situations. However, the schema may limit insight—the act of pulling together various facts into novel, functional relationships. In this sense, experience and the created schema can inhibit innovation and contribute to the persistence of behavior which once was adaptive but has become obsolete.

Again, we must emphasize the inherent arbitrariness of the entire phenomenon. There is no particular virtue in holding or changing a given schema except relative to the environment over time. This, in turn, is an uncertain base, the perception of which is confounded by linguistic bias.

Stupidity thus results both from and in perceptual limits on learning which prevent a system from recognizing its own intrinsic limitations. A new idea is not judged objectively by an independent standard but is regarded primarily as a challenge to the prevailing ego/social system. This is an emotionally based, usually subconscious reaction. Only secondarily can the cognitive content of new information be processed consciously on something like its own merits.

When pondering the passing of many great human institutions down through the ages, one must conclude that most failed to adapt to changing conditions. What is not so obvious is that the new conditions were often produced by the institutions themselves. Turnover of organizations is inherent in the human conditions in that a schema tends to limit values to those appropriate to the circumstances present when it developed. These values sustain the status quo by preventing recognition of problems created by the impact of the institution on its environment. This perceptual failure occurs concurrently with the general schematic restriction on the development of any novel modes of thought or behavior. Indeed, one of the sad ironies of life is that most innovators must fight the system in order to improve it. Very few organizations encourage excellence, so most transcendent achievements first had to overcome entrenched opposition from the establishment.

Although we all delight in the triumphs of the crackpots who contributed to the advance of civilization, it is impossible to appreciate the tragedies of those who failed not because they were wrong but because they could not overcome the built-in idiocy of their cultural environment. We cannot even imagine how much better life might have been for all of us. However, when stupidity reigns supreme, the establishment stifles critical analysis so as to thwart improvement and protect the schema for as long as possible. Such was the case in 1929 when, months before the crash, Alvin T. Simonds sent an article to **Nation's Business** suggesting a business decline, only to have the article rejected because it was "Pessimistic". At that time, financial houses hesitated to forecast declines in business, as they tended to lose good clients and win enduring enemies by objectively interpreting the facts.[17]

It is important to note that accuracy was treated as an irrelevancy in this case. Agnosticism in the general business community was promoted by wishful thinking. This is but a single example of the blind egotism so common in stupidity—the reluctance to perceive unpleasant realities.

*

Along with its linguistic/perceptual mechanism for preventing recognition of reality, stupidity has another ally which inhibits effective coping with problems. This is the mechanism by which social life establishes conflicting standards for rational behavior. That is, stupidity is actually encouraged by the basic nature of group interaction.

First of all, no one is perfect. Stupidity is grounded on this basic fact. The point is not that we all make mistakes because we are not perfect but that we cover them up for each other because we know sooner or later it will be our turn to goof up. In considering stupidity, we need not belabor maladaptive, incidental "Noise" in the human system—the errors people make from sheer inadvertence, fatigue or accident. But if we do not belabor them because they are not symptomatic of any significant, underlying behavioral principle, it is important to note that society politely hides our imperfections behind a self-deceptive illusion of mutual assurance.

Secondly, when they interact, imperfect people are not even trying to be objective, or honest, or to learn about themselves. They are usually trying to prolong a social relationship. This provides, for example, the basis for the cozy relations of the media and their sponsors, which may be fine for the sponsors but which necessarily makes the credibility of the media at least suspect. Usually, of course, they overcome this potential image problem with sincere pronouncements and very thorough coverage of events not in the sponsor's worst interest.

Most social groups exist for two related functions: group maintenance and goal achievement. The relative importance of these two functions will vary with conditions, and with compromise the normal state, most people live in a genial, casual pursuit of some particular achievement. As sacrifice is the nature of compromise, one of society's inherent stupidities is that goal achievement must often be traded off so as to perpetuate an organization whose expressed purpose is to accomplish that goal.

It is in this dual nature of group function that one finds pressures for both accuracy in and distortion of knowledge. To maintain a group, some accuracy may have to be sacrificed, making goal achievement a little less likely or more difficult. The ultimate in the chronic stupidity of institutional life is, of course, that maintaining the group may become an end in itself. In such a situation, cognitive incest obliterates any pretense at logical justification for self-sustaining acts.

Groups undergoing this process begin to separate from reality and define their own existence when the proper handling of and response to incoming information demands socially intolerable adjustments of group procedure and structure. This trend is climaxed as social inertia comes to disrupt effective reaction to the external milieu.

Civil service bureaucracies are notorious centers for such useless workfare programs. These repositories for the dysfunctional contribute nothing to the nation's health or wealth. It would be absurd even to suggest a scale for measuring their monumental waste and pathetic inefficiency. However, if they are an overall drain on society, they contribute indirectly to the self-respect of a nation which, in its stupid magnificence, provides a place of employment for the hopelessly inept—the government.

Within the formal context of written laws and rules, daily routine of most social life, institutional and otherwise, is regulated by norms—social standards for acceptable behavior, dress, manners, modes of speech, etc. These norms encourage stupidity by providing a systematic pattern of reinforcement conducive to conformity for its own sake. It is the acceptance and approval of members which first induces and then sustains a common schema and its system of values that form individuals into a group.

Life in groups is a given of the human experience. The newborn must learn all that is needed to survive, and it is the birth group that provides protection and information as this process of socialization proceeds. Not only does the initiate learn a particular language (with all its perceptual limitations), but he also develops a sense of belonging which precludes criticism of the fundamental assumptions of his culture. People may be critical when ideals are not realized, but they rarely criticize the ideals themselves. To do so automatically classifies one as an outsider, and most people would prefer to belong than be critical.

The process of maturation is one of falling into the opinions of those in one's immediate surroundings. It is noteworthy that this is only indirectly related to reality. Truth comes to be whatever conforms to the verbal environment as the member comes to believe in the assumptions of his peers rather than regarding them as hypotheses to be verified. This may entail some cognitive constraint, but submission by the individual consolidates the collective mental habits of his egocentric group.

When socialization completes this process of mental control, a schema will not be altered unless an external reward is more appealing than the discomfort of changing the schema is emotionally wrenching. People rarely change just for the sake of accuracy, unless they have internalized objectivity and learned to abide by the respect for data demanded by a disciplined methodology like that of science. Only the more superficial things (like fashions) change just for the sake of change.

When attempts are made to comprehend behavior in terms of maximizing positive outcomes and minimizing negative results, the importance of the internal reward system is often underestimated. Only such a system could account for fiascos like the Edsel, the Bay of Pigs invasion of Cuba and Watergate. The psychological basis for such idiocy is the positive feedback system that socialization and the schema create and maintain.

Conflicting or contradictory data from the external environment is deflected or deflated by the belief system, which develops into a fundamental religion. Any objective analyst may easily discern all kinds of logical inconsistencies and perceptual absurdities in someone else's religious schema, but that type of analysis is invariably based on a rational evaluation of factual data. Actually, devoutly held schemas are functional not because they effectively define and address particular problems but because they help bind self-deceptive people together. This emotional/social dimension as it contributes to group cohesion is usually overlooked by rationalists, thus making their analysis flat and somewhat irrelevant. However logical, neat and smug self-contained texts in cognitive psychology may be, they usually omit this central point and leave the reader with the same vaguely empty feeling he would have were he to see a production of **Hamlet** without Hamlet.

Although the term "Religion" is traditionally defined in reference to the supernatural, it will be used in this discussion to refer to any compelling belief system, whether the object of the schema is supernatural, natural or man-made. Thus, much of this consideration of stupidity will be dealing with "Secular religions", such as beliefs in Democracy, Capitalism, Equality, Freedom or whatever. Our concern is not with the nature of the belief's object but with the nature of the belief. If a belief is unreasonable, it usually is so because it is a compromise synthesis of reality cum mentality. Such a condition may be functional and is a normal, acceptable method of balancing the many factors which interact in our social lives. When this compromise is itself compromised, the process of schematic crumbling is simply too ambiguous in the early stages to be defined as such, so it is defined to suit the viewer. Only when the process nears completion, can it be labeled as clearly stupid.

The basic requirement of all religious organizations is not that they be logical but that they keep in touch with their members. Keeping in touch with the external environment is secondary or perhaps coequal. This commitment to the group does not really make the system less sensitive overall, but it might seem that way, as attention must be directed inward as well as outward. Also, the data that are gathered from the outer world are processed not in their own right but in terms of the internal schema. Naturally, to an external observer (who himself can never be totally objective), the responses of the system might appear irrelevant to the given conditions, but what he often fails to consider are the further "Givens" that are not elements of his own schema.

One of the basic mistakes made in evaluating behavior as stupid stems from the assumption that people are really trying to achieve a particular goal—even one in their own best interest. Many people function more in a particular way than toward a particular end, even though the way may be self-defeating. For example, some fool may be committed to being honest rather than to making favorable impressions: he is simply honest and lets impressions take care of themselves. Such a person might lose out to an imposter, if both are applying for the same job, but the specific goal of getting the job is secondary to his basic commitment to honesty.

The gutters may be filled with people like that—too dumb to deceive in a world of scams, but honesty and objectivity do not always stand in the way of success. William Howard Taft was an amusing example of remarkable insensitivity in social relations. For example, he mentioned Grant's drinking problem in a eulogy to the former President. He spoke to be accurate, not to obtain a particular effect[18] and nevertheless managed to become President and Chief Justice of the Supreme Court.

Although situation ethics may carry most individuals far in a world of superficial impressions, groups need not only belief systems but statements of those beliefs as rallying points for their sense of identity. These pronouncements are the "Creed" of the group. They are not guides for behavior of the members but verbalizations which promote group cohesion by providing superego-satisfying justifications for whatever must be done. Thus, the military claims that "Peace is our profession", and courts somehow get themselves associated with statements about "Justice". Such creeds have a self-deceptive, hypnotic effect on group members and inhibit the development of any sense that what they do is maladaptive. At best, creeds may make people knowledgeable but unaware, as the kind of knowledge gained is used to 1.) sustain the group schema, 2.) sustain the group, and 3.) help the group cope with its environment.

This creed rarely fools our classic outside observer. He is usually quite quick to note when a given group is behaving in ways contradictory to its expressed values, and he then makes the mistake of asserting that the members are stupid, in that they are engaging in behavior inconsistent with their creed. Once again, we return to the nemesis of arbitrariness—by what standard is stupidity to be judged? The creed? The observer's creed? Goal achievement? Despite obvious incongruities, people may decide unconsciously that it is in their emotional "Best interest" simply to hold on rigidly to their creed rather than try to adjust their ideas to fit either their actions or incoming and possibly disturbing bits of information about reality.[19]

If identifying the "Best interest" of a party is difficult for anyone, concerned or not, then we should not be surprised at the persistence of maladaptive behavior—even if no one knows what it is. The internal reward system of the self-sustaining schema can promote a course of action totally irrelevant to anything in the perceivable environment. As maladaptive behavior persists, pride becomes a prime motivating factor for perpetuating what is arguably a mistake—that is, people would rather go on being wrong than admit it and take corrective measures. If the war in Vietnam might possibly once have been winnable or even justifiable for the United States, those possibilities passed away years before the fighting wound down to its disgraceful conclusion.

The military effort in Vietnam actually turned out to be unusually stupid, in that it was idiotic in two different ways at once. It induced internal conflict while becoming an international debacle. Often, stupidity is found where a system disrupts itself. Alternatively, a conflict between systems (e.g., countries, religious groups, etc.) may be induced by stupidities that are mutual or complementary, so what might begin as legitimate competition can degenerate into misunderstandings, recriminations and worse. In terms of laying an egg, Vietnam was a double yolker.

In the context of the stupidity of a system struggling against itself, one appreciates the good nature of people like Barry Goldwater, who once suggested he might sponsor a Constitutional amendment which would require all decisions of the Supreme Court to "Make sense". Of course, the Court would have found it quite difficult to function effectively with such an unreasonable restriction,[d] and in more general terms, "Making sense" is about the last thing a human system should be expected to do, however pleasing it may be to analysts who prefer logic to life.

Arbitrariness notwithstanding, there are basically only two types of stupidity. By far the most common is that of principle—a system too committed to itself to adjust: its reward system becomes so internalized that it ceases to respond effectively to external change. The other type is, as one might expect, the exact opposite: this is the hypersensitive stupidity of overreacting not only to incidentals in the environment but perhaps to fantasies as well. This type usually leads to chaos, with opportunism of the moment substituting for development by a guiding schema. Both types have their places in the dynamic disorder of the human experience.

Once again, it is necessary to point out the compromise nature of the human condition. When an organization has to trade off a logically perfect system which makes sense with itself in order to find a balance with the psychological needs of imperfect people, social reinforcement will shape the behavior of those sharing common assumptions, values and beliefs. If this is a less than ideal process, it is at least consistent with the general biological principle of replacing living systems which were once but no longer are the best adaptation to an altered environment. The peculiar thing about human systems is not that they create so much of their own environment, but that they usually create one in which they cannot survive with their belief systems both honored and intact.

One specific form of rigid stupidity as induced by social norms deserves special mention because it has been identified and studied so intently. "Groupthink"[20] is a very intense form of stupidity as it works its magic on a small, tightly knit band of people too committed to their common schema to save themselves. The Kennedy-condoned Bay of Pigs invasion remains the classic example of groupthink in all its stagnant glory. All the elements of stupidity became concentrated in the White House as the best and brightest set about creating the perfect disaster. It exemplifies the most dangerous of all possible combinations: smart people in positions of power behaving stupidly.

If it is possible to be too cooperative, then groupthink is both possible and probable. It occurs when a decision making group is highly cohesive, insulated from outside opinion and working on a policy already strongly

---

d Actually, there is little reason to believe the Supreme Justices would heed such an amendment any more than they have the existing Constitution when making their decisions.

Society: Isolation

endorsed by the leader. Under such conditions, no member is likely to risk his group status or membership by pointing out flaws in the considered policy. In the absence of external feedback and internal criticism, anything less than the perfect plan is sure to go awry.

Not only is there this cognitive drawback based on the tendency toward uniformity of opinion among members of an isolated group, there is also an inherent danger in modern bureaucratic systems that leaders derive some sort of perverse satisfaction and prestige from being removed from reality. In accordance with Reedy's Law (i.e., "Isolation from reality is inseparable from the exercise of power"),[21] status seems to demand that those who make the most important decisions have information presented to them preselected and packaged in predigested form. Rather than surrounding themselves with truthful advisors as recommended by Machiavelli to his theoretically ideal, wise Prince,[22] many modern rulers content themselves with fawning sycophants. The miracle is not that such leaders make so many stupid decisions but that they make so few.

In general society, the lack of critical analysis typical of all stupid systems stems from the moral commitment of members to their group creed. As the schema becomes a religious belief, it is removed a second step from reasonable criticism. (The initial separation from logical control occurs when the linguistic system of the group inhibits negative evaluation of fundamental assumptions, since the words used to convey information convey implicit values as well.) Of course, there is something vexing about a whistle blower pointing out that the system does not work, so nothing is likely to disturb the almighty or the attitude of religious worshipers quite so much as a few practical observations.

One type of observation is that there is a mismatch between creeds and deeds. This problem is inherent in the human condition. Our verbal creed not only allows us to describe our world but also helps us work together in it. It provides us with ideals to live up to and hide behind. Also, our actions are compromises with all the many factors of life which impinge upon us. Small wonder, then, that there are often discrepancies between our verbal and real worlds. This can be stupid, but mostly it is simply an expression of humans attempting to function in a world of arbitrary compromise.

When present, stupidity is easy to recognize, as it invariably promotes what it should prevent and prevents what it should promote: that is, it is counter-productive. When ideals become stumbling blocks, preventing their own realization, there is something wrong. When, in the name of justice, we walk all over someone's rights, there is something wrong. When, in the name of fairness, we suppress the oppressed, there is something wrong. Just what is wrong is never clear, and in a world of con-

Society: Reform

flicting absurdities, we may become a bit jaded and accepting of stupidity as a condition so common that we no longer even recognize it as such.

The ultimate danger really is to be found in the extremism that such indifference permits and fanaticism promotes. Compromise and balance are the first victims when people stop caring enough to note the stupidity surrounding them, so if we accept the absurd, we deserve the disastrous. When control comes not through reason but primarily through conflicting powers, we have a tenuous future at best, and unfortunately, that is exactly our situation today. At least we have structured our domestic power conflicts so that confrontations are channeled through the halls of government and the courts. In such places, the most irrational decisions can be reached with maximal attention to decorum and minimal concern with reality. Again, the miracle is not that we get along so poorly but that we get along at all.

Invariably, failings and excesses of the establishment do engender checks on themselves. Reformers arise among the disenfranchised and proceed to add their particular brand of stupidity to those already flourishing. Usually in the names of improvement and progress, reformers become persecutors and strive to reduce life to some grand order through change. They might wreck the economy in their efforts to improve the standard of living. Or perhaps they induce riots and war in their quest for harmony and peace. In America, the purveyors of righteousness are always ready to make the country "Right" again—or for the first time—if the people can stand it and the world can afford it.

The main problem reformers must contend with is that the game is stacked against them. Almost everyone, to varying degrees, falls under the illusion that the establishment wants to be fair. It is rather incredible that anyone with an IQ exceeding his age could entertain such a notion. Perhaps this is just a backhanded tribute to the awesome power of stupidity that we can believe such a thing. The establishment wants to stay established: if it can be fair and retain final control, it will be, but prevailing institutions are basically indifferent to "Fairness".

By itself, being "Right" is of no particular advantage in a dispute. It can make a person aggravated and an aggravation, but it has minimal persuasive impact. All this shows is how powerful stupidity is as a factor in social life. Institutions promote it by being inherently conservative, trying to impede any significant changes in the status quo. As all judgments are arbitrary, anyone can be both right and stupid. In fact, many people are right and/or stupid, but it is seldom clear who is which and when. What is clear is that the establishment is indifferent to those who are right but powerless, because the mighty tend to judge everything according to their own self-serving standards for cultural stability and worldly success.

Morality: Beliefs

*

This arbitrarily based indifference to those with good ideas underlines our pervasive stupidity in social relations. By contrast, our undeniable successes in matters technical become all the more curious. It seems obvious at this point to consider the application of objectivity to the social domain in the hope that the social sciences might undercut our proclivity for individual and collective maladaptive behavior. This is well worth considering, if indeed our faith in science is justified and if the application of scientific analysis to human behavior would lead to a reduction in stupidity.

Science, in the form of the social sciences, has already proved successful in helping people learn about themselves and their institutions. It has also proved useless in providing any sort of ethic to direct the application of knowledge gained to any clear-cut, long-range benefit to humanity. Science is especially good in the narrow, immediate sense of gathering information about a specific problem or set of conditions, and the more specific the context, the better. How those data and possible solutions to problems relate to society in general is another crucial problem in itself and somewhat beyond the scope of true science. All science can legitimately contribute to the application of knowledge to problem solving is limited to projections of likely future results and sometimes sample test case studies.

As previously noted, one of the major shifts in our mental world in the past few hundred years is that we tend more and more to believe in human institutions with a religious fervor previously directed toward assumed supernatural forces. Thus, although the influence of established churches may have waned during this period, religious belief is still as powerful as ever as a factor shaping human behavior. All the horrors and cruelties which used to be the province of the devoutly sectarian (as evidenced by their witch hunts and inquisitions) have been extended and expanded upon by the devotees of secular (i.e., political and economic) institutions. It is expecting too much of science, which in its pure form is morally neutral, to combat such forms of socially induced subjectivity. Scientists can try to be objective and may make us more knowledgeable but not better.

The real problem confronting the foes of stupidity is not one which can be solved by gathering more knowledge, which is the function of scientific research. The solution will be found in the relevant application of knowledge, which is a matter of technological ethics. It is very much to our credit that we are so clever as engineers—efficient at inventing and building all kinds of sophisticated machines and contraptions. A list of major human achievements would read like a "What's What" in technolo-

Morality: Immorality

gy—moonwalks, atomic power, heart transplants, gene splicing, telecommunications, etc. But all this success in applying knowledge comes up short of humanity and leaves one with the feeling that the success is that of a detached system which has taken on a life and purpose of its own rather than that of one filling some compassionate need. Although we rejoice in the qualitative improvement in health attributable to medical science, the overall plight of humanity has been poorly served by those who apply what we know, with each plus seemingly counterbalanced by a minus and each advance accompanied by new problems.

If a worst-case scenario is needed to make the point, it is, unfortunately, all too available and all too recent. The fundamental and total immorality of the Nazi regime scars the conscience of civilization because it proved, in an incomprehensible way, knowledge does indeed make us free. It expands our ability to "Do" without providing any kind of human value or humane ethic other than operational efficiency. In fact, the most disturbing aspect of the tragedy is that the Nazis were so efficient in a cause so perverse.

If this was the most evil if not stupidest misapplication of force in the pursuit of an ideal, it seems just that much worse when we realize that it was not just technology gone mad for the sake of technology. It was the logically calculated use of the most advanced technology of the times, by the most educated, civilized culture of the times attempting to realize a policy deemed to be in the best interests of humanity. If anything like the Last Reich had occurred anywhere else or at any other time in history, it would have been disturbing enough, but at the turn of the century, Germany was the center of civilization, with the greatest of universities and a culture of such breadth and depth that it has never been surpassed and rarely equaled. In science as well as music, Germany was preeminent; in philosophy as well as engineering, Germany predominated—and this was the era when the leaders of the Nazi empire received their education.

The lesson is very simple for anyone willing to heed it. Science and technology are both methods: the one helps us learn, the other helps us do. Neither is a control system. They are both morally neutral and offer humanity no ethical precept which will protect us from ourselves. Worse yet is the realization that all the cultivated learning in the world seemed to encourage rather than prevent the most despicable abuse of power ever. It would be very stupid indeed to think that it could not happen again or anywhere else. The sad fact is that if it could happen in Germany then, it very certainly could happen somewhere else some other time. Nationalism and racism, a sense of injustice and betrayal, a frustrated feeling of superiority and most especially, an elite with a mission to purify the world by replacing diversity with righteous order—all these elements are com-

20

Morality: Problems

mon in many societies today. Again, the miracle is not that we have so much trouble but that we have so little.

Trouble we do have, of course. In contrast to our great achievements in technology, we have our dismal failures in human affairs. Poverty, starvation, disease, crime, drugs, riots, wars (real and potential) all confront us every day on the news. Science helps us learn about nature, and technology provides us with the means for effecting change, but neither provides us with the understanding we need to help ourselves. Hence, people continue to suffer in sloth and apathy—ill-housed, ill-clothed, ill-fed—while a self-content middle class smugly convinces itself it is somehow morally superior to the disadvantaged, and government charity doles out just enough useless help to keep the disenfranchised hopelessly dependent on the long spoon.

If this is the best we can do, we are indeed in a mess. Perhaps we would do better if we recognize that we and the institutions we believe in are the causes of our problems. Much psychological research has gone into the study of humans as problem solvers, which is all well and good because we can and do solve problems. However, virtually no attention has been directed toward analyzing our considerable ability to create difficulties and even less to our inability to resolve them. On the one hand, we are rather deft at dealing with natural problems; our scientific and technological triumphs are all over natural phenomena—the human body, genes, electromagnetism, space. On the other, our failures are self-generated, and we cannot correct them because those in power who created them simply do not recognize them as problems solvable within the system. Perhaps if we understood our foibles by applying the schematic model for stupidity advanced in this book, we could render human behavior comprehensible. Ethics could then be a function of knowledge rather than religious taboos in the way our technological expertise allows us to make informed rather than mystical decisions about our interactions with nature.

One example of the interaction of expertise, knowledge and ethics in human affairs is that of the increasing moral imperative for cooperation. Ironically, while technological success has promoted the growth of human populations, computers have made disruptive innovative thought more difficult and individual creative thought anachronistic. The development of new disruptive ideas is more difficult because technology is standardizing our cultural world. Conformity in dress, behavior and thought is promoted by centralized control in the fashion industry, the legal system and the media. We isolate ourselves from interpersonal contact with headsets plugged into boom boxes playing synthesized music or endure prefabricated laugh-tracks on sit-com TV. For variety, we depend on old-line fanatics, like religious fundamentalists, to upset the cultural quo.

Morality: Rights

Thus, creative thinking which promotes unity is now the responsibility of some undefined, centralized establishment. It would be nice enough if this were a planned process, with each idea adding to our collective happiness, but it is basically haphazard, with each item adding to someone's bank account regardless of long-term consequences for society in general. Without realizing what has happened, we have turned our right to be original over to the amassed media. Oddly, this constitutes one example of manic stupidity due to the lack of an overseeing schema as growth without development has produced change without progress.

A more extreme example of amoral stupidity is the way we are wrecking our environment. Thanks to our failure to plan resource development, we are killing our lakes and streams, poisoning our forests, turning rain into showers of acid and are generally strangling our life support system.[23] Once again, it is only the confrontation with our technological excesses that is forcing reason upon us. As a classic example of the neurotic paradox in action, the immediate, short-term profits which technologically advanced corporations net spur them on in their commitment to despoil the land, water and air.[24] These indulgences beget, however, protesters who assert their right to live and breathe and who gather strength from the obvious soundness of their position that if things continue at the current rate, there soon will be no environment left to despoil. Thus, the battle of those who would wreck the world in a random, chaotic, indulgent way versus those who would save it by systematic, controlled planning. With the political power structure being what it is, they will reach a compromise—to wreck it by systematic, controlled planning.

If it is rather trite today to observe that our technological excesses are challenging our morality, it is still worth noting that this development may decrease the likelihood that compromises in the future will be reached on the basis of justice rather than on the basis of power. Power sharing based on rights meant that more and more often, more and more people dealt with each other as equals, but we are surrendering our rights to the shadow establishment. This is the most compelling change at work in our culture, and it may lead us to a blasé world in which variety, which provides both the spice of and disputes in life, will be unimaginable.

In a more realistic vein, it would be nice if someday all existent disputes could be settled fairly rather than by force or formality and that all decisions reached would be functions of reason rather than irrationality. Whether we ever reach such a state will depend to a large degree on the role stupidity plays in our future. Stupidity can both prevent survival, by promoting misunderstandings, and promote it, by making us more accepting of our limitations. It is most likely, however, that stupidity will transcend survival because we do not understand our limitations. Specific cul-

Morality: The Question

tures rise, flourish and then pass away for lack of effective self-control—too much or too little. However, stupidity remains, appears and reappears in successive civilizations with such monotonous regularity that if we are to break the pattern and endure, we will have to answer to that overwhelming question never quite posed before: How can we be so stupid?

Notes

1. Kennedy, T. Quoted in **Ted Kennedy: In Over His Head** by Gary Allen. 1988. '76 Press; Atlanta; GA. 106.

2. Elliott, R. 1987. **Litigating Intelligence: IQ Tests, Special Education, and Social Science in the Courtroom**. Auburn House; Dover, MA. 72-80.

3. Krutch, J. W. 1953. **The Measure of Man**. Grosset & Dunlap; New York. 32-33.

4. Welles, J. 1981. The sociobiology of self-deception. **Human Ethology Newsletter**, III, #1, 14-19.

5. Goleman, D. 1985. **Vital Lies, Simple Truths**. Simon and Schuster; New York.

6. Haas, H., Fink, H. and Hartfelder, G. 1959. Das Placeboproblem (translation). **Psychopharmacology Service Center Bulletin**, 2, 1-65. (U.S. Public Health Service).

7. Becker, E. 1973. **The Denial of Death**. Free Press; New York.

8. Pitkin, W. 1932. **A Short Introduction to the History of Human Stupidity**. Simon and Schuster; New York. 8.

9. Mowrer, O. 1950. **Learning Theory and Personality Dynamics**. Ronald Press; New York.

10. Kelman, H. 1965. Compliance, identification, and internalization: three processes of attitude change. In **Basic Studies in Social Psychology** edited by Proshansky, H. and Seidenberg, B. Holt, Rinehart and Winston; New York. p. 142.

11. Chase, S. 1966. **The Tyranny of Words**. Harcourt, Brace, Jovanovich; New York.

12. Maslow, A. 1963. The need to know and the fear of knowing. **J. of General Psychology**, 68, 118-119.

13. Terrace, H. 1966. Stimulus control. In **Operant Behavior** edited by W. Honing. Appleton-Century-Crofts; New York.

14. Luborsky, L. 1990. **Understanding Transference**. Basic Books; New York.

15. Piaget, J. 1954. **The Construction of Reality in the Child**. Translated by M. Cook. Basic Books; New York. \

16. Neisser, U. 1976. **Cognition and Reality: Principles and Implications of Cognitive Psychology**. Freeman; San Francisco, CA. 53.

17. Pitkin. **op. cit.** 430.

18. **Ibid.** 368.

19. Ortega y Gasset, J. 1957. **The Revolt of the Masses**. Norton; New York. 156-157.

20. Janis, I. 1982. **Groupthink**. Houghton Mifflin; Boston, MA.

21. Reedy, G. 1966. From a mimeographed paper prepared for a conference at the Center for the Study of Democratic Institutions. Cited in **The Imperial Presidency** by A. Schlesinger, Jr. 1973. Houghton Mifflin; Boston, MA. 214. Also see Reedy, G. 1970. **The Twilight of the Presidency**. New American Library; New York.

22. Machiavelli, N. 1513. **The Prince**. (First printed in 1532.) Chap. 23.

23. Wagner, R. 1971. **Environment and Man**. Norton; New York. Chaps. 7, 9 and 10.

24. Darlington, C. 1970. The Evolution of Man and Society. **Science**, 68, 1332.

II. Defining Stupidity

Naturally—that's how! We can be stupid just by being ourselves. In fact, this book is based on two fundamental contentions: we cannot really understand ourselves without understanding stupidity, and if we understand stupidity, we will understand ourselves. Although the focus of this work is on stupidity, it is really a study of how the human mind functions. Sometimes it is "Intelligent"; more often it is "Stupid", but most of the time, it just plugs along unobtrusively in a manner unnamed because it is so common as never to have been named anything at all. Regardless of the labels used, our characteristic interactions with the environment are all directed by the same basic mental process—the process by which our schemas shape perception, cognition and behavior.

In defining our mental life and shaping our behavior, the schema so routinely causes people to act in their own worst interests that stupidity can be considered one of the few, true cultural universals. Geniuses display it; superior people flaunt it, and the average person is never without it.[1] Nevertheless, it thrives unnoticed in humanity's closet of shame. As this is the age when gays, blacks and even women have come out of the closet, perhaps it could also be the age when stupidity is acknowledged, confronted and even understood. Considering its impact on history, stupidity certainly deserves a hearing which is at least fair if not equal to that granted intelligence.

Traditionally, historians have pleased their readers with accounts of humanity's wondrous progress. These generally placed humans, as Mr. Clemens' boy Sam once observed, "Somewhere between the angels and the French". Likewise, psychologists followed the path of greatest acceptance in their concentration on intelligence to the total disregard of stupidity. Considering how little intelligence and how much stupidity there is, it really is incredible that this imbalance in the literature has existed for so long.[2] Whatever the cause for this condition, it cannot be that stupidity is not a fit topic for scientific investigation, because if it is not, then neither is intelligence. However, the one is totally neglected and the other virtually pounded into the ground. If we really want to have a full understanding of the human experience, we will have to acknowledge and examine that which is both embarrassing and shameful.

The Literature

Fortunately, our knowledge of stupidity is not limited to what historians and psychologists have not written about it. Herodotus noted that man was robbed of reason by "Infatuation". Of course, in ancient Greece, deities were responsible for everything, and in this particular matter, it was the goddess Ate who was responsible for infatuation, mischief, delusion and blind folly[3]—apparently everything contributing to maladaptation but stupidity. She rendered her victims "Incapable of rational choice" and blind to distinctions of morality and expedience. (It is worth noting this awareness of the moral dimension of Ate's influence.)

In the Christian tradition, stupidity, blunder and folly were glossed over by Jesus[4] in deference to the sensibilities of his followers, who were remarkably ignorant.[5] Criticism of human idiocy was discouraged, and Christians came to regard the truth about a fool as a type of indecent exposure and strictly taboo.[6] What other major religions of the world have to say about stupidity will not become clear until the beckoning field of Comparative Stupidity comes to flower, but the Christian attitude certainly contributes greatly to the nearly empty shelves in Western libraries where the hundreds of books on stupidity should be.

Those shelves are, fortunately, only "Nearly" empty, because there have been a few pioneers who dared delve into stupidity despite the taboo. First, of course, there were a couple of Germans. In 1909, Dr. Leopold Löwenfeld had **Über die Dummheit** published. In this work, stupidity was not defined from a medical viewpoint, but rather its broad forms were classified as multi-dimensional functional failings of a faulty intellect—meaning dullness, weak character, inattention, misperception, poor judgment, clumsy associations, bad memory, etc. One of the sexes[a] and one of the races[b] was less stupid than the others, and although the book was updated in 1921, even World War I could not shake the author's conviction about the sexual/racial distribution of stupidity. He might have inferred, for example, that white men were superior in stupidity, but he settled for everyone else being generally inferior in intellect.

Following Leopold's lead, Max Kemmerich had **Aus der Geschichte der menschlichen Dummheit** published in 1912. A Teutonic cure for insomnia, this work examines stupidity in a Biblical context and is essentially an attack on established religions. Max's emphasis on a belief system was well placed, but his work is intolerantly narrow in that he recognized the Bible as the only legitimate standard for belief and behavior.

a Guess which!

b " "

The Literature (cont.)

In 1919, psychologist Charles Richet had **L'homme stupide** published. He dodged the issue of defining or classifying stupidity but dealt with the idiocies of drugs, wealth, feudalism, slavery, war, fashion, semantics, superstitions, etc., etc. This is more a witty compilation of thoughts and examples than a scientific treatment of the phenomenon and ranged so far afield that some subjects bear only a tenuous connection with the topic.

Dr. István Ráth-Végh, a retired Hungarian judge, contributed three books to the shelves. Like most other contributions, they are neither comprehensive nor analytical but do comprise 800 pages of source material for any reader of Hungarian in need of examples of idiocy grouped under convenient headings. Originally published at the rate of one per year from 1938 through 1940, only the first found its way into English: **From the History of Human Folly** (1963).

The first book in English on the topic was **A Short Introduction to the History of Human Stupidity** (1932), by Walter Pitkin. Like many books, it was misnamed, being really a breezy essay on human folly, and failed, unfortunately, to generate any general interest in the topic. Then in 1959 came Paul Tabori's **The Natural Science of Stupidity**[c]—a superficial if entertaining collection of anecdotes culled from history—and in 1970 John Fischer's general cultural review **The Stupidity Problem, and Other Harassments**.

Although the term "Stupidity" does not appear in the title, **Groupthink** (1982), by Irving L. Janis, belongs on the shelves next to the volumes just cited. It is concerned with a specific cause of stupidity but has some general value to anyone interested in the topic and provides a number of good case studies of how leaders make both faulty and sound decisions.

Finally, Barbara Tuchman's book **The March of Folly** (1984) rates a place with the others. Although she honors the taboo against the word "Stupidity", preferring the cumbersome "Woodenheadedness" and newspeakish "Unwisdom", her book provides more case studies of leaders caught up in themselves. (Much of the material presented in Chapter VI is derived from examples analyzed by Mr. Janis and Mrs. Tuchman.)

When considering "Stupidity", it is important to distinguish between the term and the phenomenon. The term may be used to designate a mentality which is considered to be informed, deliberate and maladaptive. However, because of the existing taboo, this is seldom done. Usually, the term is used like an extreme swear word—a put-down for those deemed intellectually inferior, although this tactic normally reveals more about the attitude of the user than the cognitive abilities of the designate(s).

---

c Republished as **The Natural History of Stupidity** by Barnes & Noble in 1993.

Belief

As a disparaging term for members of an outgroup, the word "Stupidity" often indicates little more than a biased evaluation of behavior. If they do "X" it is stupid; if we do "X" it is smart or necessary. For example, political enemies voting to reduce the federal deficit may be considered socially irresponsible, while our cronies do the same thing because it is a fiscal imperative. As the same act may be interpreted as both stupid and reasonable (or brilliant), we do indeed live in a perceptual world of "A" and "Not A". Further, changes through time may alter prejudiced evaluations, so the label "Stupidity" may express nothing more than a temporal estimate made according to arbitrary standards subjectively applied to existing conditions.

As a phenomenon, stupidity is most often a limited and limiting experience pattern[7] (or, sometimes, one that is overexpanded and overextending). In any case, it is caused by a belief blocking the formation or function of one more relevant to given conditions. Something going on in the environment is not matched in the cognitive world because the existing schema is too emotionally entrenched to permit an accurate appraisal of incoming data. First and foremost, the mind is an instrument for belief —not for knowing nor for learning but for believing—and usually, it functions to maintain a schema, regardless of how debilitating that may be.

There are really two dependent aspects to schematic stupidity: one is that a schema induces stupidity, and the other is that a schema is stupid. Almost every schema induces stupidity in that a schema is a belief system which inhibits the formation of competing beliefs, hostile ideas and discomforting perceptions. Oddly enough, even a schema of "Open-mindedness" can be stupid if it inhibits the development of clearer perceptions and an appreciation of the better ideas among those available. This is the chief drawback of the liberal schema, which tends to treat all cognitions, beliefs, forms of behavior and everything else equally.

As for a schema being stupid, every one of them is by one standard or another, in that each is a compromise of the beliefs upon which a society is based, the ideas it promotes and the behavior it permits. An internally consistent schema may be repressively flat to the point of boredom for those who hold it while being maniacally disruptive to those around them. If a schema cannot motivate people to do anything more than just believe and exist, it and they may lose out to more inspiring belief systems of competing groups. At the other extreme, schemas which dominated and then died litter the byways of history. It is really this motivational dynamic of our social nature which makes our verbal schemas inherently maladaptive and us so chronically stupid.

It would be much easier for us to understand and accept this were it not for our conceptual legacy from the Age of Reason. In the eighteenth

Rationalism

century, it was presumed that people sought to understand their world and would eventually achieve an accurate and internally consistent picture of its complexities. Rationalists thought that people dealt with reality in an analytical, reasonable manner, with emotions under the direction of cognitive factors.[8] Although there are very few sworn Rationalists left, many students of human behavior are still encumbered by the flattering assumption that people are reasonable and wise—as in **Homo "sapiens"**, meaning wise.

In fact, confusion as to the relationship of wisdom to knowledge impeded our understanding of ourselves for years. Two hundred years ago, Rationalists believed that as we learned more about our world we would become wiser. That belief is no longer tenable. Knowledge accumulates; wisdom does not. For all our vaunted skills in communication, we still learn pretty much as do rats, with little wisdom passed on from one generation to the next and even less developed through education. Worse yet, each generation finds a new way to mess itself up because we do not behave even like knowledgeable rats. As knowledge accumulates, so do misconceptions, superstitions and idiotic ideas and beliefs of all sorts.[9] These do as much to shape our behavior as do immediate circumstances, since it is through our cognitive world that the stimuli we perceive are interpreted.

The Rationalists could not comprehend the nature of stupidity, intelligence or humanity because they viewed the universe as an expression of ideals in logical conflict with their opposites—good vs. evil, God vs. the Devil, etc. They did not perceive healthy behavior as a balance or blending of social needs with environmental conditions and group goals. Nor could they appreciate how wasteful it was to divine philosophical systems which were internally consistent but functionally useless because they existed only in splendid isolation. In fact, it was exactly such effete thinking that characterized the unenlightened Germanic revival of the ancient Greek tradition of impractical philosophy in the eighteenth century.

In that age, France ruled the land, England ruled the seas, and Germany ruled the air. The Teutonic schemas were beautiful in their logical consistency, but they did not relate to anything real, and although Kant never quite got around to saying so, there are only two valid criticisms of pure reason—one is that it is pure; the other is that it is reasonable.[10]

Unfortunately, the scientists in their structured roles and carefully controlled labs have been unable to do any more than the Rationalists to render analysis of the nebulous concepts of human nature and intelligence "Realistic", functionally valuable and intellectually valid. As psychologists have been unable to formulate an operational definition of intelligence, they have had to settle for trying to solve the problem of "Prob-

Problem Solving

lem solving". This is assumed to indicate intelligence and can be broken down into a number of identifiable components.

First, a situation must be perceived as a problem. The perceived facts must then be coded in a conceptual shorthand (words) which lend themselves to mental manipulations. Relevant facts may then be integrated in an assembly reflecting functional relations. The problem can then be divided into parts through controlled dissociation. Finally, a solution can be found through imaginative integration of verbal symbols into a new synthesis leading to an improved relationship with the environment.[11]

This concise summary of the problem solving process contrasts sharply with a comparable consideration of the many faces of stupidity. At the grandest level of generalization, behavior may be guided by an inappropriate schema. However, even when a relevant schema is operative, it may be misapplied in any number of inventive ways. First, information may be ignored. If perceived, the perceptions may be faulty. If accurate, they may be misinterpreted. If correctly interpreted, they may be disorganized. If organized, they may be manipulated in a faulty fashion (not at all or too much) by an imagination which is too weak or too strong. Poor language skills can contribute to the formation of sloppy symbols and clumsy conceptions. Inattentiveness can lead to the confusion of unrelated events, or there may be an inability to isolate factors from events which are concurrent but unrelated. The behavioral response may not be tested, or it may be poorly tested. It may be illogical (and therefore irrelevant) or too logical (and therefore unappealing).[12]

Unsuccessful behavior is obviously likely to result from any error in the problem solving process. Mistakes might cancel each other out but more probably compound each other. Of course failure might also result from the influence of unknown factors on those known and understood. More important, lack of success might be due to the fact that the people involved are not even seeking a solution to the given problem. If they do indeed perceive a problem as such, they might simply make an emotional response which is directed more toward relieving tension than finding a long-term solution to the situation confronting them.

It is crucial to bear in mind that the use of the term "Intelligent" or "Stupid" to describe a problem solver depends on the degree of success or failure perceived. In this matter, as in so many others, humans have proved to be rather biased judges. Our bias is inherent in our schemas, which make us both arbitrary and subjective.

We are arbitrary in the selection of criteria by which we judge. For example, a person may be judged a "Success" according to wealth, status, power, health, number of children, etc. The selection of the specific criterion used is culturally predetermined by the judge's background and completely arbitrary (in that two judges sitting side by side may disagree due to their backgrounds) and often irrelevant (i.e., stupid).

The fact that we are so consistently arbitrary has two major implications for the student of stupidity. The first is that the only thing we can really know about ourselves is that we cannot really know anything about ourselves. Over 100 years of unbiased scientific studies have conclusively demonstrated that we are arbitrary creatures incapable of making unbiased studies, particularly of our own behavior. If you need evidence of our arbitrary nature, review the more than 250 competing and often conflicting theories about human nature which have been proposed by behavioral scientists. Taken together, these indicate only that human behavior is so varied that it can be interpreted according to any number of standards to support any number of causal explanations.

The second major implication of arbitrariness is that it practically guarantees we are going to be stupid **because** it inhibits our recognition of what stupid behavior is, especially when we are involved in it.[d] One of the few consistent things about people is that we very seldom interpret our own behavior as stupid. Were we to do so, there would undoubtedly be much less stupidity. However, as judging behavior is such an interpretive process, we tend to favor explanations which confirm our sense of self-esteem.

More specifically, judgment is biased[13] by the existing schema, with arbitrariness and subjectivity contributing to the usually self-confirming result. First, criteria for judgment are arbitrarily selected, and then, within that limited context, subjective judgments are made. To continue with the example cited above, a politician would probably judge success by the criterion of power, whereas an industrialist might judge by wealth. Of course, wealth lends itself to objective measurement, in that money can be counted, but clever accountants can render financial affairs subjective by a little creative finagling.

In general, whatever stupidity is, it is induced by the biased judgments a person's schema imposes on his experiences and perceptions, as is illustrated by a probably apocryphal anecdote about a confrontation between an alcoholic ballplayer and his reform-minded manager. The manager called the player into his office one afternoon and placed an earthworm in a glass of water. The worm wriggled around quite happily until placed in a second glass containing alcohol, whereupon it promptly shriveled up

---

d In a similar way, our subjectivity makes it possible for us to indulge in behavioral excesses. Most cultural trends (development, stagnation, exploitation, etc.) become stupid as they go to excess, and they commonly go to excess because those responsible for them are too emotionally involved to judge their effects objectively.

Intelligence?

and died. "See that?" exclaimed the manager. "Sure," replied the player. "If you drink, you won't have worms."

The single, obvious lesson to be drawn here is that there is no single, obvious lesson to be drawn from what we perceive and do. Each person draws his own conclusions to suit himself, and this is where the behaviorists' model fails. Although success is a reward and failure is a punishment, just what exactly is being rewarded or punished (and even what constitutes success or failure—or even what constitutes a reward or punishment) is never quite clear, since we can draw the damndest conclusions as to what is going on in our perceptual world. Usually, the mind shapes perceptions according to a given emotional disposition, with experiences commonly teaching us lessons which are inherently biased toward the existing schema. As we are inclined to assume credit for anything positive and attribute blame elsewhere for anything negative that occurs around us,[14] we tend to become better adapted to ourselves than to our environment. It is this positive feedback system between our judged actions and beliefs which induces us to persist in behavior which others construe as stupid but which we consider as necessary or intelligent.

In the biased world of arbitrary judgments, it is easy to label an act as "Intelligent" if it can be and is construed as successful. However, the evaluation of a person's mentality according to the results attained by his behavior can be grossly misleading. Consistent with humanity's tendency to flatter itself, we often attribute to intelligence significant discoveries simply because they are considered major achievements in the development of civilization. Many of these were really just accidental and in no way due to foresight, planning or directed thinking. No one sat down to discover fire. America was discovered by Norsemen blown off course, Columbus searching for east Asia and Frenchmen following the cod.[15] Every step Dalton took to his atomic theory was either wrong or logically inconsistent,[16] and the discovery of penicillin was made possible by sloppy lab technique. None of these exemplifies intelligence, but if they do not, then to what does the term "Intelligence" refer?

"Intelligence" is the ability to process information efficiently—meaning, in behavioral terms, that data are related to relevant, effective reaction strategies. The amount of knowledge in a system can by indicated on a scale extending from agnostic (having no data) to gnostic (having all relevant data), with ignorance being the aversion to gather more. Overall efficiency of the system is measured relative to the achievement of "Appropriate" goals, whether they are explicitly intended or subconsciously hidden. The functional strategies available as possible coping responses are determined by past experience and perceived circumstances, and people are labeled "Intelligent" when the strategy employed in problem solving suits their skills and proves to be successful. Thus, in a general sense, "Intelligence" is the label applied to the successful application of a schema relevant to a given problem in a particular context.

By way of contrast, the term "Stupidity" is often used to indicate a behavioral strategy that failed, although all failures are not necessarily stupid. For example, a failure really does not reflect stupidity if it was due to the influence of unknowable factors. Failure may properly be regarded as stupid when it is caused by the application of an inappropriate schema or the misapplication of an appropriate schema to a problem. (Of course, a compounding occurs when an inappropriate schema is misapplied.) Earlier, we reviewed briefly the mechanical malfunctioning (i.e., ignoring data, misperceiving data, faulty symbolizing, etc.) which can contribute to maladaptive behavior. However, our most profound interest is not in the incidental breakdown of relevant schemas but in the inherently deleterious nature of the social psyche which tends to make all belief systems and their behavioral sets maladapted to each other and the environment.

Although the labels "Intelligence" and "Stupidity" are easy to apply in everyday life, efforts to elucidate the underlying schematic process have yielded little but confusion for centuries on end. Perhaps it is time to consider the possibility that something is wrong with the questions being asked or the questioners asking them. One obvious problem is that the questioners have human minds, which means that analysis tends to be both linear and biased. When using words, as most of us do, people can think of, at most, only one thing at a time.[17] This is the source of logic (thinking in ordered steps), and it puts us at a disadvantage when trying to understand the complexities of nature. Of course, our triumphs in unraveling the secrets of the physical universe have been possible because we can hold all other conditions steady while we selectively alter one variable at a time and observe dependent reactions. However, this approach is clearly of limited value in the study of the living world, in which the dynamic interdependence of systems is really the proper subject for investigation. On the other hand, when we use mathematical symbols rather than words to facilitate complex, computerized thought, the resultant models fail to reflect the entirety of the human condition because of our inability to quantify social values and spiritual intangibles.

We would be most successful in understanding ourselves if we not only asked the right questions correctly but had no predetermined criteria for defining our results. Nevertheless, this investigation of how the human mind works will emphasize stupidity. Why stupidity? Because it is ubiquitous! Because it is eternal! Because it has been neglected and ignored! Because it is found in overwhelming abundance in every phase and facet of the human experience, except as a topic in psychology texts and journals where it is overwhelming by its absence.

Thus, this will not be a balanced account of human behavior but an attempt to redress an existing imbalance. We will consider people not only as problem solvers but as problem creators. We will analyze not only how people succeed but how they fail. We will examine how human behavior can be both adaptive and maladaptive, and our profoundest discovery will be that intelligence and stupidity are not opposites but siblings—that they contrast with one another like two faces on the same coin.

When people interact with their environment, their behavior is directed by a schematic cognitive program. A particular act can be construed as "Intelligent" or "Stupid" depending upon the perceived degree of success achieved, but while these labels indicate opposite evaluations, they do not indicate different cerebral programs. Nor should stupidity be viewed as a disruption of an "Intelligence mechanism". There is a coping (or responding) mechanism in action, and it can be construed as stupid and/or intelligent depending upon the circumstances and the judges. This coping mechanism is multidimensional, but we shall focus on three arbitrary/subjective facets important to understanding stupidity—information processing, (mal)adaptation and relevance.

When considering the ways by which the human mind processes information, it is imperative to remember that the normal cognitive state is that of self-deception.[18] Our self-deceptive nature tends to make us stupid and, more to the point of our analysis here, certainly complicates the relationship of knowledge to stupidity. If people simply do not have relevant information available to them in a perceivable form, they are agnostic. However, if they ignore available information to the impairment of schematic accuracy, they are being self-deceptive and probably stupid. Likewise, if they misinterpret information, they are being "Data stupid", although there may be some social advantage to certain cognitive indiscretions. The person who ignores warnings of an impending disaster exemplifies the condition of being data-dumb. Military history, particularly, provides a litany of warnings unheeded or misconstrued.

The relationship of knowledge to stupidity is very circumstantial. Usually, the more one knows about a situation, the more successful his behavior is likely to be, but there is certainly no advantage in being overloaded with useless information. Worse yet, a person may worry himself sick if he is unfortunate enough to know about a threatening situation over which he has no influence whatsoever. Thus, having knowledge can be maladaptive, particularly if one has no coping response available.

If the relationship between stupidity and knowledge is circumstantial, that between stupidity and ignorance is usually reciprocal. Ignorance often exists because a schema blocks learning relevant to survival. On the other hand, stupidity may keep people ignorant by inhibiting behavior which would permit corrective learning. Instead, a positive feedback system may then make behavior increasingly maladaptive to the environment.

Data processing systems are most maladaptive when they make dysfunctional associations among bits of information. Stupidity is thus made more likely when there is not enough information (a party is to some degree uninformed), when there is too much (overloaded) but most commonly when it is wrong (misinformed). Stupidity also results when information that is present and correct is misemphasized or misinterpreted. Of course, more profound kinds of stupidity are produced from a complexing of different possible source errors—e.g., a misinformed person misinterpreting inaccurate data.

Just as many factors related to information processing may render a schema maladaptive, so is the determination of "Maladaptation" another very arbitrary/subjective facet of the general coping mechanism of the mind. For example, although a person may know his drug addiction is maladaptive over the long haul, getting the next fix is most compelling and in his immediate, short-term best interest. While it may be to a company's advantage to control more than a fair share of resources, this may be maladaptive for its supporting culture. Since determining maladaptivity depends so much on the arbitrary selection of the referent time scale and the standards and perspectives for judgment as well as the subjective evaluations of the judges, it, like "Knowing", turns out to be a rather imprecise guide for determining whether or not an act is to be deemed stupid.

When attempting to determine whether an act is adaptive or maladaptive, subjective judgments may be predetermined by the arbitrary selection of the referent itself. Is behavior maladaptive for an individual? His reference group? The environment? Behavior can be maladaptive relative to any or all of these referents. A system can be internally inconsistent, in which case it is maladapted to itself. It can pointedly disrupt communication and adjustment to other human systems, and it can prevent accurate feedback from the environment, to the long-term detriment of the capacity of nature to sustain the human experiment.

In any situation, there are thus three concentric fields for behavioral adaptation. The first is an individual system—a person, business group, team, etc. The next is the social context of the supporting culture—other individuals and groups. Finally, there is the ultimate arbiter of fitness—the physical environment. An intelligent policy is one which is advantageous to the performer, beneficial to humanity in general, and at least not detrimental to the environment. The development of the telephone might serve as an example of an invention which was a success all three ways.

Excesses

Mr. Bell and his family prospered; society was provided with speedier communication; and, except for some unsightly wires, no major negative impact on the environment was suffered. Usually, of course, a policy engenders new problems as it solves the old by emphasizing success in the first, limited category at the expense of the others.

Thus can a policy be both adaptive and maladaptive. In a short time span, a pattern of behavior can be construed as adaptive by those who profit from it while it is condemned by those who must endure it. Over a longer time span, individuals may alter their judgments about a policy as they become aware of unexpected and clearly negative results. As a bottom line, "Self-interest" is really the final criterion of judgment, and stupidity is behavior counter-productive to the welfare of the performer.[19] However, as the Shah of Iran, Ferdinand Marcos of the Philippines, and Nicolae Ceausescu of Romania found, the pursuit of one's own best interest may be maladaptive in the extreme.

The American industrial complex is a prime example of a dynamic association of similar organizations concentrating on their own short-term enhancement while contributing to the demise of the common life support system for general society. The government's response to the pollution and exploitation of our natural resources was the Environmental Protection Agency. On non-recycled paper, it was an ideal solution to a real problem. In reality, it was taken over by the industries it was designed to control. Its record in promoting pollution and the desecration of nature is unsurpassed in the annals of government. It is most easily dismissed as a misnomer: it should be called the Industrial Protection Agency or the Environmental Pollution Agency.

If it is difficult to generalize about and define maladaptation, it may be quite easy to recognize. Commonly, a behavioral trend goes to a self-defeating excess. Technological overdevelopment, political repression and human exploitation are all examples of maladaptation induced by the inherent tendency of cultures to function as positive feedback systems. Such excesses usually indicate a power structure caught up in the neurotic paradox: excesses are promoted as entrenched values both reinforce established patterns of behavior and render criticism less likely and less effective. In most cases, a dominant subgroup controls its supporting culture and may be living beyond the carrying capacity of the general society.

Maladaptation usually indicates that the coping mechanism really is not "Coping" but is simply responding in counter-productive ways. In a more common but less spectacular fashion, nonadaptive behavior indicates that the coping mechanism is responding in wasteful, irrelevant ways. As indicated above, the determination of relevance/irrelevance requires both arbitrary decisions and subjective judgments. The arbitrary criteria by which relevance may be judged are: context, personnel (the people who act and/or judge) and purpose.

The context of an object or behavior does much to determine—indeed, it practically defines—just what its relevance is. With regard to an object, as Winston S. Churchill observed: "A baboon in a forest is a matter of legitimate speculation; a baboon in a zoo is an object of public curiosity; but a baboon in your wife's bed is a cause of the gravest concern."[20] As with baboons, so with behavior. For example, the purpose of a doctor asking, "How are you?" may vary with the setting. In his office, it is likely an initial professional inquiry: on the street, it is probably a cultural throwaway.

Of course, context is not merely a matter of physical location. Behavior is invariably interpreted in a conceptual context, but it is the observer who arbitrarily selects the context in which relevance is judged. Thus, a patriotic hawk construes a Congressional vote for a large defense budget as laudable, whereas a frugal-minded economist would regard the same act as fiscal madness. The one views the purchase of vast amounts of military hardware and the maintenance of a sizable military force as necessary for national security; the other considers the money spent as an intolerable drain on our financial resources.

In a similar way, arbitrary personal considerations play a major role in evaluating the relevance of behavior. The critical factor is the relationship between the actor and the observer. If a friend and an enemy do the same thing, two different interpretations are likely. In terms of the example just cited, a political ally voting for a large defense budget is patriotic, whereas an opponent doing so is a reckless spendthrift.

There is often a real cultural loss when attention afforded an innovation and its considered worth (relevance) are both only secondarily determined by its inherent worth. The status of the innovator may either add to or detract from the value an offering is accorded. This social dimension is a major determinant in groupthink: e.g., when a leader sponsors a proposition, it is likely to receive a favorable reaction from his followers.[21]

The final criterion by which relevance is judged is that of purpose. Survival is a basic purpose of life, but when it becomes an end in itself, development ceases and is replaced by stagnation. When the purpose is simply to survive, human behavior is shaped by an opportunistic schema which is consistent only in the ease with which it yields to immediate circumstances. In such cases, life is a moment to moment struggle for short-term existence, with no thought given to long-term ramifications of behavior. Such a schema might be labeled "Meism/Nowism" as any other morality is simply an unaffordable luxury.

Misinterpretation

If behavior is not dictated by necessity, purpose can be created by a commitment to group norms. Accepting group standards can be stupid in that it defines adjustment in terms of a single, totally arbitrary value system. In general, most schemas are directed toward maintaining a status quo. Unfortunately, they may be so committed to themselves that they self-destruct. The process begins when an initially successful pattern of behavior becomes routine; when it serves to block innovation, it promotes failure. Reformers who then call for improvements in the schema are regarded as a source of distress. They are usually considered maladjusted and are not, in fact, adjusted to the cultural values society has enshrined as sacred. This particular kind of vexation is a growing problem today, as Western Civilization moves from making people equal in rights to similar in thought and behavior.

Because the judgments concerning the condition of "Knowing", the process of adaptation and the nature of relevance are so arbitrary and subjective, the coping complex is practically preprogrammed for stupidity. Indeed, tragedy often strikes when we let wishful thinking prejudice and/or prevent objective analysis of our interactions with the environment. It was just such a gratifying, self-confirming attitude on the part of NASA officials which contributed to the disaster of the space shuttle **Challenger** in January, 1986. The pleasing, working assumption was that everything was A-OK unless there was clear, uncontrovertible evidence to the contrary. The Morton Thiokol engineers responsible for the rubber seals (O-rings) between the booster rocket segments simply did not know if they would function at the low temperatures prevailing at the scheduled time of lift-off because they had never been tested under such conditions. In the absence of clear-cut data indicating likely malfunction, the engineers' expressed reservations and warnings of possible malfunction were blithely overridden by company executives and NASA administrators committed to the launch schedule and hence predisposed to assume the seals would work. Unfortunately, this proved to be an unwarranted assumption.[22]

In a more positive vein, we may derive some psychological and social benefits from the arbitrary and subjective ways we misinterpret our behavior. We commonly indulge ourselves by holding self-serving, inconsistent, unrealistic beliefs which characteristically contradict our behavior. With such cognitive aids, people can live in mental worlds which transcend reality and, to the extent that some healthy fantasies are realized, improve their circumstances. Such cerebral bootstrapping is common in humans and provides positive support for the coping mechanism which also can be so maladaptive.

For better and worse, the normal human mentality protects us from ourselves so that we cannot recognize the irrationality of our belief systems nor the inconsistencies between them and our behavior. What kind of inconsistences? We are rewarded for lying and cheating, although our superego value system tells us we should be fair and honest. We are advised to be meek and humble by the powerful and mighty. A person really could be justly accused of being stupid just for doing as he is told. Usually, most people are street wise enough to resolve such paradoxes pragmatically by seeking tangible rewards and leaving ethical considerations to the empty-handed.

Although recognizing stupidity is a very arbitrary/subjective process, it is quite easy to cite the conditions thought to characterize stupid behavior. Stupidity is commonly considered possible only when and where behavior is optional. If conditions have deteriorated to the point that a maladaptive course of action is the only one available, survival and not stupidity is the only consideration. However, it may have been somewhat stupid to have become boxed in in the first place.

On the other hand, it is just as stupid (in the sense of being wasteful) to underreach one's level of competence as to overreach it. In the first case, a system fails to develop its potential because it really is not challenged and therefore is not functioning as efficiently as it might. In the second case, stupidity can lead people into an environment or situation in which they cannot function effectively because their behavioral options are unsuited to the conditions at hand. In such a situation, an overambitious system finds itself unable to cope with the problems confronting it. Life's best compromise of competence is to find an environment in which a decent level of efficiency can be sustained over a long period of time, with a reserve capacity available for coping with emergencies.

Another condition thought to characterize stupidity is "Counter-productivity". A stupid schema promotes its own demise by directing its devotees to behave in ways "Perceivably" in their own worst interest.[23] To the extent that this is a valid point, it is one of the wonders of humanity that such behavior can clearly be so common. Nations sleep while their enemies march. On the other hand, paranoids defend themselves in the face of nothing. Companies squander millions on an executive's pet project while rejecting products or improvements which would net them millions and more. The crux of the matter is that stupidity is perceivable as such by all but those engaged in it at the time. These simply cannot perceive their own behavior as stupid because it does not appear to be so in terms of their own schema.

While failing to perceive their own behavior as stupid, people usually do see themselves as morally justified as they pursue their worst interests. A sense of morality is a human universal, with the many cultures differing only as to the specifics of their various ethical codes. Further, in each and every case, language plays a major role in determining the standards available for evaluating the morality of behavior.

In an absolute sense, there is, unfortunately for all the world's Pollyannas, no simple and direct correlation between success and any one system of (im)morality. Any trite generalization in this regard would have too many exceptions to be of any real value. At best, it might be said that an honest person puts himself at a short-term disadvantage when dealing with liars, cheats, phonies and frauds. These, on the other hand, run the risk of finding their nefarious successes hurt them in the long run.

Thus, stupidity can be viewed as a short-term adaptive strategy, in that it allows a degree of adaptability denied any strictly rational behavioral system, if indeed any such thing ever existed. To the extent that schematic rigidity inhibits the adoption of corrective measures to reduce the causes of existing problems, a system runs the risk of breaking rather than bending. Every living system is going to experience a certain amount of stress; it is in danger when behavior becomes increasingly maladaptive as stress increases.[24] This occurs when the schema ceases to be a guide for successful coping with the environment, establishing itself instead as a stumbling block to functional responses. In such situations, new stimuli may elicit an outmoded reaction pattern or perhaps none at all. When a schema finally does break down under stress, it ceases to be a guide at all, so even consistent stimuli may elicit chaotic responses.

In searching for intrinsic causes of human imperfections, it is most reasonable to begin with a consideration of genetics. Although stupidity is a behavioral universal, this cannot be taken as proof of a genetic basis for the trait, as it could be the legacy of a common culture or, more probably, a function inherent in culture. Most emphatically, stupidity is not mental retardation, which is caused by the many factors which limit the cognitive skills of those who test poorly on conventional IQ tests. Such factors may be genetic or chemical, as in the cases of drugs or poisons. Retardation may also be caused by head injuries and infections.[25] However, all such restrictions on the development of normal mental functions are irrelevant to the topic at hand. Stupidity is not a restricted form of intelligence but a normal mental function in its own right and an expression of our cultural rather than our genetic heritage.

There are, of course, any number of environmental factors which promote maladaptive behavior, but they really do not contribute directly to stupidity, as caused by an irrelevant schema. Some of the environmental factors which reduce adaptability are climate, diet and disease. In addition, other factors, like fatigue, age and drugs may play roles as well.[26] It is interesting to note that all the above factors hit the smartest hardest. The dull may get a bit duller, but the brilliant can suffer greatly. Thus, society loses not only by a drop in general responsiveness of everyone but particularly from the loss of creative ideas from the bright.[27] In this way alone do such factors contribute to stupidity.

Geography, for example, can play an indirect role in the development of stupidity.[28] Usually, seacoasts are areas of cultural interaction. Where transportation is difficult, as in the mountains, or where distances are forbidding, as on the plains, beliefs are less likely to be challenged and become more firmly entrenched. Of course, in a relatively constant environment, fixed beliefs may be quite functional, but when change does come, adaptation is then all the more difficult.

Climate has a more direct role in effecting stupidity. The oppressive heat and humidity in the Middle East and much of India no doubt played a role in the development of the fatalistic indigenous religions. An accepting, passive life style is adaptive to such stultifying and sultry conditions in that it keeps one from overheating, but it hardly encourages inventive enterprise. The tropics are stupefying in that they afford too much food and comfort naturally and provide too little stimulus for people to develop their potential.

By way of contrast, the moderate and varying climates of the temperate zones encourage people to interact vigorously with the environment as they make continual adjustments to changing seasons. In the past, for much of the year, work was a way to keep warm, so the climate encouraged an active work ethic. As working is a way of learning, by being actively engaged with the environment, a culture tends to thwart the development of stupidity.

On the other hand, the harsher the environment, the more stupidity is promoted, in that one cannot afford to be too sensitive to the rigors of his surroundings.[29] Thus, insensitivity to the point of callousness can be an advantage, with the hypersensitive sometimes breaking down under climatic and work induced stress duller compatriots may hardly perceive.

As if cultural stupidity is not enough, people have a tradition of deliberately stupefying themselves artificially to help them escape self-imposed stress. While there are reports of birds, elephants and monkeys selectively eating fermented fruit (presumably for the effect rather than the taste), people drug themselves en masse. Alcohol is one of our milder stupefiers and may have made civilization both necessary and possible. The standard saw is that nomads settled down to cultivate grain for food, but an alternative explanation is that they grew grain for the production of alcoholic beverages. The escape afforded by alcohol from the long-term stress of concentrated associations of town life may have permitted the development of civilization.[30]

Extremes

Even without artificial stupefiers like alcohol and narcotics to help them, people routinely achieve irrelevance by adhering to or seeking out a maladaptive schema. When indulging in such stupidity, they usually display certain symptoms characteristic of their condition. As mentioned above, ignorance commonly enjoys a reciprocal association with stupidity: this can take the form of a positive feedback system in which ignorance begets stupidity which begets further ignorance. Other symptoms of stupidity are often opposite extremes bracketing functional means. Stupidity can be due to as well as cause both insensitivity and hypersensitivity. If confusion is a stupid state, clarity in the expression of trenchant thought can be offensive and thus stupidly disrupt social coordination and cooperation. It may be equally stupid for a person to be either too slow or too fast in reacting to a situation.

However, under extreme conditions, any of the normally stupid extremes may be the operational ideal. Sometimes, we must be fast, callous, reckless or otherwise intemperate. Judging when conditions are abnormal enough to require the abnormal response is one of the ultimate subjective tests anyone can face. In such a situation, the standard rules no longer apply and emergency measures must be adopted if the system (individual or group) is to survive. Whatever the conditions, stupidity is the failure to apply the appropriate, relevant schema effectively.

While considering extremes, it is interesting to note that humans are extreme in their cultivation of stupidity. It is found in the animal world but is limited in both degree and kind. In more general terms, some students of human nature aver that there is nothing qualitatively distinctive about our species: according to this view, we are just a particular blend of many traits commonly found, although in different proportions, in all animal species.[31] Thus, our nutritional needs, bodily functions and behavioral habits are all considered typically animal—perhaps extreme in some cases, as with learning, aggression and stupidity—but not distinct in kind from our fellow creatures.

An alternate view is that we are indeed distinctive. Just what the distinction is has long been a subject of speculation. The "Soul" is one of the longest-lived attributes which is alleged to separate us from beasts which seldom kill their own kind and never en masse. More notably, language is thought to be a distinguishing human characteristic, and it is—as long as it is defined as the way humans communicate. Stupidity happens to be one of those many types of behavior which we share with our relatives. We have just perfected it and, thanks to language, given it a distinctly human twist.

The common feature in all cases of stupidity is that a given program of response blocks a more relevant reaction. In insects, the program may be very limited and keyed tightly to a few critical environmental stimuli. Differences may appear among the caste groups of social insects like bees —workers work, drones drone, etc.—but within each caste, there is remarkably little individual variation.

The nest building behavior of the digger wasp provides a classic example of the inability of an animal behavioral system to adjust to altered conditions. The usual routine of the female is to dig a nest, kill some form of prey, drag the victim to the nest, place it in the nest, lay eggs on it (the larvae from which will feed on the carcass after the eggs hatch), and then close the nest. This sequence might be considered the insect's schema for action, and it is usually quite effective, as long as there is no scientist around to play God. In the event of divine intervention with any step in the ritual, the rest of the behavioral program will be continued blindly, although it has been rendered pointless. If, for example, the prey is removed from the nest after the eggs have been laid but before it is sealed, it will be sealed anyway, dooming the offspring to a tragedy of larval dimensions.[32] The only reason this is not considered a classic example of stupidity is that the wasp has no choice in the matter. It is preprogrammed to follow a set pattern of behavior, with no adjustment to information feeding back from the environment. Once the schema starts the sequence of action, it runs to completion.

In contrast to the preprogrammed nature of insect behavior, vertebrates are characterized by an open genetic program. The responses of adults of a species will thus be similar to the degree that they share similar genes and experiences and different to the degree that the general patterns of behavior can be refined by unique experiences of each individual. While higher vertebrates can be individualistic, social behavior of vertebrates in general has been promoted and achieved by 1.) enriched communication systems, 2.) precision in recognizing and responding to individual group-mates by the learning of idiosyncratic behaviors, and 3.) the formation of subgroups within the general society. Usually, vertebrate behavior favors individual and in-group survival at the expense of the extended society.[33]

It is important to note that the process of learning, which is so crucial to the vertebrate way of life, is preconditioned in many species by a biological disposition to learn actions that are crucial to survival. This is the phenomenon of "Preparedness"[34] and is exemplified by the facility with which birds learn to fly and people learn to speak. It suggests that organisms may be preprogrammed to learn certain behaviors as part of their normal developmental process.

While "Preparedness" indicates a positive legacy from an organism's evolutionary past, the Garcia Effect demonstrates that there are biological predispositions in some species to favor the learning of certain lessons over others in the lab.[35] The average pigeon will learn to peck a disc to obtain food but will not learn to peck a disc to avoid a shock. For a rat, the same learning pattern is found: it can learn to press a bar to obtain food but cannot learn to press a bar to avoid a shock.[36] "Preparedness" and the Garcia Effect suggest that learning can be promoted or inhibited by a preprogrammed mental set in an organism. This is the effect of the schema on humans—it makes learning of certain things easier and others more difficult.

Outside the lab, animals of all kinds may be fooled by mimicry and deceitful displays of members of their own and other species. Birds, for example, may be tricked into playing hosts to the eggs (which usually look something like their own) and young of the scores of brood parasites which infest the avian world. In the case of the cuckoo, the hosts end up rearing the parasites' young to the exclusion of their own.[37]

Beyond showing the ability to cope more or less successfully with reality, higher vertebrates evince the cognitive capacity to live in a world of fantasy. This was demonstrated experimentally by B.F. Skinner's "Superstitious pigeons",[38] or so we like to believe. The birds came to make idiosyncratic jerking movements in response to randomly scheduled food reinforcement, behaving as if they thought their actions caused the production of food. Likewise, the "Rain dance" of Jane Goodall's chimpanzees[39] suggests a mental ability to associate effects with noncauses. Of course, in this case as well, the behavior does not necessarily indicate the cognitive world of the performers. The animals may simply be displaying emotion and releasing tension without presuming to influence that great chimp in the sky who makes it rain. However, it is reasonable to assert that such behavior indicates mammals can carry maladaptation to new levels of confusion.

In general, the mammalian life style emphasizes extended learning in fewer, slower developing individuals in contrast to more rigid behavior patterns in swarms or schools of quicker developing insects or fish. This necessarily means there is a premium on the adaptability of the individual in times of crisis, rather than a reliance on numbers to carry the species through. However reliable they may usually be, the patterns of behavior which are learned in the routine of daily life may be maladaptive in a short-term emergency situation. Adjustment of behavior to novel necessity is very much a learned process typical of the more adaptable mammals, like the primates[40] and particularly ourselves.

As with all of our other special traits, human stupidity is the culmination of a long train of development shaped by our evolutionary past, but meaningful generalizations about our psychic evolution are difficult because we are a compromise of all the incongruities of life. For example, our ancestors had to be adaptable but not too adaptable. They had to be calm, accepting, thick-skinned and slow-witted to survive the harshness and boredom of daily routine.[41] In contrast to this long-term disposition, on the other hand, they had to be responsive to emergencies and ready to adjust quickly when circumstances demanded a speedy and novel reaction. This basic duality of a long-term/conservative, short-term/innovative mentality made each step in cultural adaptation an optimistic gamble at best, as it rarely was absolutely clear at the time of decision if conditions warranted a new policy to deal with the problem at hand.

If balance was the key to survival, it was a balance of extreme potentials subjectively applied to naturally and culturally selecting conditions: e.g., sensitivity to environmental stimuli is necessary for survival, but either extreme (i.e., hypo/hypersensitivity) can cause a stupid response. Insensitivity provides a basis for stupidity in that what we do not know can indeed hurt us, so one measure of stupidity is what we fail to consider—what we fail to perceive, refuse to learn or omit from reckoning.[42]

At the same time, and in exactly the same way, insensitivity eased the way, for what we do not know cannot worry us. For example, insensitivity toward killing, blood and suffering was of survival advantage in our not so distant past. To the extent that fighting and killing determined survival, brutality was a necessity and sympathy a luxury.[43] Further, to the extent that people were inured to suffering, suffering was an acceptable way of life and death. Thus, the power of dullness made our last million years such a struggle and contributed to our acceptance of our struggling condition.

However, with the mean of sensitivity as the balanced ideal, those who reacted to cold, hunger, abuse and injustice died out.[44] Those who were insensitive to such conditions endured and transmitted their passivity to their descendants. This selective pressure was somewhat balanced by the simultaneous elimination of those insensitive to immediate threats and dangers. Thus, the human psyche was shaped for long-term tolerance and acceptance of difficult conditions while being responsive to short-term challenges of the moment.

The wonder of human culture is that anyone manages to grow up with anything like sanity and sense. Consider the fact that most people start life with the handicap of parental love. Of all forms of emotionally induced blindness, this is the blindest, and most of us get a double dose. As with others who love, parents are blind because they want to be, and for nearly two decades, the child is helpless to escape the best efforts of his parents to distort his self-image and sense of importance.[45]

Whatever limitations culture may have, it certainly is efficient at transmitting stupidity from one generation to the next (as well as developing it anew). Children receive a basic lesson from their parents and other adults who gain some peculiar pleasure in denying reality to them. It is quite common to say to a small child, "What a big boy you are".[46] Statements contrary to the obvious may be more comforting than the truth—"My, what a scrawny little runt you are!"—and have the added advantage of preparing the child for the adult world in which accuracy is commonly sacrificed to diplomacy.

In the first year, the child forms a basic information processing schema. This is the first step in the construction of a general religious belief system which will guide and limit future behavior. Also at this time, the child develops a fundamental sense of trust or mistrust,[47] which is another source of future stupidity: later on, the individual will find himself mistakenly trusting the untrustworthy or suspiciously dismissing honest people with sincere intentions.

A cognitive correlate of trust is the concept of object permanence, which is formed by the age of 18 months. By this age, the child can represent by mental image objects no longer in sight. The underlying, supporting assumption is that objects are consistent—that they remain the same not only when viewed from different angles or distances but even when they cannot be viewed at all. Thus, different perceptions can be associated with a presumably constant object.[48] This has potential for stupidity, in that objects sometimes do change and yet people will cling to their original images rather than adjust to an altered reality.

The age of two years is the age of language, with actions and objects being represented by verbal as well as visual symbols.[49] Classifying and grouping the symbols is accomplished according to the specific language of the social group. This is the process by which information is sorted and organized into categories which may or may not reflect relevant relationships found in the environment.

Along with the development of a child's cognitive world of ideas, a sense of rules and order also develops and undergoes transformation with maturation. For a young child, a rule is reality and is sacred because it is traditional. Even some adults never get beyond this stage, and, indeed, the basic rules of life, whatever they are, do not change. The older child comes to realize that stated rules are expressions of mutual agreement. They are seen to function by promoting social cooperation through individual constraint.[50]

Although the idea of rules may change, the system of assumed world order the young child inherits from his parents is a moral necessity to him. As he matures, he will be forced to resort to reason when the sacred and obligatory rules are challenged by people with other rules or by an amoral environment. He then may be pulled in a number of directions while trying to impose unity on the chaos of this experience.[51]

For all their inventive play, young children are really basically conservative. They hate change, as anyone who has dared change a word in a bedtime story well knows. Their cognitive expectations are very precise, with routine providing a sense of safety in a world which is often strange and unpredictable.[52] Generally, the more uncertain the external world appears, the more tenaciously the schema is held. It is important to note that the schema provides a sense of security beyond its functional capacity to provide accurate predictions of events. Whatever its flaws, it becomes the "Cognitive map" of the individual's reality and contains 1.) the worldview, 2.) the self-concept, 3.) the self-ideal and 4.) ethical convictions. Although it can cause stupid behavior by the way it both functions and malfunctions, its common presence indicates that the schema must also be, to a significant degree, truly adaptive.

Notes

1. Pitkin, W. 1932. **A Short Introduction to the History of Human Stupidity**. Simon and Schuster; New York. 21.

2. **Ibid.** 20.

3. Tuchman, B. 1984. **The March of Folly**. Knopf; New York. 46.

4. Matthew V, 22.

5. Ripley, G. 1839. **Letters on the Latest Form of Infidelity**. Boston, MA. 98-99.

6. Pitkin. **op. cit.** 25.

7. **Ibid.** 129.

8. Proshansky, H. and Seidenberg, B. (eds.) 1965. **Basic Studies in Social Psychology**. Holt, Rinehart and Winston; New York.

9. Pitkin. **op. cit.** 165.

10. Kant, I. 1781. **Kritik der reinen Vernunft**. (J. M. Dent & Sons; London. Translation)

11. Pitkin. **op. cit.** 40.

12. **Ibid.** 41.

13. Lewicki, P. June 23, 1992. Quoted in "Your Unconscious Mind May Be Smarter Than You" by D. Goleman. **The New York Times**. C11.

14. Lau, R. and Russel, D. 1980. Attribution in the sports pages. **J. of Personality and Social Psychology**, 39, 29-38.

15. Pitkin. **op. cit.** 14.

16. Holton, G. Jan. 1953. On the duality and growth of physical science. **American Scientist**, 41, 91.

17. Pitkin. **op. cit.** 286.

18. Lockard, J. and Paulhus, P. (eds.) 1988. **Self-deception: An Adaptive Mechanism?** Prentice Hall; Englewood Cliffs, NJ.

19. Tuchman. **op. cit.** 5.

20. Halle, K. 1967. **The Irrepressible Churchill: A Treasury of Winston Churchill's Wit**. World Publishing; New York. 153.

21. Janis, I. 1982. **Groupthink**. Houghton Mifflin; Boston, MA. 142.

22. Kolcum, E. Mar. 3, 1986. Morton Thiokol Engineers Testify NASA Rejected Warnings on Launch. **Aviat. Week and Space Tech**. 18.

23. Tuchman. **op. cit**. 5.

24. Smith, R. Sarason, I. and Sarason, B. 1982. **Psychology: The Frontiers of Behavior**. Harper & Row; New York. 487.

25. **Ibid**. 388.

26. Pitkin. **op. cit**. ix.

27. **Ibid**. 82.

28. **Ibid**. 307.

29. **Ibid**. 50.

30. Muller, H. 1966. **The Loom of History**. Oxford University Press; New York. 39.

31. Durbin, M. 1973. Cognitive anthropology. In **The Handbook of Social and Cultural Anthropology** edited by J. Honigmann. Rand McNally; Chicago, IL. 447-478.

32. Evans, H. and Eberhard, M. 1970. **The Wasps**. University of Michigan Press; Ann Arbor, MI.

33. Wilson, E. 1975. **Sociobiology**. Harvard University Press; Cambridge, MA. 381-382.

34. Seligman, M. 1970. On the generality of the laws of learning. **Psychological Review**, 77, 406-418.

35. Garcia, J., McGowan, B., Ervin, F. and Koelling, R. 1968. Cues: their relative effectiveness as a function of the reinforcer. **Science**, 160, 794-795.

36. Bolles, R. 1980. Ethological learning theory. In **Theories of Learning: A Comparative Approach** edited by G. Gazda and R. Corsini. Peacock; Itaska, IL.

37. Meyerriecks, A. 1972. **Man and Birds: Evolution and Behavior**. Pegasus, Bobbs-Merrill Co.; Indianapolis, IN.

38. Skinner, B. 1948. "Superstition" in the pigeon. **J. of Experimental Psychology**, 38, 168-172.

39. Goodall, J. 1971. **In the Shadow of Man**. Houghton Mifflin; Boston, MA. 52.

40. Washburn, S. and Hamburg, D. 1965. The implications of primate research. In **Primate Behavior: Field Studies of Monkeys and Apes** edited by I. DeVore. Holt, Rinehart and Winston; New York. 620.

41. Pitkin. **op. cit**. 80.

42. **Ibid**. 54.

43. **Ibid**. 99.

44. **Ibid**. 67.

45. **Ibid**. 438.

46. Freud, A. 1966. **The Ego and the Mechanisms of Defense**. International Universities Press; New York. 84.

47. Erikson, E. 1974. **Dimensions of a New Identity: The 1973 Jefferson Lectures in the Humanities**. Norton; New York.

48. Piaget, J. 1932. **The Moral Judgment of the Child**. Macmillan; New York.

49. **Ibid**.

50. **Ibid**.

51. **Ibid**.

52. Smith, **et al. op cit**. 366.

III. The Schema as Adaptive

The brain of an infant may be the blank tablet envisaged by Locke,[1] but as it develops into the mind of an adult, it is shaped by both experience and language. As the character of the maturing individual becomes defined, the mind shapes experiences decreasingly according to immediate stimuli themselves and increasingly according to linguistic interpretations of and emotional reactions to perceptions. Thus, the environment does not dictate human behavior but provides a context for its expression.

The basis for interpreting environmental stimuli is the schema—the cognitive program (Ger: **Weltanschauung**) which acts as a template for perceptual experience and provides expectations and explanations about objects and their relations to each other.[2] As a frame of reference for information, ideas and behavior, it defines the mental life of the individual.

Although social intercourse plays a role in structuring both ideas (i.e., verbal concepts) and behavior (physical action), there is often a discrepancy between expressed creeds and attendant activity. If it helps to visualize this discrepancy, think of the schema as a vee with the verbal attitudes of the data track represented by one arm articulating at a point with the other arm representing the normative attitudes of the behavioral track. Daily, routine behavioral acts and comments overlap at or near this point of contact. Moving from the point of congruence toward the open end of the vee, the correlation between the two tracks drops as circumstances become more challenging and the person becomes more self-conscious. The distance between the two arms represents the emotional potential built up by a person trying to maintain a positive, superego image while doing whatever must be done to cope successfully with the real world.

When the emotional involvement is minimal (near the point of the vee), there may be no awareness that a discrepancy between creed and deed exists at all. If the discrepancy is more marked, the defense system falters, and the person experiences the emotional discomfort of cognitive dissonance until behavior can be redirected into more appropriate forms or redefined in more acceptable terms. In extreme cases, an event may be so totally unexpected that there is no reaction, emotional or physical. Such a situation is incomprehensible in that it cannot be evaluated and dealt with within the context of the existing schema. During such an experience, a person may freeze like a rabbit transfixed by headlights.

While providing basic notions about principles of nature and theories about how the world works, the schema both fosters and inhibits further learning. It is particularly good at promoting learning of refinement, whereby established expectations are confirmed and reinforced and responses made more subtle. However, learning of novelty is made less probable and more difficult by preset patterns of thought which limit an individual's range of cognitive adjustment. Thus, the schema encourages self-corrective, fine tuning of itself even in cases where it remains a basically maladaptive behavioral program.

The learning process can be broken down into two interrelated steps: assimilation and accommodation.[3] Assimilation is the perception of stimuli and the incorporation of experience into an existing schema; it is accomplished by assigning an object or phenomenon to an established cognitive category, as defined by the individual's vocabulary.[a] Accommodation is the change or modification of the schema due to the assimilation of new information. Minor adjustments and modifications of the schema are very common and occur with little or no awareness or emotional disturbance. The resulting schema is the individual's attempt to reorganize his experience into a system which provides both some assurance of predictability and a basic strategy for behavior.

However, as an individual matures, the presence of the schema tends to dominate the process of assimilation by defining perception in progressively restrictive terms and by the formation of attitudes which evaluate perceived data. Attitudes determine whether a given fact is construed favorably or unfavorably. This point is easily demonstrated by a play on a standard form of humor: "I have some good news and some bad news: the Yankees won last night". This is good news to Yankee fans, bad news to anti-Yankee fans, and not particularly amusing to anyone.

There are three factors which may contribute to the formation of attitudes. First of all, attitudes may be rooted in a person's need to know about the environment. Such attitudes are data based and provide a verbal knowledge system to which incoming bits of information are compared or contrasted. Attitudes may also be adopted because of externally applied social rewards and pressures of normative group influence. Finally, atti-

a There are, of course, nonverbal schemas—e.g., those which permit us to interpret physical forms, body language, music, etc. However, as our prime concern here is with interpersonal stupidity, we will concentrate on verbal/behavioral schemas.

tudes may be expressions of the value system of the individual and provide him with the self-satisfaction of internal rewards.[4]

Along with their function of evaluating information, attitudes also act to promote the achievement of goals deemed to be worthy, to maintain self-esteem and to express views. Most important of all to students of stupidity, attitudes determine what a person considers to be his "Best interest". This is crucial if stupidity is deliberate, informed, maladaptive behavior—that is, behavior counter to one's own best interest.

The determination of "Best interest" thus turns out to be quite an arbitrary process. The basic problem with such an evaluation is that judgment is so "Attitudinal". For example, the extreme case of homicide may variously be considered a crime (murder), necessity (self-defense), heroic (combat) or simply accidental: the evaluation of the act depends very much upon the circumstances and the attitude of the judge.

It is by interacting with the environment that people reveal their attitudes—the beliefs, values and ideas which the reference group's language and norms have molded into a schema. Socialization internalizes this system so that it defines who and what a member is and does. As a young person matures or an initiate conforms, external rewards and punishments become anticipated and behavior adjusts to preconceived expectations.

It is important to note that the creed of a group functions as a unifying force.[5] Political and economic systems (e.g., democracy, capitalism, etc.) are often misconstrued as descriptive of how societies interact with their environments. Actually, along with behavioral rituals which are also binding, such systems are concrete expressions of ideological creeds which promote group unity. When the system's values are internalized, the individual feels himself to be part of a homogeneous group of people comfortable with themselves regardless of what they are doing.

One of the inherent drawbacks of intense group loyalty, however, is that it can interfere with logical analysis of problems.[6] The unacknowledged goal of most groups is maintenance of the schema. Reason is used to rationalize, and perception is skewed to favor the schematic quo. Conformity is the standard and intellectual integrity a threat to short-term, immediate complacence.

To achieve and maintain a healthy balance, there must be a dynamic trade-off between the short-term social needs of the group and the long-term intellectual imperative of information. This inherent compromise is typical of the human condition and displays itself as emotional conflict, suppressed or expressed, in all but the total conformist. One of the saving graces of a schema is that it can easily make minor adjustments—changes which reduce rather than arouse emotional tension. Accumulated minor adjustments can add up to a significant schematic alteration which

Language: Categories

would be traumatic if forced in one step. This process is comparable to the gradual evolution of one species into another by the accumulation of genetic mutations.

Minor adjustment make it possible to retain the schema while behavior adapts to novel circumstances. This is ideal for a stupid society, as it permits vague and ambiguous leaders to do somewhat more or less than they should while their followers can believe their cause to be sacred. As new behavioral norms emerge, so too may an identity crisis or conflict gradually evolve as traditional values are de-emphasized for the sake of group cooperation in new circumstances. The mechanism of successful schematic adaptation to novelty is, usually, largely language dependent, as it is language that provides the basis for our cognitive life, including the expanded mental capacity to be both very intelligent and very stupid.

Language probably evolved as a means of promoting group cooperation, but as a correlated side effect, it shaped the human psyche by the very nature of words. These are really audible symbols which represent selected, generalized aspects of the environment. In this sense, language is a code,[7] with each particular language necessarily biased and restrictive as it defines perceptions in terms of the specific culturally determined categories to which the encoded symbols are attached.

It is the linguistic requisite for categorizing which makes the human way of experiencing nature different from that of all other species. While making the human psyche unique, our verbal tradition prohibits "Freedom of experience" from the human condition, as no one can escape the subjective impact that the specific verbal values of his given reference group imposes.[8] Each language segments the environmental continua (motion, color, sound, etc.) into various arbitrary categories. Collectively, these provide the cognitive context in which members of the language group think, feel and evaluate experience.

Although categorizing permits the streamlining of some perceptions for the sake of mental efficiency, there are drawbacks. For example, every group is somewhat compromised by the very human tendency to indulge in "Stereotyping".[9] This is a process of "Overgeneralizing" to the point that important discriminable experiences are treated equally.[10] As we go through life, we fill out our verbal categories with discrete items or events. When we deal with people, for example, certain salient characteristics which members of some perceived group share in common (skin color, language, religion, etc.) are considered determining factors in evaluating the group in general. For the sake of expedience, individual variation may then be ignored and generalizing carried to the extreme that all people who can possibly be placed in a given pigeonhole are lumped together mentally under the label for that category.

51

Language: Definitions

Not only do we lose information to stereotyping, but the many groups of people become separated from each other because their different languages segment the common environment into different categories. Sad to say, when people in "Opposing" cultures experience the same stimuli differently, they often squabble about their perceptions and reactions rather than enlightening each other with complementary views of the world. Only in superficial matters can alternative interpretations be accepted as interesting or humorous without being threatening. On the other hand, most of history's great religious and military conflicts had their origins in perceptual/philosophical differences of competing groups which found they could not live in both the same and different worlds.

Such conflicts underscore the point that language functions as a "Defining system" for people.[11] It is through words that "Relevance" is determined for each of us by our culture, with behavior being shaped by the structuring of our reactions to what we construe to be relevant. What may really be relevant to one's best interest may not be identified as such by a necessarily biased language system.

This bias of the language system is based on the descriptive categories and labels used to construct a person's cognitive world (the verbal arm of the schema). As the schema is formed, accuracy and objectivity of perceptions are sacrificed for and by euphemisms. These enhance self-esteem by giving favorable interpretations of the actions of the individual and his reference group and negative stereotypes to rivals and opponents.

For example, in dealing with Vietnam, the Johnson administration began with a humanistic way of thinking and talking about the war but ended up following the lead of the military. The change to a detached attitude and then to a dehumanizing outlook was facilitated by the use of euphemisms. "Gooks" were to be converted into "Body counts" by "Surgical air strikes" which were to precede "Pacification".[12] It was as difficult to argue against such strategy as it was easy to misjudge American's best interest in those terms.

A few years later, the Nixon administration had a similar problem judging its own best interest and literally got hung up on the terminology of "Executive privilege" and "National security". The Nixonians were also easily disposed to use derogatory terms for the enemy—meaning the press, liberals and practically everyone else.

In contemporary American society, social integration is all the rage, although it is so commonly accepted as a goal that it is hardly ever even mentioned amidst the rhetoric about "Civil rights", "Affirmative Action", "Women's lib" and "Discrimination". The abuse of this last term in current language is most revealing about prevailing ambiguity in defining acceptable means of achieving an implicit goal.

Language: Attention

Although it is a synonym for "Distinguishing", "Discrimination" has been equated, through long historical association, with "Segregation". What we now have in the field of "Civil wrongs" is a rash of Affirmative Action laws which require discrimination as a means of achieving integration. Racial discrimination was supposed to have become legally unfashionable in the mid-1960's, but those passionately committed to integrating society have taken over the means of their historic adversaries, so now race is routinely required to be a consideration in hiring and promotional procedures. In the pursuit of "Equality", the Constitutional mandate of "Equal protection of the law" has been subverted, and contrary to a ruling of the Supreme Court,[13] minority groups have become special favorites of laws which have become means for compensating them for past experiences and current conditions.

Along with defining experience, language shapes the schema by directing attention[14] to certain facets of the environment which are deemed important by the verbal value system. Each language system has an inherent tendency to emphasize certain experiences while others are trivialized. Thus, accuracy of overall perception and objectivity of interpretation are sacrificed to verbal appeal as people focus on particular stimuli at the expense of others.[15] Of course, events of expected significance receive the most attention and analysis—particularly if they pose either a serious threat to the schema or an opportunity for a triumphant achievement worthy of the Superego Seal of Approval.

Language further serves as a memory system,[16] in that categorized, encoded experiences act as a basis for comparing the present with the past and for projecting future expectations. Naturally, the process of memory formation is systematically skewed off by omitting some events that happened and including others that did not. Thus, some aviation accidents (and even more so, near misses) can be redefined out of existence while fantasy provides a rosy picture of what self-serving experts at the FAA (Flying Accidents Administration) can trick themselves into interpreting and believing. The worst that can be said about language in this regard is that it allows people to remain firmly in touch with their delusions.

While examining the role language plays in the formation and functioning of the schema, we have considered it as a system for encoding, categorizing, stereotyping, defining, focusing and memorizing. We should not forget that it also functions as a communication system, making the individual's schema a product of and contributor to the group creed. As a means of sharing experiences, language is quite efficient, but as a means of permitting people to talk to and about themselves realistically, it is too biased to allow accurate self-analysis.

53

As a belief system, the schema promotes coping with some problems while limiting the ability to recognize even the existence of others. The schema promotes coping with acknowledged problems if the discrepancy between verbal beliefs and necessary behavior is emotionally tolerable, so in such situations, both individual and group efficiency is enhanced. However, when the discrepancy is so pronounced as to make people self-conscious, and when coping has to be treated as heresy, psychological and social disruption result from the delusive mental set of stupidity.

Interestingly enough, living out the expressed creed—that is, living up to the ideals—can also be aggravating to the devout who flout their beliefs in daily life. Christ was crucified for fulfilling prophesies and embodying ideals. Like most great rebels, he endeavored to live up to stated standards; unlike most, he did. For example, his kicking money lenders out of the temple was an expression of his intolerance for organized impurity. Such a person may be a great model for the dispossessed but is very dangerous for the establishment, so he was betrayed by the leaders of his own community. In this case, they responded in a manner representative of any leaders who would be displaced if their promises were realized, and they had no difficulty recognizing what course of action was in their own best interest.

In the absence of whistle blowers, who are usually crucified to the degree that they live up to the creed, language maximizes the potential of a social group to cooperate at whatever is accepted as necessary. Ironically, it promotes cooperation among members by inhibiting an appreciation of exactly what it is they are doing or to what extent they have either over- or underdone it. Hence, although it normally functions as a screen between people and their environment, language can become a barrier if perception and cognition become skewed off and distorted for the sake of biased values.

In the two dimensional world of the schema, information from the reality of the behavioral environment is often redefined by the social imperative of language. An individual may find himself experiencing momentary cognitive dissonance[17] when finding incoming data from the world of "Doing" contradicting or conflicting with his ideology—the system of ideas built on his established beliefs. The usual reaction in such a situation is to "Save the schema" at the expense of learning about and adjusting to the environment. Thus, numerous Freudian defense mechanisms (e.g., rationalization, repression, suppression, etc.) function to keep individuals content with their superego value systems, albeit at the cost of improving the schema.

Physical reality may be a better source of information, but social values are preferable,[18] as they are comforting and reassuring even while they are misleading. The social world is really a symbolic environment of subjective judgments, all routinely condoned and defined by the prevailing language system. Incoming perceptions are compared to the established schema, and if a way of fitting them in can be found, it will be. If none can be found, the data are usually rejected by the defense mechanisms mentioned above. In more extreme cases, undeniable perceptions may force an uncomfortable awareness on an individual (or discussions in a group) which eventually lead to a new, more inclusive schema.[19] This changing of one's mind is the last resort, however, particularly if it tends to isolate an individual from his social group.

A group is defined as "Individuals who share a common set of norms, beliefs and values" (i.e., a schema). The behavior of any member is usually of consequence to all other members,[20] and for most people, the social support of the group is vital in that it defines existence. A sense of belonging is one of the most compelling factors in the human experience and the feeling of isolation a tempering sensation unpleasant to most. The vast majority of people do almost all their learning in the immediate presence of others who serve as teachers or role models. Thus, socialization proceeds as initiates learn appropriate behavior and correlated linguistic values which make group members out of an assembly of individuals.[21]

Norms function in the formation of the schema by providing social reinforcement (positive and negative) to the development of both the linguistic value system and the behavioral control system. It is group norms which define group values by shaping the language, attitudes, sentiments, aspirations and goals of the members. These give the in-group a sense of identity and a degree of solidarity proportional to the hostility which may be directed toward conflicting out-groups.[22]

Norms function to induce conformity wherever social organization is found. They provide the means group members use to exert subtle and indirect pressure on each other to think and behave appropriately. They are the customs, traditions, standards, rules, fashions and other unofficial criteria of conduct which organize the interactions of individuals into the codified behavior of group members. In fact, the initiate becomes a member to the degree that he focuses on the norms of a specific group and guides his actions according to them.[23] Identification is complete when the norms become internalized and function as subconscious reward systems. They then serve as the criteria that sustain the attitudes and objectives of the group as members' judgments and interpretations of perceptions tend toward conformity. The result is similarity if not uniformity of thought and action[24]—a condition which can be regarded as normal or intellectually depressing.[25]

The Reference Group

Of particular importance in formation of the schema is the role norms play in shaping the attitudes of group members, since attitudes are the evaluative components of the schema. That is, it is through social norms that words come to be evaluative labels with positive or negative connotations for group identity and survival. Usually, group attitudes are formed as members concurrently share experiences.[26] Such common experiences provide the basis for the formation of attitudes which express the emotional values of and make certain words loaded terms to members (e.g., "Liberty" to revolutionaries, "Good Christian" to the local holy and "Old Siwash" to loyal grads).

These loaded terms and the attitudes they signify provide standards of thought, expression and behavior for the individuals who consider themselves members of the group. Norms and attitudes then become mutually reinforcing because the attitudes of the group, expressing its essential values, provide strong psychological pressure on members to honor the norms by conformity. In fact, norms and the verbal attitudes they engender make it very likely all true-blue members will think, feel, believe and behave in socially acceptable, predetermined ways about relevant objects and events.[27]

When a group determines the set of values an individual uses for judging behavior, it is known as his "Reference group". By shaping verbal attitudes with emotionally ladened terms, the reference group provides a standard or base of comparison for evaluating one's own behavior as well as that of others.[28] As identity with a group develops, a self-conscious sense of obedience to expectation is replaced by a devoted commitment to common values. The fully functional member is a collaborating component of the group and contributes to perpetuating group norms by cooperating with colleagues.

Of course, a reference group is all the more effective in imposing its values on members if it surrounds their heads with halos and arouses in them a sense of holiness. The emotional attitudes then become even more effective in promoting conformity to norms as they assume the mantle of moral righteousness. Beliefs condition the existence of any social group and become all the more firmly entrenched if they are sanctified as they are inculcated into the schemas of the devout. The most effective beliefs structure both the consciousness and the conscience of group members.

Along with shaping verbal attitudes into ethical values, group norms serve to regulate the behavioral actions and interactions of members by providing both a communication network and social support for each individual. The best that can be said for the functional value of norms is that they promote group cooperation. If they do this, the beliefs they promote and sustain will gain the status of inner ideals. Once a belief is en-

The Gold Effect

sconced in the schema to the point of unilateral respect, it defines "Moral realism" which supports and transcends the "Verbal realism" of attitudes expressing its basic values.[29] This process can go to an extreme, as co-operating members all sharing the same values reinforce their common beliefs about reality.

With such social support, a new or altered schema may achieve mass acceptance if it once is established in the minds of a simple majority of group members. This self-promotion of a belief system through intensifying reinforcement is known as "The Gold Effect", having been first described by Professor Thomas Gold, F.R.S.[30] The process is akin to genetic drift in that in cultural life, a field is dominated by a factor (an idea rather than an allele) not because it is superior to competing items but simply because it is more common. This fact alone enhances the likelihood that, in cultural life, a self-reinforcing fad will become a mania. In terms of schemas, a popular belief can become extremely popular even if popularity is not directly dependent upon accuracy or veracity.

Such an extreme may be ideal, if the standard of success is group cohesion. A legitimate goal of any society is to keep disputes within reasonable bounds, which is exactly what the common value system of a shared schema renders more probable. Being a human system, it rarely achieves an ideal 100% efficiency rating, but the schema, as formed by common norms, does function to reduce frictional conflicts within a given group. Many cultures provide forums (soapboxes, letters to editors or Congressmen, public hearings, etc.) where the disgruntled can vent their emotions without much likelihood of anything being settled or disturbed. A classic example of this phenomenon is the Song Singing of Eskimos—a ritual in which two disputants compose insulting songs which they sing as loudly as possible at each other.[31] Although nothing may be settled by such rituals, they do reduce psychic and social tension by permitting people to express their grievances and release their emotions.

If coping with given problems is too difficult within a static, well defined value system, a group may sacrifice its standards for the sake of cohesion. For example, students unqualified to receive diplomas may get them anyway, so as to avoid hurting their feelings. This tactic of inflating academic symbols does not really address the problem of learning, but it has a positive, short-term effect on some images and is therefore good public relations. In general, a lag or tension is characteristic of a dynamic schema, as new behavioral norms conflict with a preconditioned, if outmoded, verbal value system.

Of course, the cultural impact of any particular schema is diluted by the many interpretations it receives from the individuals and subgroups which compose most reference groups. For example, the grand "Western

Cohesion

schema" is subject to national variations which define the citizens of the Western nations on the international scene. Further, the American variant is subject to different interpretations on the domestic scene by businessmen and laborers, policemen and preachers, Christians and Jews, etc.

This process of schematic interpretation is somewhat complicated by the dynamic interactions of the given reference group with its environment. When the group is threatened or impacted by external forces (natural disasters or conflicts with competing groups), the schema serves as a rallying point, commitment to it intensifies and cohesion is enhanced. The rampant patriotism of Americans in 1944 exemplified this phenomenon: businessmen and bankers, lawyers and laborers all tended to emphasize their common nationalistic schema and conformed to patterns of thought and behavior in the best interests of their country. By way of contrast, in 1946, there was a tendency for subgroups and individuals to polarize by perceiving and interpreting events according to their own best interests within the larger context of the national supergroup.[32]

Although intense cohesion may be entirely appropriate during temporary emergencies, the forced, long-term cohesion of totalitarian states is the arbitrary concoction of leaders committed to themselves. Naturally, a standard ploy of such leaders is to conjure up or create external[b] threats and crises so as to promote cohesion and justify repression.

Cohesion can also be artificially sustained by deliberate attempts of leaders to bypass the rationale of the schema and appeal directly to the emotions of the people. Hitler was past master at arousing enthusiasm by the structured use of the irrational.[33] His favorite method was the induction of mass hysteria through the use of symbols, uniforms, marches, salutes and national games.[34] His goal was the development of an ethnic/racial pride, and his incredible success in achieving that goal was due to his dealing directly with the attitudes of his followers. He provided something they valued and wanted to believe in—themselves. The logical implications of the Nazi ideology had their own appeal to some but were largely (dis)missed by most.

If we shift our focus of attention from the schema to the individual person, we find that each is partisan to many schemas, as each of us is a member of a number of different reference groups. A person is a citizen of a country, an employee of some organization and a member of a family. As a member of each group, the individual has at least one role to

---

b Looking at it the other way, the Arab countries surrounding Israel have promoted its survival by posing a long-standing, ineffective threat to its existence. Were they to leave it alone, it might self-destruct from internal bickering.

Roles

play and has an appropriate schema to guide his thoughts and actions as he shifts identity: e.g., a man can be a son to his father while being a father to his son. At each level, from supergroup to subgroup to individual and for each role, there is a schema to be adopted and applied by people cast in roles that shift with issues and circumstances.

For the sake of contrast, it is interesting to note the fundamental difference between human roles and insect castes.[35] In highly social insects, an individual is a member of a caste, which is a "Life role". It is a soldier, a worker, a queen, etc. for all of its adult life. Determination of caste membership may be genetic, as in the case of the haploid drones of bee colonies, or environmental, as exemplified by the queens, which develop under the influence of royal jelly. Also note that in all groups of animals where cooperation is vital, it is accomplished by role playing. Only in herds, flocks and schools (of fish) can masses of equal individuals be found, and such groups are characterized by the lack of differentiation of members, with at most only leader/follower designations.

Among humans, anarchy and mass riots are the exception and indicate a breakdown of traditional norms. People are peculiar in that they usually compete for sharing. They have roles and rules for this phenomenon of cooperative conflict, and the winners and losers are usually pretty clearly defined in terms of a commonly accepted and disproportionate reward system. The rules are laws and norms which define how the role players should interact.

Within a group, the emphasis must be on cooperative role playing. There are leaders and followers, thinkers and doers, rule makers and rule breakers. There may be any number of roles, all usually defined in terms of their mutual interactions.[36] For example, in an educational institution, administrators, faculty members and students all have interacting roles to play relative to each other. Such interactions can be formally defined by laws or rules as well as informally regulated by norms and taboos. In all situations, of course, there is considerable room for individual variation, depending on the personalities of the particular players. However, the basic principle is that all members of a group share a common schema which they interpret according to their specific roles.

These differences in schematic interpretation give the various, interacting role players the sets of guiding expectations they need to gain the rewards and avoid the sanctions of the reference group. Conformity to expectations is usually the best policy, as it promotes cooperation within and among groups. "Rights" and "Truth" usually have little meaning and less impact on decisions about behavior. Most of these are made subconsciously and follow neural paths of least resistance leading to social paths of greatest acceptance. Along with the language of the major reference group, each subgroup has its own identifying jargon to help its members define their place and fulfill their roles. Also, role players have little rituals—manners and mannerisms—which facilitate communication and cooperation within and between groups at all levels of organization.

Thus, the strategy most conducive to successful role playing is one of conformity to reference group norms. "Fitting in" is usually something of a "Lube job"—a matter of confirming existing beliefs by telling people what they already know and doing what they expect will be done.

A given individual has, of course, many roles. In fact, a person has exactly as many roles as there are groups about whose opinion he cares. Unfortunately, playing roles in different groups can occasionally create dilemmas and contradictions in behavior—especially when one tries to be loyal to conflicting reference groups.[37] A common type of role conflict occurs when one role offers immediate, material rewards while the superego value system of another reference group twinges the conscience. An example of this might be the Christian businessman who wrings his hands over the ethics of making a cutthroat move to advance his career in the corporate hierarchy. A person experiencing such a role conflict has to choose or compromise between external rewards and basic morality.

In many cases, an individual may not be aware of the inconsistent or contradictory demands different roles may be making on him, since the human mind has a great ability to compartmentalize roles into particular settings. Thus, a person may be a good Christian on Sunday, a successful businessman during the week and himself on Saturday. Most of the time, such distinctive role programs can be separated subconsciously so that psychic duress is minimal or absent.[38]

Occasionally, an individual may be forced to alternate between conflicting roles. An example of this might be a student who plays teacher for an interim. Generally, this is not much of a problem, as most competing groups are usually distinctly separate with few, if any, common members: not many businessmen are also members of a union; nor are there many Jewish Christians nor many sailors in the army. However, a person trying to alternate conflicting roles does have a problem, as meeting the expectation of one group may cause censure by the other.[39]

Such problems may remain potential, however, and not even apparent under routine circumstances. If there is any inconsistency in behavior, it may pass unnoticed as the conflicting roles normally are separated by time and/or space. A business executive who moonlights as a card carrying musician can play such conflicting roles comfortably enough. On the other hand, a crisis may force a person to choose a role—forcing recognition of who he really is. During a disaster, public servants may favor

The Self

their families over their jobs. Of course, this is a crucial conflict if the job is related to relief efforts and public safety.[40]

As a person shifts roles with changing circumstances, certain attitudes and elements of behavior remain constant and define the "Self".[41] As a manifestation of the individual's core schema, the self consists of perceptions, motives and experiences fundamental to identity. Moving outward from this central, consistent essence of character, each person has multiple, superficial attitudes and behavioral programs designed for the various roles to be played—each slightly different and each relating to a different reference group. Behavior in any situation is an expression of the self drawn out by the given role applied to specific conditions.

Expression of the self by role playing may not always be healthy.[42] Although it is normal for people to play roles, in that most people do so most of the time, it can be distressing. If playing a particular role means hiding one's real self, then that is the price that must be paid for the social reward of acceptance. While it may be psychologically distressing to hide from a required role, it can be socially deleterious to bury oneself in a role.[43] Roles and situations are often said to dehumanize or "Deindividuate"[44] the people caught up in them, but it is very human for individuals to take narrow roles to uncritical extremes. Even the happy state of "Being oneself" in a congruent environment can be both ideal and injurious, if the role has become limited or the environment artificially contrived. An example might be the archetypical "Pig" policeman who loves to push people around and gets away with it as long as official word of his abuses can be contained within the precinct.

Expression of the self is also affected by the fact that each role has as many dimensions as it has functions. For example, the leadership role has two interrelated functions—goal achievement and group maintenance. Goal achievement requires organization, motivation, sanctions and concentration on relevant environmental factors. Group maintenance depends on mutual respect, trust and friendship of members. A responsible leader accomplishes a given task while maintaining or enhancing group identity usually by being a good role model. However, there is a duality intrinsic to many roles and an inherent ambiguity in determining just how effective any leader really is.[45]

Of course, personality plays a part in what kind of leader a given individual is, as a comparison of Generals George S. Patton and Dwight D. Eisenhower makes clear. Patton was goal oriented and one of our best combat commanders; Eisenhower was more the diplomat skilled at maintaining group cohesion. It was the Allies' good fortune in World War II that both found their appropriate niches and played their proper roles.

Ambiguity

For a group to realize its goals, the leader must coordinate the roles individual members play. One way to succeed in this respect is to build on the fact that members sharing a common schema will tend to assume mutually supporting roles which promote cohesion. Although their specific behavioral roles differ, members will interact effectively if there is common agreement about the desired goal. For example, in team sports, the players at various positions have different roles which will interrelate smoothly as long as everyone is committed to the ideal of winning.

Unlike sports events, when games end and teams disband, many challenges a society faces are eternal[46] and are dealt with by groups which seem as perpetual as the problems they never solve. A potential problem of and for such permanent groups is that they become committed as much to maintaining their roles as they are to fulfilling them.[47] For instance, disease is certainly older than medicine, but the medical profession is well enough established to have structured ambiguous roles for its practitioners. This was demonstrated by the reaction of the American Medical Association to a rash of malpractice suits which recently plagued its members. A number of possible reforms were suggested to reduce such suits—not malpractice, mind you, just malpractice suits. For example, one suggestion was to shorten the period a patient would have to file such a suit. This would be fine for the doctors, if not their victims, and it shows that one of the roles doctors play is directed toward keeping themselves in business as they attempt to play the role of healers.

If there is ambiguity in this kind of role playing, it is because there is ambiguity in life. Ideally, doctors would be acting in their own best interests simply by acting in their patients' best interests. Of course, most of them do this most of the time, but that is not enough in our contemporary, legally oriented society. There is an inherent ambiguity in the expression "Health profession". Medicine is a business, so most doctors play two roles, looking after their own wealth as they look after their patients' health.

For the student of stupidity, the important point is that the ambiguity of "Best interest" is due to the arbitrary nature of role dependent judgment. This can make it difficult to determine whether or not a particular act is stupid or not. A person may act in his own worst interest in one sense while playing out the requirements of a conflicting role. Even within a given role, a person may have to emphasize one aspect of it to the neglect of others. A resultant decision or act may be deemed stupid by a judge who considers that which was sacrificed to be more important than that which was accomplished. Even a person's intentions provide no reliable standard, as they may be misguided and shortsighted and ultimately work against him. All things considered, "Best interest" turns out to be quite unreliable as a guide for evaluating stupidity. Such a judgment is usually ambiguous because it is invariably based on an arbitrarily selected standard, so stupidity is thus often induced because a person can easily find some emotionally appealing standard to justify his actions to himself and will then persist in behavior which may work to his actual detriment.

In the face of ambiguity, one may fall back on a more general schema to find a basis for defining a proper role, reducing perceived conflict and establishing a program for response in confusing circumstances. In American society, the official schema is the law. Laws provide guidelines for behavior and courts arbitrate when conflicts cannot be settled informally. Of course, the law itself is as ambiguous as lawyers can make it,[48] so Americans often fall back on business principles as guides for judging behavior. For example, for hospital administrators, the crucial criterion for admittance is not a prospective patient's state of health but his ability to pay. When a person goes to a clinic, he needs to take his lawyer and accountant. Treatment begins only after payment is guaranteed and forms for medical irresponsibility are filled out. (It is a virtual Godsend that the law of "Malice of intent" which gives the media license to libel does not also apply to the medical profession.)

Ambiguity is compounded by the fact that, in most cases, a role is shaped by a schematic compromise of means with ends. Most people have general goals (happiness, wealth, etc.), and most behavior toward these goals is guided by general constraints (laws and ethics). That is, as most of us seek to achieve our goals, certain forms of behavior are proscribed and others condoned. Only in extreme cases is a schema dominated by an "End" to the point that a totally unscrupulous person (like a Hitler) would do literally anything to attain it. Likewise, only in exceptional cases (like loving Christians) do people live by a schema which defines success in terms of how they behave rather than what they achieve.

If there were less ambiguity in life, people would be clearer about their goals and more easily find appropriate means of achieving them. The schema is a general guide which provides a quasireligious ethic for behavior. This may or may not be consistent with the goals, which are determined largely by the emotionally loaded terminology of the reference group.

For example, in the field of civil rights, the change from discriminating against blacks and women to discriminating for them marked a great change in attitude toward the races and sexes but no change in attitude toward discrimination. The goals flip-flopped from segregation to integration, while the means, however ill suited to the new end, remained the same. In this specific case, the change in attitudes toward minority groups was accomplished as awareness of the inconsistency between idealized

Adaptation

goals and behavioral reality made people uncomfortable with their traditional values and norms. Majority group members transcended their psychological inertia when they realized they would be more comfortable with accommodation than with continued resistance to social pressures.

When values become tarnished by the realization that they have ceased to be serviceable, and problems of the street overcome nostalgia, beliefs change. We saw this in the South in the mid-60's, and we see it in eastern Europe today. Norms and attitudes are recast into new molds as schemas are altered in response to problems which can no longer be ignored. A schema provides a set of beliefs (which pass for an understanding about the universe), a program for directing behavior and, most important of all, a sense of identity. As a guide for a person attempting to cope with an uncertain environment, the schema is adaptive until being oneself becomes too costly in terms of schematic values. Then the attitudes which define the self must change if the schema, in even a modified form, is to survive at all. Of course, to the extent that the schema inhibits effective adjustment to the environment, it is clearly maladaptive.

Notes

1. Locke, J. 1690. **An Essay Concerning Human Understanding**. Bk. II, Chap. I, Sec. 2.

2. Hamilton, D. 1979. A cognitive-attributional analysis of stereotyping. In **Advances in Experimental Social Psychology** edited by L. Berkowitz. Academic Press; New York. Vol. 12, 53-84.

3. Piaget, J. 1932. **The Moral Judgement of the Child**. Macmillan; New York.

4. Proshansky, H. and Seidenberg, B. (eds.) 1965. **Basic Studies in Social Psychology**. Holt, Rinehart and Winston; New York. 104.

5. Arnold, T. 1937. **The Folklore of Capitalism**. Yale University Press; New Haven, CT.

6. Proshansky and Seidenberg. **op. cit.** 616.

7. Smith, R., Sarason, I. and Sarason, B. 1982. **Psychology: The Frontiers of Behavior**. Harper & Row; New York. 215.

8. Whorf, B. 1956. Science and Linguistics. In **Language, Thought, and Reality: Selected Writing of Benjamin Lee Whorf** edited by J. Carroll. MIT Press; Cambridge, MA.

9. Lippmann, W. 1922. **Public Opinion**. Harcourt, Brace; New York.

10. Brown, R. and Lenneberg, E. 1958. Studies in linguistic relativity. In **Readings in Social Psychology** edited by E. Maccoby, T. Newcomb and E. Hartley. 3rd ed. Holt, Rinehart and Winston; New York.

11. Sapir, E. 1964. Cited in **Language in Culture and Society: A Reader in Linguistics and Anthropology** edited by D. Hymes. Harper; New York.

12. Janis, I. 1982. **Groupthink**. Houghton Mifflin; Boston, MA. 111.

13. Bradley, Jus. J. Oct. 15, 1883. **United States v. Singleton**. 109 U.S. 3.

14. Brown and Lenneberg. **op. cit.**

15. Herskovits, M. 1950. **Man and His Works**. Knopf; New York. 542ff.

16. Durbin, M. 1973. Cognitive anthropology. In **The Handbook of Social and Cultural Anthropology** edited by J. Honigmann. Rand McNally; Chicago, IL. 450.

17. Festinger, L. 1957. **A Theory of Cognitive Dissonance.** Stanford University Press; Stanford, CA.

18. Festinger, L. 1954. A theory of social comparison processes. **Human Relations**, 7, 117-140.

19. Kuhn, T. 1970. **The Structure of Scientific Revolutions.** 2nd ed. University of Chicago Press; Chicago, IL. 15-22.

20. Proshansky and Seidenberg. **op. cit.** 377.

21. Smith, et al. **op. cit.** 197.

22. Sherif, M. 1958. Superordinate goals in the reduction of intergroup conflict. **American J. Sociology**, 63, 349-356.

23. Sherif, M. 1965. Formation of social norms: the experimental paradigm. In Proshansky and Seidenberg. **op. cit.** 461.

24. Proshansky and Seidenberg. **op. cit.** 378.

25. Kierkegaard, S. 1849. **The Sickness Unto Death.** (Translated by W. Lowrie. Anchor; Garden City, NY. 1954. 166-167.)

26. Proshansky and Seidenberg. **op. cit.** 101.

27. **Ibid.**

28. Kelley, H. 1952. Two functions of reference groups. In **Readings in Social Psychology** edited by G. Swanson, T. Newcomb and E. Hartley. 2nd ed. Holt, Rinehart and Winston; New York.

29. Piaget. **op. cit.** 280.

30. Lyttleton, R. 1979. The Gold Effect. In **The Encyclopedia of Delusions** edited by R. Duncan and M. Weston-Smith. Wallaby; New York.

31. Hoebel, E. 1954. **The Law of Primitive Man: A Study in Legal Dynamics.** Harvard University Press; Cambridge, MA.

32. Converse, P. 1965. The shifting role of class in political attitudes and behavior. In Proshansky and Seidenberg. **op. cit.** 339-349.

33. Toland, J. 1976. **Adolf Hitler.** Doubleday; Garden City, NY. 139.

34. Fest, J. 1970. **The Face of the Third Reich.** Pantheon; New York. 83.

35. Wilson. E. 1975. **Sociobiology.** Harvard University Press; Cambridge, MA. 554.

36. Proshansky and Seidenberg. **op. cit.** 383.

37. Killian, L. 1952. The significance of multiple-group membership in disaster. **American J. Sociology**, 57, 309-314.

38. Proshansky and Seidenberg. **op. cit.** 383.

39. **Ibid.** 384.

40. Killian. **op. cit.**

41. Shaver, K. 1981. **Principles of Social Psychology.** 2nd ed. Winthrop; Cambridge, MA. 277.

42. **Ibid.** 271.

43. **Ibid.** 277.

44. Zimbardo, P. 1970. The human choice: individuation, reason, and order versus deindividuation, impulse, and chaos. In the 1969 **Nebraska Symposium of Motivation** edited by J. Arnold and D. Levine. University of Nebraska Press; Lincoln, NB. 237-307.

45. Proshansky and Seidenberg. **op. cit.** 387.

46. Hart, J. 1982. **When the Going Was Good.** Crown; New York. 120.

47. Thibaut, J. and Kelley, H. 1959. **The Social Psychology of Groups.** Wiley; New York.

48. Abel, R. 1989. **American Lawyers.** Oxford University Press; Oxford.

IV. The Schema as Maladaptive

However adaptive a schema may be, it will also be maladaptive[1] to the extent that built-in biases compromise data so that perceptions will conform to expectations and desires. In addition, a schema's behavioral program (which presumably was adaptive when formed) might become maladaptive as conditions change. If fundamental conditions change significantly, maintaining a schema may be maladaptive. On the other hand, altering behavior to fit fantasies may also be maladaptive. Just when and how much change is needed are very subjective matters, and the schema is inherently biased about maintaining both its integrity and existence.

In general, schemas tend to be conservative, with norms organizing behavioral systems into rituals that prevent effective responses to significant change. Habits may originate as functional patterns of behavior but later may serve more to promote group complacence than group competence. At worst, such rituals become sacred and form the trappings of a religious system, with the devout satisfied just to repeat habitual responses.[2] The rituals may then serve as reinforcing rewards in and of themselves without reference and often without relevance to the environment.

Such rituals can be a major stumbling block in rapidly developing organizations in that new problems emerge which are unrecognized so their solutions remain beyond the ritualized coping mechanisms of the establishment. A case in point was Henry Ford's car company in the 1930's and early '40's. What it needed was a modern system of corporate administration which could guide it through the challenges induced by changes of styling in the marketplace, labor problems due to the Depression and the growth of government controls accompanying World War II: what it had was a leader who clung stubbornly to an antiquated system which was totally unequal to the demands of the new era. The result was that Ford slid into third place in sales behind General Motors and Chrysler.[3]

It is patently stupid to hang on to a dysfunctional schema while leaving obvious needs unattended. However, rather than dropping old schemas and creating new ones suited to emerging conditions, groups usually bend traditional schemas to new purposes. While this gives a society a sense of continuity, cultural identity may become confused as organizations and institutions take on new and perhaps incongruous roles. For ex-

Irrelevance

ample, capitalism does not feed the hungry; it feeds those with money; charity and welfare feed the destitute. Thus, it has been for relief efforts sponsored by both church and state to assume the burdens of an economic system ignorant of the suffering it fosters by indifference.

This process of adapting institutions to new purposes is a normal part of cultural life. Generally, people are disposed to use whatever is at hand (be it a tool, organization or idea) to deal with a problem. This approach may be effective in resolving an immediate problem, but it means that the item may come to have a function different from if not at odds with its original role. The resulting cognitive state may then become one of schematic dissonance, with language strained to match up altered behavior to established values. In the extreme, a system becomes irrelevant to itself.

As in the case of cognitive dissonance in an individual, tension will motivate society to achieve consonance. In both cases, the schema will strive to save itself, so if challenging data or disturbing perceptions cannot be ignored or rejected, words will be redefined so as to convert dissonance into confusion. The discrepancy between behavior and superego values will thus be reduced at the expense of identity. While an appearance of continuity with the past is maintained, words are revalued to lend verbal support to prevailing behavioral norms.

Thus, there are three methods by which we can induce irrelevance: 1.) adhere to an obsolete verbal value system while adopting new behaviors, 2.) adhere to obsolete behavioral norms while professing new values, and 3.) devise a compromise conflict between necessary behavior and converted values. All three are maladaptive in their own ways, but the compromise conflict condition is by far more common than the two extremes, as it disperses stress over both fields.

The first method is the English mode of clinging to tradition while moving toward resolution of real problems. The history of the House of Lords is an admirable example of a traditional system retaining its tradition and little else while Commons tends to reality. The second method is that of the phony liberal who agrees that change is necessary but never gets around to it. A folksy example would be the American who, in the 1960's, agreed that the schools would have to be integrated—someday. The third method (i.e., compromise) is one of virtuous pragmatism: one adapts as necessary and makes it appear to be ideal. An example of this process is found in the optimist who tries to convince himself and anyone who will listen that necessity is "Right on", this is the best of all worlds possible at this moment, and current behavior is the realization of historic tradition and religious morality.

All three methods reduce dissonance by distorting information—by denying reality and/or inventing fantasy. This distortion is the mechanism

Criticism

by which the schema responds to induced dissonance, and it makes people inherently stupid. It is apparently impossible for any culture to be accurately adjusted to its past traditions, superego values, behavioral norms and external reality. Compromises are made somewhere and may shift around depending on conditions. Thus, society may be adjusted but not "Accurately", in that incoming information about how the system interacts with its environment will be distorted to favor the short-term survival advantage of the group in power. This is but another example of how the neurotic paradox contributes to stupidity.

This systematic distortion of information makes human societies characteristically self-deceptive, with people disposed to believe they are living up to their ideals, particularly when they are not. The existing schematic dissonance is usually subconscious, due to the misleading nature of words, so society stumbles smugly along while at odds with itself, its environment and its equally stupid neighbors. In fact, the only really effective control of development comes not from inside but from physical limitations (what cannot be done) and competition with other groups which are also out of touch with themselves.

In general, internal criticism is of limited value as a control mechanism for growth and development of a social system. There usually tend to be few, if any, effective critics within any organization. When not dismissed out of hand as a crank or an outsider, anyone with valid criticism is made an outsider, as ostracism is a common reward for honesty, accuracy and integrity. Thus, criticism without power is largely wasted, producing little but woe for the bewildered critic himself.

Perhaps there are so few effective critics because anyone with any brains at all quickly finds that most human organizations just are not set up for effective criticism. The basic working assumption is that everything is just fine. Outside criticism is deflected and internal feedback is supposed to be positive reinforcement from "Yes men" promoting their careers by corrupting the mighty. At best, criticism has a place on the fringe, where cranks and comics can be tolerated as amusing diversions.

The resistance of organizations to criticism is inherent in the human condition. Criticism is invariably disruptive, since group spirit, if nothing else, is disrupted when unrecognized problems are made explicit. Such disturbances are unwelcome to those in power. While a critic may think he is performing a service by calling attention to an obvious problem, he is often treated as if he caused it.[a] Actually, critics should be considered society's early warning systems, sensing symptoms of problems before

---

a In day to day terms, this would be like treating someone who reports a fire as an arsonist.

anyone else does and making coping easier than might be possible later. However, the need of the establishment to maintain the appearance of internal order and the image of competence among those in power is most compelling and makes appreciation of legitimate criticism difficult at best. Thus, opportunities for correction and improvement may be sacrificed for the sake of a pleasing facade.

Leaders can achieve a sense of order by providing all members of the reference group with a social milieu which distorts their cognitive world toward acceptance of the status quo. Being inversely proportional to the size of the group, the strength of this general phenomenon of misdirecting thinking by social support becomes most intense in a leader's own tightly knit coterie. The result is groupthink, which in its pure form is characterized by cognitive complacence and promoted by blissful ignorance. Actually, groupthinkers are only half ignorant—they ignore only contradictory information. Confirming data get all the attention which can be lavished upon them by sycophants, who have surrendered their independence of thought to the group karma. The reluctance of members of the clique to voice objections to approved policies usually leads to an illusion of unanimity and a false consensus. Both of these are built less on raw data than on misinterpretations by members committed to the appearance of group perfection.

Whether in the concentrated form of groupthink or in the more diffuse forms of general stupidity, misinterpretation of data inhibits effective adjustment to problem situations. All situations are not created equal:[4] one may invite a favorable interpretation while another begs to be ignored. Situations which demand that the perceivers make psychic adjustments may be considered "Problems". These are solved if the adjustment is anticipated as being to the advantage of the adjustors.

One of the main problems people have is that a schema which functions in solving a problem may hinder the solving of problems created by the initial solution. Thus, the very human catch phrase, "If you think we have a problem now, just wait until we solve it". This goes a long way toward explaining the dysfunctional attitude of America's mighty corporations toward pollution: the companies formed to exploit our natural resources are basically indifferent to the mess they create for everyone to live in because there really is no profit in cleaning it up.

This type of problem creating belies the basic assumption of behavioral scientists that behavior is adaptive. Maladaptive behavior is thought to be anomalous—some kind of breakdown of the normal adaptive mechanism. Along with the inevitability of death and the impressive predominance of extinction in the fossil record, the record of failure of human civilizations confronts us with an unsettling question: how can any mechanism which is supposed to be adaptive be so incredibly bad at its job? Much as we prefer to accentuate the positive and optimistic, it appears that life is characterized by mechanisms built-in for the demise of systems. Life goes on, but the organisms, societies and species pass away.

In the case of our own species, it is primarily through misperception that we become maladaptive. Misperception is limited, distorted and/or inventive data gathering. It is a feature common to schematic systems and makes stupidity a normal part of the human experience, since stupidity is based on the subjective nature of perception, which requires the observer to be actively involved in the process.[5]

First of all, people select information stupidly. Any individual or organization takes in only a fraction of the data available. Since information gathering must be limited, it might be ideal if it were selected at random, so that it would reflect accurately the general state of the environment. However, perception is a directed process, with certain elements in the surroundings receiving inordinate attention and others being ignored. At best, this can permit the system to function effectively in a limited milieu in which attention can be directed toward phenomena considered relevant to acknowledged problems. At worst, the system puts itself out of touch with the general environment.

If stimuli fit the perceiving schema, in that they conform to expectation, they barely register and are promptly dismissed. This accounts for the overwhelming majority of informational bits which are picked up by any system—they are simply too routine to warrant one's attention. A good example of this process is the oblivion of a driver to most of the stimuli continually bombarding him as he goes along. As long as everything fits expectation, with traffic patterns in the normal range and the road right where it belongs, the driver may be unaware of even his own presence.[6]

However, the perceiver will immediately pick up on any aspect of the environment which does not quite fit the schema. Anything exceptional will be noticed and, if necessary and possible, adjustments will be made. In fact, the schema may adjust itself a little to allow for future variations similar to any experienced.

Beyond this normal range of perception and adjustment, however, the schema can be a limiting and debilitating factor when it prevents appreciation of events which would be emotionally distressing if acknowledged. This is the basis for the fabled ostrich strategy for avoiding awareness of threats or other unpleasantries. Such selective ignorance of stimuli is characteristic of the schema as a mechanism for misperception and a program for stupidity.

Paranoia

This selective ignorance is the result of the schema's "Perceptual defense", which acts as a filter through which stimuli must pass. This defense protects us from the anxiety that would be aroused by perceiving threatening stimuli. The physiological basis for this process is that the threshold level for threatening or anxiety-arousing stimuli is higher than that for neutral stimuli.[7] Of course, this kind of defense can be stupid, if knowing would help or permit coping. Ignoring warnings is not much of a way to defend oneself.

In the mind of a paranoid, on the other hand, fear creates threats. This exemplifies the role the schema can play in creating misperceptions by projecting itself onto stimuli. The process of perception is not accomplished by analysis of discrete bits of information in independent isolation. It is effected by the building of a picture of the environment. As one might suspect, the picture constructed is not based on the data, all the data and nothing but the data. As indicated above, data which do not conform to the existing gestalt contribute little, so modification is based disproportionately on information which confirms the schema as well as some invented material which makes an experience easier to accept and retain.

This is the process by which fantasy provides data to fit the schematic gestalt so as to improve a bit on reality. In the act of misperception, people routinely add their own knowledge to data they do receive from the environment[8] and compound the mixture with a bit of imagination. As many jurists have found, witnesses may testify to perceptions which are really more impressions created by their own schemas. In a light vein, this process provided the basis for Mark Twain's comment that he could remember everything that happened and some things that didn't.

The verbal arm of the schema really is a cognitive construct which consistently contributes to perceptual misinterpretation. Incoming data are used to solidify or modify the schema so as to make it more refined if fundamentally unsound. Thus, the schema is inherently conservative, with conflicting data misinterpreted or blended with some fabricated facts to fit into existing definitions and patterns of thought.[9] If the discrepancy between the new stimulus and existing schema is too great, the data may be totally rejected out of hand. In extreme cases, the whole system may freeze, as when the rabbit is transfixed by headlights.

Along with contributing to misperceptions of the environment, the schema tends to limit expectations of behavioral results. A certain effect is usually desired when one undertakes a course of action. That desired end is commonly anticipated, and its perception is favored over other possible effects. This problem is particularly important when actions can have long-term, negative consequences. A prime example would be the difficulties created by the use of the insecticide DDT. True, the poison accomplished its intended purpose of killing agricultural pests and carriers of disease, but it had other, unanticipated consequences as well—it spread throughout the environment and concentration within predators as it passed up the food pyramid to the decided detriment of a number of species including our own. These results were as unexpected as perception of them was unwelcome.

This process of misperception in turn depends on associating stimuli and cognitions by constructing elaborate complexes which integrate incoming data with the existing schematic network of related elements. As entering information connects with a known element, it becomes part of the schema. In general, it is easier to learn material which is consistent with the schema, since the more elaborate the connections, the better the material will be remembered. However, by categorizing perceptions via verbalization, limitations are placed on possible associations and general relevance of behavior.

Accordingly, as the schema develops, it becomes directional, bending incoming data to its own support, deflecting conflicting data, misinterpreting situations and generally making itself decreasingly accurate as a representation of the totality of reality and increasingly a source of self-gratification for the beholder. This means that human affairs do not tend to work out for the best; they tend to work themselves out according to their own natures, whatever they are.[10] Responses become less and less relevant to environmental stimuli and more and more reflections of biases of the schema. In addition, even the initial successes of a schema may work against it if it is rigorously applied to situations beyond its range of definitions,[11] thereby leading to reactions which are irrelevant. Thus, maladaptation is virtually inherent in any system which is committed to maintaining its integrity while imposing itself on reality. This is the basis for the general capacity of human organizations to self-destruct.

This self-destructive tendency is primarily a result of a failure of self-perception. People simply do not see in themselves traits they do not wish to see.[12] If specific acts must be performed, they may be misinterpreted by the agent into a favorable verbal context so as to minimize embarrassment, shame or anxiety. People may also make themselves feel better by projecting their own problems or shortcomings on to others.[13]

In this process of promoting a positive self-image at the expense of accuracy, both negative and positive reinforcement systems are at work. There is ample experimental evidence that negative feedback lowers self-esteem making further confrontations with the self aversive[14] and less likely, thus making further criticism less likely. On the other hand, positive feedback enhances self-esteem and promotes self-confrontation in situations where one excels. The net result of these two factors is that positive feedback is increased and criticism reduced, thus distorting the self-image toward one more favorable than warranted. Although this may make people feel better about themselves, it does not help them adjust their behavior to their overall environment. At best, image enhancement is accomplished and accompanied by specialization, so that people deliberately limit their experiences to situations with which they can cope effectively. Thus, a degree of success is achieved by circumscribing reality.

Of course, one of the great stumbling blocks to understanding is the presumption of the "Reality principle".[15] This is a legacy of the rationalist tradition which posits that people live in a real world which they test to decide logically when and under what conditions they can safely satisfy their needs. If there ever was a case of fantasy, it is the reality principle. The schema keeps people ignorant toward and therefore uniformed about certain undesirable aspects of the environment. More important, negative feedback about oneself tends to be subverted or disrupted. Naturally, a certain amount of objective information does pass through the perceptual and ideological filters so that people can cope with culturally approved problems. Finally, there is the element of fantasy in the schematic world which makes behavior potentially independent of actual circumstances. To the extent that the schema tests reality, reality often fails the test. As for logic, people usually resort to that only after an act or decision so as to rationalize an emotionally preferred response.

As misleading as the rationalists' reality principle is the liberals' principle of "Open-mindedness". The inhuman ideal that people are or should be equally open to all information presented to them must necessarily be compromised so that they can achieve some kind of balance between a decent exposure to potentially good ideas and a wasting of time. Not only may a system be too open or too closed to communication, but the compromise struck is usually more biased than balanced. Communication is a selective process with the schema ignoring offerings deemed irrelevant and snapping up pleasing material all before evaluation. There is something of a Catch-22 in this situation, in that one must, for example, waste time reading a book in order to determine that it was not worth reading. Worse yet, the pre-screening techniques people commonly employ are usually based on irrelevant criteria—like the book cover. As for personal communications, people self-consciously committed to the pecking order of life are often prejudiced to ideas according to the status of the source: the higher-ups have good ideas; lower-downs do not.

When the ego interferes with effective learning, it serves itself poorly. Stupidity is a common result when the schema imposes itself on reality or disrupts contact with it. The problem is that these are things the schema routinely does. It sustains its integrity by distorting perceptions and selecting information according to maladaptive ideologies. Developing a semirational system of ideas for screening out data and inhibiting communication may be self-serving in an immediate sense, just as it may also be self-defeating over the long haul. When information is rejected by a schematic defense for being inconsistent with existing ideas or when its content is judged more by the communicator's prestige than its own inherent worth, a case of stupidity is probably in progress.

Another factor contributing to the development of stupidity is a false sense of the "Self".[16] The theoretically ideal self is an organized, consistent set of perceptions and beliefs. Unfortunately for idealizing people, most selves are disorganized and inconsistent. This just happens to be the invariable result of the compromise nature of the schema. People live in a gritty world of real, immediate problems which must be solved pragmatically, and in coping, they are somewhat restricted in perception by the language of and in means by the norms of their reference group. When there is conflict among these interacting aspects of the human condition—when one perceives the necessity of acting in a manner not condoned by society, the self will blend short-term immediate survival with some kind of justification comprehensible to anyone concerned enough to care but not objective enough to be critical.

Along with the basic duality of the individual/social self is the duality of the static/dynamic self. The intrinsic compromise in the latter case is one of balancing self-preservation against self-seeking behavior.[17] Self-preservation is a basic, fundamental aspect of life: in human terms, it is expressed as a conservative dedication to the status quo. Self-seeking behavior, on the other hand, is directed toward self-enhancement by providing for the future. Many crucial decisions in life require a person to take a self-conscious risk in trading off security for opportunity. In general, younger people tend to be self-seekers; older people tend to be self-preservers, since their schema tends to favor its established ways as it becomes more entrenched through the years. At the moment of decision for an individual confronting a particular problem, the only thing clear to an observer is that this is but another of the very arbitrary/subjective dimensions of the human condition. Just which strategy will be employed or how much risk will be taken depends very much on who is making the decision and who is taking the risk.

Oddly enough, self-seeking is promoted by social support. Enhanced self-assurance encourages people to assert themselves as individuals, so when the reference group provides favorable reinforcement (approval) to members, it makes independence more likely. The self-confidence engendered by commonly perceived success makes one willing to attempt further endeavors.[18] This may in fact disrupt the group and can lead an in-

Feedback

dividual to overreach his ability, but this is the price that must be paid for being open to the possibility of individual enhancement.

The motivation for such difficulty stems largely from the self-approval made possible by the biased structuring of the feedback system. Data contradictory to a flattering self-image are blocked or interpreted so that behavior can be viewed in an emotionally acceptable context.[19] It is interesting to note that it is one's emotional need that sets the standard to which reality is molded. It is difficult to overestimate the role that such a mechanism can play in misdirecting behavior. Sustaining reinforcement can be generated internally so as to maintain the independence of a particular pattern of behavior from moderating influences of the environment, while much of the potential negative reinforcement from the environment simply does not penetrate the system.[20]

The worst result of this disruption of feedback for the sake of self-image is that it really can motivate people to make errors. It separates people from their environment and makes them relatively independent so that they can pursue their own notions without regard for their relevance or the negative consequences engendered. A classic example of this process in action is the manner in which dissidents are suppressed by totalitarian regimes. Such tactics are usually simply denied by the establishment or, alternatively, justified because of the disruptive nature of the criticism. Policies of suppression may do nothing to solve existent social problems, may even promote internal hostility against the rulers but also may promote a positive image for leaders, so long as knowledge of such suppression can also be suppressed.

If there is a simple rule of thumb for judging the stupidity of a system, it must be its reaction to valid criticism. The stupider people and institutions do not want criticism. If that includes everyone, it is because we are all a bit vain. More to the point, when negative feedback is suppressed, rejected, conveniently misinterpreted or referred to a committee, stupidity is in progress. If things are not working out, there is usually, unfortunately, the all too handy alternative explanation that problems are all someone else's fault. This is the scapegoat philosophy of life and perpetuates almost as much stupidity as is produced.

Fortunately for sensitive egos, people do not have to acknowledge criticism in order to react to it. Corrective reactions may be undertaken without anyone admitting anything was wrong. The accompanying verbal response to warranted but unwelcome criticism is usually to the effect that, "We have not done anything wrong and will not do it again".

On the other hand, we must also bear in mind the fact that hypersensitivity to criticism can also be debilitating. The process might be thought of as an intensification of the feedback loop, with fantasy perhaps adding some totally unwarranted criticisms. This type of stupidity is more common among individuals than organizations and may tend to shut a person off from participation in life.

By way of contrast, when in harmony with their own limitations, people can be happily stupid,[21] preferring ignorance to the pain of learning. If people really do not want to know something, it probably is because they sense that learning it might be upsetting. In such instances, stupidity has reached its maximum potential for the system, which is as limited as it can be. As usual, a balanced appreciation of criticism and compliments is healthiest, with extreme biases tending toward stupefication.

For whatever purpose, to produce effective and enduring changes in thought and action, it is necessary to alter the self-identity of those involved. Major renovation of personalities, also known as brainwashing, can be accomplished by stress which undermines social relationships within a reference group. Consensual validation of norms, attitudes and values is thus disrupted, and established ways of thinking and acting are discarded.[22] This may be fine, if the original personality complex was so bad that it could be replaced by something clearly better. The reason why such a program[b] is not routinely applied to inveterate criminals in penitentiaries must be that they have internalized their own attitudes to the point that they each make up a reference group of one. The only thing to be gained by tinkering at this point would be emotional disruption and a resistance to knowledge, accommodation and improvement.

In the case of powerful leaders, the sense of identity (value system) may be rendered immune to alteration by aides who insulate their mentor from reality. The strong man's attitudes may then become symptomatic of neurosis. When dictators revel in or deny their brutality, stupidity has gained both another victory and victim. Dealings with such leaders should be conducted not by ambassadors but by psychiatrists. Not only do tyrants have difficulty recognizing limitations of their power, they also have difficulty controlling their actions. Rather than adopting new attitudes or altering behavior, the mighty tend to place excessive reliance on the modes of thought and action which brought them to power: rather than being adjusted, these stand-by methods are usually extended, often making aggravated social and political conditions even worse. Finally, control becomes tenuous as unacknowledged forces build to the point that the leader can no longer remain oblivious to them.

---

b At least it could be tried. Right now, most American prisons (which could be relabeled "Personality Renovation Centers") are institutions shaped by business and labor interests which are increasingly concerned that when doing government contract work, inmates in the Federal Prison Industry program are causing unemployment in the private sector.

Bias

The desire to be unconscious is very much underestimated in and by nearly everybody. Most people have their lives set into routines so that they do not have to be aware of themselves or anything else. Who really remembers last Thursday? Was there anything really distinctive about the trip to the office yesterday? If not amused, people get annoyed when a crank points out that the routine could be improved. Whether it could or could not be is secondary or even irrelevant. What really matters is that it could not be improved without changing it, which means people would have to adjust to something new. Usually, this would make them self-conscious and uncertain and probably make them feel a little awkward. In their public lives, most people do not like to feel like graffiti in motion, much preferring to feel nothing at all.

Consistent with the desire to be unconscious is the desire to be unaware of contradictions between one's beliefs and behavior. Inconsistency in this context is apparently quite acceptable—much more so than would be the anxiety which might accompany self-revelation. Most people prefer to avoid the limelight of self-confrontation, going about their business as best they can without dwelling on their shortcomings. If their behavior can be misconstrued into a favorable context, good enough. In fact, humanity thrives on the difference between reality and its most acceptable interpretation. Precision is just too much to expect from people struggling in a world in which motivation is as important to success as accuracy in perceiving compromising situations. Thus, the schema which promotes successful coping also inhibits self-improvement. This is a contradiction inherent in the human condition.

As the schema attempts to match the perceptual with the behavioral world, it perforce exists in an emotional setting which both defines and is defined by cognitive elements. This process of mutually defining interactions of facts and feelings provides a dynamic basis for interpreting events and evaluating behavior. Cognitions are interpreted according to a given emotional state which, in turn, may be altered by those or future ideas and actions. In fact, it is this emotional dimension which makes the schema so subjective in its assessment of incoming data. Certain objects and experiences elicit specific emotions—love, hate, fear, etc.—which may promote biased reactions to many important impinging stimuli.[23]

It is important to bear in mind that adjustments or maladjustments of the schema are usually determined as much by emotional factors as by any objective value of cognitions themselves.[24] Most minor adjustments are both easy and accurate in that there is little or no emotion involved and they keep the schema, such as it is, attuned to slight alterations in the environment. However, there is invariably major emotional resistance to changing one's mind, as it really becomes a matter of changing oneself. This can be emotionally wrenching and is usually effected only as a last resort, after all other psychic tricks of refuting and misinterpreting data have been exhausted. Finally, there is the extreme when an experience is so totally bewildering in its unexpectedness and excessiveness that it "Blows your mind" right off the emotional/cognitive scale. An example of this might be a bad accident which leaves one physically untouched but mentally stunned beyond response.

It is largely the emotional vector attached by words to data which determines how perceptions and cognitions will interact to affect adjustment of the schema. The irrelevance of so much behavior is really an expression of the commitment of the schema to itself, since existing terminology defines the emotional context in which stimuli and responses are construed. This is really the foundation of stupidity—the emotional commitment to the schema. It inhibits objective "Reality testing"[25] because any emotionally disturbing discrepancy between expectation and perception is simply interpreted to mean reality failed. Needless to say, such an approach to life is at least as successful in creating as in solving problems.

Problems arise as the schema acts to maintain a subjective world which minimizes anxiety. Disturbing input is reduced and probably replaced with fictions and fantasies. As objectivity and anxiety are sacrificed for independence from reality, a degree of dysfunction is promoted. Improved group cohesion may compensate for loss of contact with the environment and even oneself, but all that means is that self-deluding people are all the more cooperative in effecting inefficient policies. At worst, stupidity can create or be characterized by delusions which produce anxieties and difficulties where none really needs exist. Once again, we find this duality of extremes, as when stupidity can prevent or cause anxiety by the schema under- or overreacting to reality.

Adverse conditions often create anxiety, in that people are not sure they can cope with the problems confronting them. Having or finding an explanation for their plight reduces their sense of helplessness and vulnerability by plausibly identifying the cause of their distress and providing a course of action for resolving the crisis.[26] It is important to note that the explanation does not have to have much real effective value in terms of external conditions. If it makes people feel better about themselves and their situation, that is a lot. It may not be enough, but it provides a practical basis for a religious belief which, if it does not disrupt learning, may permit the development of a functional coping strategy.

Such beliefs shared by a reference group constitute their religious system. It does not matter that verbal expressions are at odds with the behavioral norms of the group—as when the Crusaders killed for Christ. The functional value of the common schema is that it binds the group together. A positive feedback system comes into play as highly cohesive groups provide a source of security for members, reduce anxiety and heighten their self-esteem. As cohesion increases, so do the group's capacity to retain members and its power to bring about conformity to its norms.[27] All this can occur with an indifference to consistency and effectiveness. Just believing and belonging sustain each other quite efficiently. Of course, as mentioned above, the self-assurance derived from belonging may induce some group members to undertake self-seeking behavior that might disturb the group, but this is a distinct counter-current within the general trend of conformity for the sake of emotional security.

Much as the feeling of belonging can act to reduce anxiety, it can also generate anxiety in individuals who feel compelled to maintain a false front for the benefit of members of their reference group.[28] The simple analysis of such a situation is that the person really is not a member of the group but for some extraneous reason feels obliged to conform to its norms. An example of this might be a homosexual who feels pressured to dress and act according to the dictates of the general, straight society. Groups often maintain irrelevant standards for their members' compliance, and intolerance for variation is itself taken as a sign of belonging, as when witch hunters wrapped themselves in the flag during America's periodic "Red scares". Most group members regard diversity as suspicious rather than as a source of strength, so cooperation is usually promoted by people playing their given roles without displaying their unsettling idiosyncrasies. Cohesion thus tends to make groups rather narrow and, for all their self-induced efficiency, limited in outlook.

Not only does group cohesion tend to narrow the schema, the belief systems of normal humans are also slightly off center, as objective accuracy has been sacrificed for enhanced esteem of members. This is why "Be realistic" and "Be yourself" are such dubious bits of advice for a person having difficulty relating to others. The assumption that normal society is reasonable and realistic is part of the Rationalists' legacy and is patently erroneous. For someone who is trying to adjust to society, the goal is not an ideal state of mental health but one of adapting to the particular quirks and notions of a given reference group.

The normal human condition is a state of compromise between two competing tendencies—one to test and the other to deny reality.[29] Actually, denying reality is an extreme; misconstruing it through the misinterpretive power of words is the norm. Of course, adding a touch of fantasy can further reduce any anxiety which might be induced by accurate perceptions of the environment. Thus, prevention of anxiety and promotion of group cohesion combine to produce a schema which is both more and less than a reflection of reality. Irrationality helps the slightly neurotic

Delusions

normal people adjust to each other even as it prevents them from knowing themselves or achieving a long-term adjustment to their limitations.

In Freudian terms, stupidity is a defense mechanism which keeps culturally forbidden desires at a subconscious level. It is bad enough that the mechanism for informing us about our environment is disrupted, but stupidity also isolates us from ourselves. All we are likely to know about our society and ourselves is that which is culturally acceptable. Consequently, much conscious knowledge is only obliquely related to a restricted reality, being limited by subconscious biases and thus often irrelevant to the solution of existing problems.

In fact, all defense mechanisms appear to be stupid to the degree that they maladaptively distort reality[30] and may not be necessary relative to external conditions anyway. For example, the judgments paranoids make are commonly based on fear and may both justify and continue that emotional state rather than function to reduce a real threat. On the other hand, members of an overconfident, insulated group can become arrogant and careless when temperance and caution are in order, creating problems that otherwise would not exist. Stupidity really is due to a mismatch between the external demands of the environment and the internal attitude of the schema.

Delusions are classic examples of psychic defenses which, in excess, can be stupefying. At any level of intensity, they provide a person with faulty interpretations of reality to which the victim will cling despite all kinds of contradictory evidence.[31] The schema becomes delusive through a combination of insensitivity and fantasy. Excessive insensitivity to the most obvious facts contrary to an egotist's plans and desires most often leads him to ruin.[32] Likewise, the fabrication of gratifying data can be immediately pleasing while serving to entrench a misleading schema. Of course, excessive amounts of energy may be used to impose delusions on facts, but this is usually, in the long run, a maladaptive strategy.

Even when a schema is inadequate, delusions may make it appear to be functional. A pointedly maladaptive schema may become firmly established as a delusive individual ignores signs of difficulty and conjures up signs of success. This intensification of self-identification is defensive in that the person is his schema. Ineffective as it may be, without it, the individual is lost. In such a case, the person is really in a losing situation, in that he cannot survive as such. To survive, he must adopt a new schema, since the one he has will not adapt. However, by doing so, he would no longer be himself.

The basic principles of ego defense which function and malfunction for individuals may also be applied to groups. The delusion of "Protective destruction" which shaped American conduct in the Vietnam conflict was an idiotic case in point: any time you have to destroy something in order to save it, it is time to back off and reevaluate the situation and yourself. In a more global sense, perhaps our collective epitaph will read, "In order to survive, they self-destructed", for we seem bent on creating an environment in which we will all achieve the perfect equality of extinction.

Such a headlong rush to do things, whatever they are and whatever the consequences, is characteristic of the manic, so we are all manic to the extent that we act without thinking. This impatience of leaping while looking is a combination of suspended thought and an inner drive to action. It is interesting to note that clinical manics are often hypersensitive, having acute senses of sight, hearing, etc.[33] It is as if being too sensitive induces stupidity in that the thought process is bypassed, and a direct if irrelevant connection is made between stimulus and response. If it is possible to have human life without a schema, this is it, and the possibilities for stupidity with this "Ready, fire, aim" mentality are boundless, as it is by definition always a case of sheer action without guidance or control.

The opposite extreme of excessive control to the exclusion of action is the condition of repression, and it can be as stupid as mania—the one as quiet as the other is explosive. Just as denial is a defense against external threats, repression is a defense against internal threats.[34] The schema excludes potentially threatening thoughts or feelings from awareness by preventing their verbal or behavioral expression. At the level of the individual, the Oedipus complex[35] was one of Freud's favorite repressions. A totalitarian society may also be repressive—prohibiting demonstrations and speeches which might call attention to problems. Of course, repression is a great way to maintain order based on the appearance that all is well, and it reduces the demand to cope with any underlying problems. However, these may surface eventually, although often in forms unrecognizable to the conscience in individuals or to the leaders in society.

As a defense mechanism, repression can make us feel a bit more pleasant by helping us forget disturbing events. In extreme cases, this process produces the clinical condition of amnesia, which occurs when people cannot subconsciously accept the reality of their own circumstances and behavior.[36] If we ignore for the moment the possible complications of brain damage due to physical trauma (a blow to the head, etc.), any great psychological trauma—a bad traffic accident or combat experience—may be lost on the schema, which simply is not set up to process the data presented. The mind then picks up normal functioning after the trauma has passed, to the exclusion of memories of everything that occurred before. The schema survives at the expense of knowledge, leaving the amnesiac functioning without knowing who he is.

While classical defense mechanisms may be, in moderation, effective means for coping with external stress, there are no defense mechanisms which reduce internally generated stress (as, for example, when a paranoid perceives threats which do not really exist). When the schema becomes maladaptive to the point of being primarily self-sustaining or self-destructive rather than responsive to the environment, a condition of mental illness exists, as behavior is more likely to reinforce than reduce the source of stress. Such self-generated stress is produced when the schema motivates, misinforms and leads one to behavior which is irrelevant to the resolution of external problems or the improvement of internal mechanisms of reaction and control.

Although all mental illnesses are stupid, stupidity itself is most similar to the clinical condition of neurosis—i.e., unrealistic behavior[37] which is maladaptive, self-defeating and frequently punished by society. The major difference is that stupidity is often rewarded by society. People usually engage in any form of behavior because of some sort of immediate reward, even if it is simply a smile or pat on the back. In the case of neurosis, social rejection and failure to attain goals may be the prices paid in order to be free from assumed emotional strain.[38] In the case of stupidity, social acceptance may cause the failure to attain important goals, this being the price paid for the psychic satisfaction of belonging to a group.

Sometimes, a schema may break down under routine conditions due to a lack of sustaining reinforcement.[39] This is the condition of depression, an extreme case of "Doubt" induced by a failure of reality to live up to expectations. No one ever wrote a story about a little engine that was not sure or could not be bothered, but it would have been about saving energy until the apparent pointlessness of behavioral feedback could be constructed into some kind of sensible schema. In the meantime, a stupid passivity would have prevented effective responses to the environment.

In extreme clinical cases, fantasy may produce hallucinations to compensate for missing stimuli. This is often the experience of schizophrenics, whose schemas can provide emotionally required comfort and help[40] and/or terror and threats missing from the external world. In this sense, their subjective world is a decided distortion, for better or worse, of reality. Of course, their behavior takes on a degree of independence from and irrelevance to their surroundings, but that is the price paid for the creation of a far, far different world from that which most of us recognize. In schizophrenics, the orthodox sensory channels break down[41] and input is created internally which both expresses and justifies the existing emotional state of the individual. In schizophrenic political systems, the orthodox channels of communication break down so that protests become messages transmitted from within to an establishment unreceptive to suggestions or criticisms. Such insulation simplifies the immediate world of the leaders but also promotes the accumulation of long-term discontent throughout the general society.

Nietzsche noted that madness[c] is the exception in individuals but the rule in groups, and certainly there is often something mindless in conformity. Freud noted people in a group may act like children—suspending mature judgment and common sense when caught up in the mass psychosis of blindly following a charismatic leader.[42] Indeed, lack of vigilance and acceptance of excessive risks are common when members of a reference group band together to support a mutual sense of overconfidence. In the inner circles of government, a leader may pressure advisers to rubber-stamp an ill-conceived program, but he might rather simply exert subtle influence to prevent them from exercising their critical judgment,[43] with the net result in such instances usually being pointedly maladaptive.

The madness of a group, like that of those who followed Adolf Hitler or Charles Manson, derives much of its impetus from social support. Madness of the individual, like that of Hitler or Manson, often develops when a creative person is ostracized by general society. Obviously, in the two examples mentioned, the individuals warranted ostracism not just for being different, but for being diabolical. However, society is not usually very discerning in its wariness of people who fail to conform to expectation. It is also worth noting that general creativity can develop in those ostracized. As they are estranged from a schema they never really identified with anyway, those on the fringe may well develop schemas of their own. Whether this leads to madness, genius or some mixture of the two is but another matter for arbitrary judgment.

Inventive genius is due to the creative fantasy of introverts often incompetent to grasp even the simplest precepts of social life. Beethoven, for example, lost all effective contact with the social and business worlds before he was thirty years old. He was totally devoid of sympathetic insight and inhabited a world of his own into which no one else could penetrate. Except for a few disastrous occasions, he left others to live their own ways in their own worlds.[44] To put it bluntly, Beethoven was pretty damned stupid in nonmusical matters. This was the price of his genius.

Henry Ford had little in common with Beethoven, except that both were totally inept in their interactions with ordinary people. Beethoven misunderstood people because he lived in a world of tones and emotions;

---

c And he was something of an expert on the topic. It is not clear if he made this observation before or after he went happily insane, but as it is a concise, accurate statement, it must have been afterward.

Creativity

Ford had the same problem because he lived in a world of steel and over-alls.[45] This inability of the great to relate to ordinary minds shows up in sports as well: no[d] great baseball player has been an effective manager. Such people do so much so naturally and well that they have difficulty relating professionally to those who are struggling to learn and to whom performing is in some way a conscious effort.

Further, the development of creativity and genius seems to depend very much on such noncognitive factors as personality, motivation, up-bringing, etc. Although a certain level of mental ability is necessary for mastery of a body of knowledge, independence of thought is really the factor which permits the creative person to move beyond mastery to inventive genius.[46] Most geniuses work to greatest advantage when least embroiled in human society.[47] Mozart, for example, created best when completely himself,[48] because excellence is a subjective, personal experience rather than a social phenomenon. It is not a commodity which can be bought or sold; nor is it a matter to be settled by arbitration or reached by mutual consent; nor can it be imposed on anyone by force. The genius provides an alternative perspective to that of the accepted schema,[49] and he reaches that pinnacle of perception by building faith in his own beliefs about a phenomenon in which he is totally absorbed. The inventive genius deliberately isolates himself from society so that he can deal exclusively with a limited amount of information independently.

It is important to note the contribution of stupidity to genius. For the creative person to achieve independence of thought, he must, to some degree, make himself oblivious of his surroundings as well as of prevailing explanations and assumptions. One recipe for creative thinking is a peculiar blend of daydreaming and concentration. The first step is to get the eyes out of focus so that disruptive external stimuli are reduced.[50] This reduced awareness of the environment gives imagination a chance to wander. When, in such a state, the mind can fix upon a new idea and concentration on it and its ramifications can be carried to logical or even absurd extremes. If this brings one closer to the solution of a problem or opens new vistas for personal or cultural advancement, then the brief lapse into stupidity was worthwhile.

As might be expected, there are different kinds of genius. The sensational form is the schemabuster (like Beethoven or Ford) who breaks convention to redefine the world. Geniuses of this type are usually people of

---

d The only exception might be Rogers Hornsby, who was for a while, interestingly enough, a playing manager. Even his lifetime won/lost record, however, was under .500. (By the way, the converse is also true: the great managers had been poor to mediocre players.)

Crackpots

flair and great insight. By way of contrast, there is the conventional form of genius who really abides by the rules—the formal, stated standards—and makes them work. Louis Pasteur is an example of a person who creatively applied the rigors of experimental investigation to unconventional assumptions. His results conclusively demonstrated basic principles of life and disease so convincingly that these replaced age-old myths with knowledge and understanding.

There are also different types of genius in another sense: those who work independently of people and those who get people to work for them. The first type is the artist/inventor. The second is the leader/messiah. The one frames a schema which accurately reflects reality or expresses an aesthetic state. The other offers his followers a schema which answers their needs and motivates them to live for the realization of their beliefs. Both Abraham Lincoln and Adolf Hitler were gifted in being able to articulate what many around them just felt. For whatever purpose it is used, this ability must be recognized as a kind of genius.

It is hardly surprising that the decision to label a particular creative person a crackpot or genius is one of the more arbitrary judgments people presume to make. Of course, since people usually use their own schema as the standard for evaluation, they tend to regard any deviation from expectation with a certain amount of humor or trepidation and interpret it irreverently. The general rule is that a crackpot is someone who makes a concerted effort to find a new way to be stupid, whereas a genius is a crackpot who just happened to be right.

All such arbitrary judgments would be easier to make and there would be much more concurrence in them were we not so amazing in our ability to learn. This is one of those general animal capacities which humans have taken to a dubious extreme. We can learn just about anything. The problem is that we are not limited by reality to learning just what exists or occurs. Our schemas may keep us from learning what is while helping us, by illogical extensions, learn things that are not.

The creative mind which invents new possible relationships among objects or combinations of them may be committing an act of genius or stupidity, depending on whether reality can be brought into conformity with the new ideas. However, that mind will be labeled "Genius" or "Stupid" according to its conformity to the demands and desires of the reference group. The act of reorganizing cognitions in itself is of no particular value, except that it expands our potential for understanding and controlling the environment. Just how efficiently we do this and whether for good or evil depends on our cognitive abilities and the morality of our own conventional standards for evaluation.

One very real drawback to this process of learning by evaluating new creations is that there are so many mistakes, errors and blunders made along the way. Not only may new ideas or inventions be faulty, but the standards for evaluating them may be faulty (or inappropriate): ergo, the long human tradition of disasters born in absurdity, vice and folly.

In this context, stupidity may be seen as the price paid for the benefits of imagination. The value gained by an occasional good idea by a mind wandering beyond immediacy more than compensates for the many useless, silly or even dangerous notions so common in our mental life. Imagination may thus be viewed as increasing the range of stupidity while providing options for cultural advancement. As mentioned earlier, some maladaptive behavior is simply inefficiency—noise in the system. However, maladaptive behavior may also be indicative of cognitions straying from the narrow confines of the conventional schema. While the initial reaction to any such deviation from the norm may be negative, every so often one such variation will catch on and be appreciated as a positive mutation in the cultural life of a group.

This method of adjustment permits social evolution in gradual steps when novel contributions are minor and perhaps limited to particular circumstances. The major leaps of genius are often cognitively as well as emotionally incomprehensible to the majority in a group. However, they can serve either as beacons for guiding future development (if they are indeed constructive) or as sirens for luring the unwary into fruitless pursuits (if they are nothing but alluring). Naturally, neither adopting novel modes of thought and behavior nor adhering to convention is in itself stupid. That evaluation is circumstantial, arbitrary and subjective.

That process of evaluation, however, is most biased toward conforming to the status quo. Language, tradition and norms all support the familiar and tend to make anything[e] new suspect. Language prejudices judgments by the nature of emotional values associated with certain terms. Traditions and norms further tend to stunt cultural development by way of the neurotic paradox, since the immediate, short-term rewards of conforming to expectation are usually most real and compelling. Accordingly, accepted behavior may be reinforced despite real, long-term detrimental consequences. The condition of a consistent, contented culture or, alternatively, one with balanced development might be ideal but not typically human. This is because the schema automatically favors itself, perverts

---

e In this regard, it should be noted the contemporary American throwaway culture is a decided anomaly, in that businesses have convinced us that throwing things away just to throw them away is something of a virtue in itself.

Judgment

the process of cultural evaluation into one of self-confirmation and tends to steer evolution toward conformity.

This is not to say that progress is impossible or just illusionary, nor that we simply have to select among various forms of stupidity. There is change, and it can be for the better, if one can set a standard for judgment. The problem is that we do not set a standard for judgment. People set any number of standards which are very much conditioned by who they are. Perhaps the miracle is not that we have so much conflict and confusion in the world but that we have so little.

If we have so consistently failed in our efforts to establish a world of peace and plenty for all, it may be because we are not trying to do that. Most people are just trying to get along. They are basically out for themselves and not much interested in improving the system. Although they may be unconsciously involved in cooperative, synergistic movements to construct more complex societies, this is, at best, half of the story. For ages, people have flattered themselves with the pleasing notion that we are intelligent, God's favorites, free, etc. Recently, analysts have carried on this tradition by emphasizing the anabolic aspects of civilization, and it is true, we can and do cooperate, and the whole can be greater than the sum of the sacrificing parts.[51]

However, there is another side to the story, and it is not as flattering as that which emphasizes our constructive nature. It is a legacy of the cynics and their intellectual descendants who viewed humanity as mean, depraved, evil and stupid. Not surprisingly, scientists have been reluctant to carry on this tradition, and those who have have not usually been well received. The shock and dismay that greeted Freud's revelations are representative of the reactions of both the public and professionals to theories about human behavior that are both sound and unsettling.

The sad fact of life is that there is a catabolic side to nature. Civilizations both rise and fall. The same schemas which promote social cohesion can and it seems invariably do corrupt learning and adaptation and thus lead to their own disintegration. The whole becomes less than the sum of its parts as it dominates to the point of preventing subgroups from carrying out their functions effectively. This is a moral rather than a cognitive failing, as people fail to do what they should, doing instead what they should not—and the term "Should" denotes a moral imperative.[52] Unfortunately, this process of self-corruption is inherent in human culture.

Notes

1. Horowitz, M. 1992. **Person Schemas and Maladaptive Interpersonal Patterns**. University of Chicago Press; Chicago, IL.

2. Weisz, P. and Keogh, R. 1982. **The Science of Biology**. 5th ed. McGraw-Hill; New York. 4.

3. Nevins, A. and Hill, F. Dec. 1962. Power is the Prize. **American Herit.**; XIV, #1, 50.

4. Smith, R. Sarason, I. and Sarason, B. 1982. **Psychology: The Frontiers of Behavior**. Harper & Row; New York. 451.

5. Kant, I. 1781. **Kritik der reinen Vernunft**. (**Critique of Pure Reason**. J. M. Dent & Sons; London.) What Kant attributed to the structure of the mind is now attributed to language. While he emphasized the way the mind turns perceptions into knowledge, I emphasize how we are misled by our learned biases.JFW

6. Kahneman, D. 1973. **Attention and Effort**. Prentice-Hall; Englewood Cliffs, NJ. 131.

7. Erdelyi, M. 1974. A new look at the new look: perceptual defense and vigilance. **Psychological Review**, 32, 109-118.

8. Sulin, R. and Dooling, D. 1974. Intrusions of a thematic idea in retention of prose. **J. Experimental Psychology**, 103, 255-262.

9. Wylie, R. 1978. **The Self Concept. Vol. 2. Theory and Research on Selected Topics**. University of Nebraska Press; Lincoln, NB.

10. Pitkin, W. 1932. **A Short Introduction to the History of Human Stupidity**. Simon and Schuster; New York. 473.

11. Johnson, L. and Ley, R. 1990. **Origins of Modern Economics: A Paradigmatic Approach**. Ginn Press; Needham Heights, MA. 28.

12. Alexander, R. 1975. The search for a general theory of behavior. **Behavioral Science**, 20, 97.

13. Sears, R. 1936. Experimental studies of projection: I. Attribution of traits. **J. Social Psychology**, 7, 151-163.

14. Gur, R. and Sackheim, H. 1979. Self-deception: a concept in search of a phenomenon. **J. Personality and Social Psychology**, 37, #2, 162.

15. Freud, S. 1927. **The Ego and the Id**. Hogarth Press; London.

16. Rogers, C. 1970. **Carl Rogers on Encounter Groups**. Harper & Row; New York.

17. Shaver, K. 1981. **Principles of Social Psychology**. 2nd ed. Winthrop; Cambridge, MA. 246.

18. Coopersmith, S. 1967. **The Antecedents of Self-esteem**. Freeman; San Francisco. CA.

19. Singer, J. (Ed.) 1990. **Repression and Dissociation: Implication for Personality Theory, Psychopathology, and Health**. U. of Chicago Press; Chicago, IL.

20. Bandura, A. 1979. The self-system in reciprocal determinism. **American Psychologist**, 33, 344-358.

21. Pitkin. **op. cit.** 500.

22. Proshansky, H. and Seidenberg, B. (eds.) 1965. **Basic Studies in Social Psychology**. Holt, Rinehart and Winston; New York. 609.

23. **Ibid.** 23.

24. Schachter, S. 1966. The interaction of cognitive and physiological determinants of emotional state. In **Anxiety and Behavior** edited by C. Spielberger. Academic Press; New York.

25. Smith, **et al. op. cit.** 472.

26. Hammond, P. 1978. **An Introduction to Cultural and Social Anthropology**. 2nd ed. Macmillan; New York. 331-332.

27. Cartwright, D. 1969. The nature of group cohesiveness. In **Group Dynamics: Research and Theory** edited by D. Cartwright and A. Zander. 3rd ed. Harper & Row; New York.

28. Smith, et al. **op. cit.** 492.

29. Freud, A. 1966. **The Ego and the Mechanisms of Defense.** International Universities Press; New York. 80.

30. Coleman, J., Morris, C. and Glaros, A. 1987. **Contemporary Psychology and Effective Behavior.** 6th ed. Scott, Foresman & Co.; Glenview, IL. 190.

31. Smith, et al. **op. cit.** 502.

32. Pitkin. **op. cit.** 243.

33. Custance, J. 1952. **Wisdom, Madness and Folly.** Pelligrini and Cudahy; New York.

34. Hilgard, E., Atkinson, R. and Atkinson, R. 1975. **Introduction to Psychology.** 6th ed. Harcourt, Brace, Jovanovich; New York.

35. Freud, S. In **The Standard Edition of the Complete Psychological Works of Sigmund Freud** edited by J. Strachey. 1950. Hogarth Press; London. Vol 3, 253.

36. Smith, et al. **op. cit.** 228.

37. Horney, K. 1950. **Neurosis and Human Growth.** Norton; New York. 166.

38. Mowrer, O. 1950. **Learning Theory and Personality Dynamics.** Ronald Press; New York.

39. Lewinsohn, P., Mischel, W., Chaplin, W. and Barton, R. 1980. Social competence and depression: the role of illusory self-perceptions. **J. Abnormal Psychology,** 89, 203-212.

40. Karon, B. and VandenBos, G. 1981. **Psychotherapy of Schizophrenia.** Jason Aronson; Northvale, NJ. 42.

41. Vonnegut, M. 1975. **The Eden Express.** Bantam Books; New York.

42. Freud, S. 1921. **Group Psychology and the Analysis of the Ego.** (Bantam; New York. 1965.)

43. Janis, I. 1982. **Groupthink.** Houghton Mifflin; Boston, MA. 3.

44. Pitkin. **op. cit.** 367.

45. **Ibid.** 222.

46. MacKinnon, D. 1967. Assessing creative persons. **J. Creative Behavior,** 1, 291-304.

47. Pitkin. **op. cit.** 368.

48. Holmes, E. 1878. **The Life of Mozart, Including His Correspondence.** Chapman & Hall; London.

49. Coopersmith. **op. cit.** 60.

50. Pope, K. and Singer, J. 1978. The waking stream of consciousness. In **Human Consciousness and Its Transformations: A Psychological Perspective** edited by J. Davidson, E. Davidson and G. Schwartz. Plenum; New York.

51. Corning, P. 1983. **The Synergism Hypothesis.** McGraw-Hill; New York.

52. Carey, A. Feb. 25, 1990. The United States of Incompetence. **Philadelphia Inquirer.** 16.

V. The Cultural Basis of Stupidity

What is culture? There are many answers, as it is different things to different people. Basically, it is a means of behavioral organization by which some of the more advanced species (especially sophisticated vertebrates) learn to interact with their environments. In our case, each society has a specific set of cultural controls—recipes, rules, plans and instructions—which provide both a method for structuring behavior[1] and a linguistic context for perceiving it. In terms of a schema, normative rules define the behavioral program of a people while language frames their common assumptions.

Culture is also a means of transmitting behavior and values across generations. Further, it is a communication system, and it has been analyzed as a means for distributing both human and natural energy. However, no one yet seems to have considered culture as a means for fostering stupidity—promoting, developing and transmitting it throughout a society and through time. Perhaps it is this as well.

As a cultural constant, stupidity is routinely transmitted from one generation to the next by the time-honored mechanism of the vicious cycle. Poorly adjusted children mature into maladjusted adults, then using the same techniques their parents used on them to raise yet another generation of misinformed conformists or malcontented sociopaths.[2] If there is some selection pressure acting to weed stupidity out of each generation, it is, apparently, easily offset by a willing disposition of people to spread it and encourage its continual, spontaneous synthesis.

For all the observing and generalizing done by cultural anthropologists, this one, true human universal seems to have escaped notice completely. In every age, land and culture, stupidity defines the hominid condition. It is both eternal and ubiquitous, although the specific forms it may take are, of course, dependent on the misperceptions and fantasies of the particular people running themselves into the ground chasing their own favorite rainbow. As a quality, it is the great equalizer of humanity, being a common element in all religions, philosophies, societies, political regimes and economic systems. No machine is built without it, and most artists—especially modern artists—depend upon it for their success. As a quantifi-

Rule Making and Breaking

able phenomenon, however, stupidity is distributed unevenly, with some people being clearly superior to others in this respect.[3]

This may be a short-term boon for society, if the dumb are failures who are unable to comprehend that the successful make and break their own rules to suit themselves. Verbalized ideals then may keep the disenfranchised in their places—exhorting them to work harder, toe the line, forgive, etc.—while the actual, functional means used to achieve specific, immediate ends are seldom acknowledged by the establishment. Unfortunately, some of the stupidest people may be the leaders, so graft and corruption in politics and subjectivity in science, for example, may have to be treated as exceptional (although self-serving behavior in government and biased attitudes in laboratories are as common as grass is to lawns). In order to protect the guilty, cultures usually reduce themselves to impracticality, so most are, at best, short-term successes which induce their own long-term demise.

Although the specific forms that contemporary stupidity assumes are our own and some of them newly minted, the general condition is part of our cultural heritage. It is the legacy of bygone eras which crushed the sensitive and favored the dull.[4] We are the descendants of those who survived the drudgery and boredom of past working and living conditions. Our forefathers were the shirkers who left the fighting to the valiant and the brave. Our ancestors were just low enough on the ladder of cultural life not to succumb to the anxiety, stress, ulcers and high blood pressure of conscientious authority.

The person of limited sensitivity and modest ambitions finds happiness relatively easily. Having found it, he strives to maintain it and becomes the enemy of progress.[5] Allied with the dull and happy are the powerful and successful, who often are not particularly happy but, nevertheless, want to retain their positions of influential unhappiness. Thus, both happiness and power are conservative forces acting to preserve the status quo by opposing objective evaluation of criticisms or suggestions which might improve the world but certainly would change it. Usually, the powerful will accept only those changes which increase their power—that is, changes which make significant change less likely.

Contributing greatly to the culture of stupidity is the willingness of people to submit to higher authorities in matters requiring intellectual effort. This willingness provides the psychological basis for the church and state,[6] with the church providing beliefs for people who cannot understand and the state providing things for people who cannot do. In their self-serving ways, these institutions feed on the weaknesses of people, making them weaker and keeping them from learning and doing things they might comprehend and accomplish. As a state religion, Islam consti-

91

tutes one of the most intense forms of cultural stupefication existent, as it concentrates human energy by promoting conformity in both belief and behavior.

In general, culture may be viewed in terms of a number of interacting component systems,[7] each of which caters to a basic human need. First and foremost (and incidentally consistent with our own unbiased emphasis on schemas), culture is a belief system; there is invariably some religious commitment to a higher order of presumed powers or conjured beings. Also, culture is a system of ideology, with a philosophy of life based on false beliefs nurtured in agnostic ignorance. Further, culture is a communication system which disseminates the misinformation upon which a political system is based. The political system in turn is shaped by an economic system (if the term "System" still applies) which concentrates wealth, power and status upon the social system's favored few while distributing poverty, misery and despair among the unfortunate many. A system of technology helps each culture wreck its environment, and a system of arts provides symbolic expressions in front of which people may hide.

In each and all of these systems, there is a subtle hint of stupidity as a common element which unifies culture into a disintegrating whole. For the past two hundred years, social scientists have been trying to impose some order of logic on the actions and interrelationships of these systems. Perhaps it is time to consider the very real possibility that both the systems and their interactions are illogical, inconsistent and maladaptive to the point that culture may be characterized as stupid.

The range and intensity of religions may differ, but having a belief system is a human universal,[8] and culture is the social mechanism for creating and maintaining the various religious systems of the world. Religion was originally directed toward supernatural spirits which presumably influenced natural events. Now, belief systems are also directed toward superhuman principles which presumably shape our institutions. Whether supernatural or superhuman phenomena be revered, the mode of religious belief is the same, and it is this process of belief—the defining feature of schemas—which determines the nature of human culture.

The psychological basis for religion is that people are disposed to worship what they cannot control. (This disposition may be represented by the formula: Control x Belief = K.) People also like to think they enter into some kind of reciprocal relationship with the incomprehensible if a system of belief, observance and ritual is established. This may provide a one-sided, imbalanced reciprocity, but it gives people the feeling that they have at least some input into the cosmic schema. In more mundane matters, people may literally "Believe in" (worship) their cultural institutions

Beliefs: Answers

(the government, economy, etc.), particularly if and when they feel they have no control over such organizations and entities—as many feel they do not in the modern world.

One real psychological benefit to having belief systems and their supporting rituals is that both can serve to reduce anxiety in times of crisis: Belief systems provide a sense of control, and rituals provide a culturally acceptable means of action. In matters of ill health, the success of curers can be explained not only by the real effectiveness of medicinal treatment and the fact that some people recover anyway, but also by the fact that stress and anxiety are reduced for some patients who really believe in the medicine man and his little rituals.[9] Thus, recovery may be enhanced even if the specific treatment is physiological nonsense.

For example, in some primitive societies, a belief in the malevolent dead provides a theory of disease. It offers both an explanation of cause (the actions of evil spirits) and a means of prevention (calling on friendly spirits). In the absence of any really effective medical means of coping with illness, such a belief and its attendant rituals permit people to face an otherwise bewildering experience with some confidence, and this, itself, can reduce the psychological distress accompanying an illness.[10] If this is a short-term gain, and it indeed may be, there may also be a long-term loss, if such a belief system and its sustaining rituals prevent people from finding a real cure or means of preventing disease.

In general, religious systems are most conspicuous among peoples who are intensely dependent upon nature and have limited technical means for controlling it.[11] This is the condition that originally led fantasy to add a spiritual element to the natural world, making the supernatural. This process was typically human—people rarely being content to generalize from just the data at hand when some more can be invented to dress up reality a bit. In sophisticated societies, people have come to misdirect their religious fervor toward their own cultural systems and even themselves. Although this may promote group cohesion and improve morale, it can inhibit both learning and adaptation. Although, in moderation, this trade-off can be adaptive, by its very nature, it tends to excess and becomes maladaptive because it is a cultural phenomenon, and culture is, inherently, a positive feedback mechanism. (E.g., technological development begets more technology; patriotism produces more patriots; etc.)

Along with beliefs, which all people have, humans also must have answers. The questions are universals: Who are we? Where did we come from? Where are we going? When will we get there? The answers form an ideology, which will be considered directly. However, if valid answers are not immediately available, they are manufactured by the schema because having an answer, even if it is wrong, is apparently more comfort-

93

Beliefs: Priests

ing than having none at all. One seldom hears the entropically futile, "We are helpless and hopeless and doomed to a pointless existence by indifferent fate"[12] or even the more prosaic, "We don't know what we're doing". If and when such answers are offered, those accepting them are not much inspired nor well disposed to pass them on.[a] On the contrary, most contrived answers tend to be self-serving and are designed to promote beliefs in both the supernatural and the people who provide the answers.

The role of "Answer man" is played by the "Priest"—a religious or secular expert who serves as an intermediary between the public and the supernatural spirits or superhuman institutions in which the people believe. The priest is really sort of a public relations specialist for the Almighty or the mere mighty. His job is to pass off reality in the best possible light and gloss over minor disasters, plagues, wars, etc. As everyone already knows, truly evil events are attributed to other powers which serve as foibles for the priests and those they represent.

Worse yet, priests are responsible for perverting noble ideals into ignoble means by the very human device of "Interpretation". This is the method by which a code of beliefs is adapted to the real needs and circumstances of society. Interpretation permits faith to continue, although necessity clearly demands that behavior contradict ideals. For example, American ideals have twice been trampled by "Real" Americans indulging in witch hunts for Communist heretics during the post-World War Red Scares. In a similar vein real Christians are supposed to love their fellow man, but "Man" is interpreted to mean "People[b] like us" when intergroup conflicts arise.

It is sad indeed to note that the teachings of great religious leaders have so often been interpreted to justify some of the most barbaric, "Inhuman" attitudes and acts in history.[13] An example of such a degraded ideal was provided by the Crusaders, who slaughtered infidels (and often the devout as well) in the name if not the spirit of Christ. It really is some kind of perverse miracle that the image of peace, purity and principle personified by Jesus could foster such fanaticism in his followers that his commandment to live in love could be so lost on the faithful.

---

a Freud proffered such a despairing answer in **Beyond the Pleasure Principle**, leaving behavioral scientists to find a way around the second law of thermodynamics—that everything ultimately goes into the dumper. Optimists can hope we will find a balance with nature, but unless we overcome schematic stupidity, I fear even that would be a tenuous balance of conflict(s) at best and hence probably not enduring. (JFW)

b Many groups named themselves "People" in their own language. This was done by the Germans, the Ainu (in northern Japan), the Inuit (whom we call Eskimos) and the Ankewehonwe (Mohawk Indians), among others.

Beliefs: Irrelevance

Obviously, stupidity is the great ally of priests and leaders when they presume to interpret a creed according to need. Stupidity makes illogical interpretations both possible and acceptable. In times of challenge, when people are most in of need a credible cause, no one would be so stupid as to point out that the schema is a drawback and should be abandoned for a better one. However justified such an assertion might be, no religious leader could make such a self-defeating admission. If the schema can possibly be stretched to cover existing events, it will be. Be they religious creeds or secular laws, schemas are interpreted rather than corrected until the system breaks down. This occurs when unwelcome perceptions of cultural disintegration in the forms of violent riots, disruptive protests or massive emigrations cannot be denied even by the devout.

Not only can interpretation reduce a prevailing schema's meaning to irrelevance, but the emotional commitment of believers to a maladaptive schema can inhibit the adoption of one that is better suited to reality. The reaction of the holy Church to the inroads of science during the past several centuries is a stupendous example of how attempts to maintain a schema can inhibit development of control over the real world. Obviously, the clergy were just trying to retain their influence among the faithful, but they therefore steadily had to renounce power as we gained understanding about natural phenomena.

The social sciences are currently directed toward rendering cultural phenomena comprehensible rather than just credible. However, most people retain their unwitting religious attachment to established political, social and economic institutions. What most social scientists fail to appreciate is that they are studying religious systems, tampering with people's beliefs and experiencing very much the same kind of rejection[c] natural scientists experienced in ages past when they tried to help people understand the natural world.

One of the peculiar things about all religions, be they supernatural or superhuman, is that so much of their substance is demonstrably false. Nevertheless, religious beliefs are the driving force of society. People would really rather believe than know.[14] Facts and knowledge pale before the values of established beliefs and cherished attitudes. Norms sanctify behavior and certify social procedures as beyond question. Anyone who dares contradict, question or even doubt enshrined cultural values is asking for ostracism. No matter how society may falter, only cosmetic or comic criticism will be welcomed. Any fundamental challenge to or ques-

---

c A case in point is the persistence of the devout in their belief that capital punishment is a deterrent to potential murderers—all evidence to the contrary notwithstanding.

tioning of basic assumptions will usually be dismissed out of hand as threats from the outside. That America is not a democracy and that the alleged "Capitalistic" economy is government regulated mean naught to flag wavers.

The basic problem with trying to reform religious institutions is that believers tend to discount factual knowledge. Facts are routinely refuted by information gathered by divination—a method of gathering unavailable information, a means of learning the unknowable[15] and a source of considerable comfort and solace to those firmly committed to the prevailing religious beliefs. This puts objective investigators at a disadvantage, as they accept the self-limiting principle of confining themselves to verifiable data. Naturally, disturbing criticisms do not carry much weight with people intractably entrenched in the holy establishment. These are more committed to themselves than to any principle of adjustment and thus tend to make any institution less and less efficient as justifiable complaints accrue unheeded with the passage of time.

Fortunately for priests, beliefs are sustained by ritual rather than relevance. Ceremonial observances provide participants with what they perceive as means of influencing their relations with supernatural or superhuman powers that are believed to control all things. Usually, participation in rituals is intended to perpetuate or improve the believer's relation to such powers. Supplication is frequent and sacrifice explicit.[16] Naturally, anything good happening to the believer after prayers is attributed to them and acts (as did the food reward to Skinner's superstitious pigeons) as a reinforcement for the ritual.

Rituals not only strengthen the belief of the individual but also serve to promote group cohesion, since religious rituals are often social events. Although rituals are not designed to effect objective change directly, positive results may follow when an inspired believer or the united group copes with problems. Thus, rituals should not be judged as stupid for being misdirected at the time of performance; their value should be assessed later when the motivated, confident individual or cohesive group acts to deal with the challenges of the environment.

While we might tend to think of rituals in a purely theological context —that is, in churches and similar institutions of spiritual beliefs—they also play a significant role in secular religions. In American politics, for example, party platforms have taken on a metaphorical meaning, being increasingly ceremonial[17] expressions of and for the devout and decreasingly programs for future behavior.[18] People applaud and cheer them in perfunctory fashion, and perhaps some good comes out of all that later on, but the ritual is certain to be repeated four years later as much regardless as because of its direct or indirect, immediate or long-range effects on political life.

If rituals are basically futile efforts to effect change in some direct and immediate sense, much of the criticism in Western societies could be considered ritualistic. First, criticism is often off the mark because it must be couched in language which inhibits accurate, relevant thinking about fundamental problems. Second, the people who are on the inside, know what is going on and could make relevant criticism are too much caught up in the system to put themselves in jeopardy by blowing whistles. Further, those on the outside usually have little influence and less power, so their expressed grievances may be safely ignored. Finally, although it is very nice that we can write our Congressman, send a letter to an editor or draft a useless book like this, anyone who thinks that valid criticism in such messages will have some positive effects probably also counts on the equally likely event of winning the jackpot in the state lottery.

Even when criticism is justified, witches or their human correlates may be targeted as convenient scapegoats by people unable or unwilling to acknowledge their own contribution to the creation of existing difficulties. Belief in witches and witchcraft is usually most intense in times of increased social tension when people are faced with a crisis they are unable to resolve by the institutional means which created it. Since witches cause misfortune, misfortune must be caused by witches, and there is nothing like a good witch hunt to permit a culture to express its frustration and release its hostility on some hapless soul. This may be unfair, wrong, irrelevant and stupid, but it certainly is most satisfying to everyone (except the witches).[19] Mostly, however, a witch hunt obscures the real causes of underlying problems and makes finding long-term solutions less likely as energy and attention are misdirected toward the rituals of chasing, catching and disposing of people who were being themselves. You need not wonder where to look for our modern witches: our prisons are full of them.

They have been imprisoned because culture transmits behavior, beliefs and rituals across generations by the process of indoctrination. Not only do individuals learn certain forms of social or antisocial behavior, but groups each invariably pick up the notion that they are the one with superior values and which alone has a private line to the Almighty. People in other groups are judged, by some standard selected just for this purpose, to be less worthy than themselves.[20] This superiority complex must have been and may still be of survival advantage in intergroup competition, for groups with inferiority or realistic complexes are not notedly common. Thus, the belief in superiority can realize itself by making believers in fact superior to those who doubt they are or know they are not.

Ideology: **Raison d'etre**

Obviously, this sense of superiority can run away with itself, cause a culture to overreach its limitations and, as happened with Nazi Germany, induce its own demise.

A slightly inflated sense of worth tempered by some sense of reality appears to be the common psychological state of most cultural groups, but even a modest sense of superiority usually is enough to make a believer feel compelled to convert others to his better ways. If conversion to the faith is impossible, the imposition of religious prohibitions is a worthy, secondary cause for a missionary.[21] It is difficult to imagine and impossible to calculate the misery presumably superior people have inflicted on others. Teaching by example is seldom enough. The presumption is to help the unwilling by forcing observance of rituals, proscribing behavior and attempting to impose beliefs on those unfortunate enough to come into contact with superiority.

Every religion is invariably accompanied by an ideology—another cultural universal which plays its role in fostering stupidity throughout the human family. An ideology provides believers with a **raison d'etre**—a logical justification for existence (although it may appear irrational if based on flaky assumptions). It describes, to their satisfaction, their relations with other people and to the universe as they perceive it.[22] Further, it provides a means of comprehending the environment, and it also serves as a guide to action[23](or inaction) so as to maintain as secure and static a psychic quo as possible. In most cases, a well developed ideology is conservative, but fanatics may tailor their own to justify extreme acts of violence deemed necessary in their value system.

The ideology finds impractical expression in the laws and explicit rules of cultural organizations. These serve to misguide such organizations, bureaucracies and formal social groups into set patterns of behavior which protect insiders from criticism as they crudely crush human aspirations. If laws are left on the books long after they are dysfunctional, if bureaucrats insist on following procedures simply for the sake of procedure, if groups cling to irrelevant traditions, somewhere an ideologue is content in the knowledge that his world is consistent with itself.[24] The failure of an organization to adapt to changes in the environment matters little to the loyal member committed to obeying rules. Of course, if anything good does befall a group, priests claim confirmation of the ideology, whereas if anything bad occurs, everyone attributes it to external forces.

People really need an ideology, just as they need food and drink. The constant attempt of humans to make principles of behavior both moral and rational indicates an inner quest for a universe with both meaning and order. While learning can be an opening and broadening experience, it often tends to be self-conforming and progressively restrictive. Ergo, the

Ideology: Explanations

cultural characteristic that a given philosophical system tends to become entrenched ever more within itself, inhibiting adaptability and repressing expressions of novelty. The unquestioning commitment to an ideology can make compromise difficult, particularly in times of challenge and change when a willingness to adjust may be needed most. Military history indeed shows that most wars have been fought over metaphysical issues rather than pragmatic problems because during intense cultural confrontations, the commitment to ideology becomes inflexible to the point of rigidity, whereas compromise is usually possible on practical matters.[25] Also, people come to fight over their different ideas of morality when they finally realize how totally useless philosophical argumentation really is.

In terms of morality, ideology malfunctions as a guide for behavior by defining right and wrong and good and evil so that people can be wrong and evil. Naturally, people like to think they are right and good (or extremely clever) and that any snafus are due simply to bad luck or unforeseeable circumstances. However, people so often bring on their own bad luck and contribute to their own demise by failing to heed clear warnings that they must usually be at least wrong and perhaps evil as well—or else being right and good is not all it's cracked up to be. The point is very simple: priestly sanctions of individual behavior and cultural institutions, economic morality, the family marriage, propriety in society, honorable leaders—all these express a "Correct ideology"[26] which, if not selectively applied to reality, may be tragically maladaptive. Further, an ideology as a theoretically abstract set of idealized answers to life's problems may be maladaptive not only for what it is but for what it is not: it can be fatally misleading when providing answers and when inhibiting questions.

An ideology is supposed to be explicatory, and, in a sense, it is. It usually does explain to members of a culture who they are, why they are, whence they came, and what they should do and be. It provides an explanation of how the universe operates, how to respond to the environment, and how the group will realize its end.[27] It does not much matter that these are all stories based as much on agnosticism and ignorance as misinterpretation and emotional conjecture.

If it is stupid enough that an ideology explains so little so poorly, it is even stupider when it prevents people from learning what it purports to explain. Having an explanation is the biggest stumbling block to getting a better one. Since people seem to need credible explanations, an ideology is constructed to be sort of consistent with itself even if it is contradictory to beliefs and behavior. When it dominates to the point of making ideas independent of and coping responses irrelevant to unacceptable circumstances, an ideology becomes a menace to its own well being as well as that of its devotees.

Communication: Language

One basic problem in such a situation is that some specific problems are simply declared taboo and left to fester because they should not exist in the first place: they confront the cultural ideal and threaten the underlying belief system. The fundamental, avoidable message is clear—society is not working as expected. Thus, taboo problems pose a threat to the ideology, as this is the rational element of the schema which provides people with the illusion that they are in control of their lives[28] and that everything is going along A-OK. Beliefs are basic and irrational, rituals are fixed action patterns for responding to perceptions, and the ideology is somewhere in between trying to organize information into some rational order that will, in Barry Goldwater's terms, "Make sense".

The fact that the ideology (set of ideas) contributes to the existence of shameful problems by inhibiting reasonable discussion of them is largely lost on everyone. Poverty and disease are but two phenomena which may be explained by acts of God, moral turpitude of the afflicted or any number of other possible causes. The explanations offered invariably conform to and confirm the basic ideology of the explainer: rebels blame the establishment while officials affix blame on the victims or immutable natural forces. The problems, however, remain and become more serious until a relevant way of coping is found by someone responsible enough to learn how to relate causes to effects and then, finally, causes to cures.

In the transformation of cultures, as indeed in their original formation and transmission, learning is paramount. In fact, learning, unlearning and relearning are all processes fundamental to the development and existence of culture.[29] This is not a uniquely human phenomenon, as many mammalian species depend upon their considerable learning capabilities in the development of their social organization and general behavior. With the basic cultural process being part of our primate heritage,[30] it is language that gives human culture its distinctive flair.

In developing the cultural capacity for stupidity to human dimensions, language proved to be a most effective mechanism in that it both inhibits awareness and subverts communication. It is language which provides us with our basic misperceptions, which culture then embellishes and disseminates. Thus, self-awareness is inhibited when language permits us to misinterpret embarrassing events into socially acceptable contexts. Although sense organs give us our first impressions of our environment, words fix our attitudes, direct the process of data selection and strongly influence the misinterpretation of information so that we may contentedly misconstrue experiences.

It is through language that "Exploitation" becomes "Development"; "Indoctrination" is "Education"; and "Destruction" is "Liberation". It is no wonder that so much stupidity is so readily accepted, as so much of our psyche is structured to prevent its recognition, and so much of our behavior is designed to reinforce evaluations of immediate success even as we sacrifice critical adjustments and long-term survival.

Criticism within a system is inhibited not only by language but also by common if unjustified assumptions. For example, in terms of terms, capitalism really cannot be effectively criticized as a system of economic profits and losses. However, in terms of the human misery of poverty sustained and needs ignored can capitalism be taken to task. Unfortunately for the poor, the term "Misery" does not happen to be in the businessman's vocabulary, so its perception rarely appears in his mind. Further, the capitalist's assumption that the system will respond to need is flat out idiotic and serves only to hide the failings of the system from its devotees. The business economy responds to capital. If there is a need and no money, as there nearly always is in starving Africa or even American slums, business does not respond. On the other hand, where there is money and no need, advertisers will be paid to create one.

Criticism is further diminished and stupidity promoted by the cultural suppression of honesty and integrity. Both are welcome if they promote group cooperation. In and of itself, however, honesty is worthless. In fact, it may even be a dangerous indulgence, as honest whistle blowers have discovered to their dismay when pointing out corruption within the system. Such criticism is regarded as disruptive, and such candor is dealt with according to Luce's Law—"No good deed goes unpunished". When leaders regard truth as a threat, anyone with a modicum of sense will suppress any inchoate urge to correct rather than confirm the establishment. At the first sign of integrity, the state totters.

It would be nice to think that cultures would develop watchdog subgroups which would promote social order. The news media are supposed to compose one such element in American society. However, when the watchdog is fed by those it is watching, its objectivity is likely to be compromised. The ideal of an independent press is a myth. News is reported honestly, accurately and fairly, if that is acceptable to sponsors, advertisers, publishers and owners, but editors are paid to keep honesty out of the media as well as to direct it toward problems deemed profitable to explore and exploit. The business of journalists is to distort and pervert truths not acceptable to the establishment. Reporters and editors are intellectual prostitutes[31] permitted to be virtuous only when it suits the corporate and political powers behind the scenes.[d] Nothing fundamental is cri-

---

d For a detailed case study, see **The Power Broker**—a biography of New York's master builder Robert Moses—by Robert Caro. The book chronicles the initial failure and eventual tically examined by the "Mythia" (i.e., myth x media): for example, the government might be criticized but not the Constitution.

For lack of effective, meaningful criticism, power does indeed tend to corrupt (as Lord Acton noted), because stupidity is a corruption of learning. For some reason, the power to command frequently causes a failure to learn—as if power can be or is a substitute for wisdom. In an ideal state, the responsibility of those in power is to govern as reasonably as possible to the mutual advantage of all. To accomplish this end, a leader had best be well-informed, heed available information, be open-minded without being empty-headed and judge all effects of policies objectively. However, it is unusual for someone transfixed by his own power to be open-minded enough to perceive that a pet policy is having unintended, negative effects, responsible enough to admit it and wise enough to replace it with a better one.[32]

Generally, mismanagement is promoted when creeds and rituals of government become so rigid as to inhibit adaptive responses. In the holy wars of politics, priests crusade and campaign, thrive and perish,[33] but even when victorious over political opponents, officials may find their reforms and policies lost to bureaucratic inertia. It often appears that the machine of government is designed to produce friction, constructed to break down and operated for those who service it. Society is there for the government—to feed it and clean up after it, to nurse it through illness and to support it when it goes out to cut its teeth on its neighbors.

The sad fact of real political life is that misgovernment may actually strengthen a regime temporarily.[34] Gaining and retaining power is what government is all about, and the idea that having power is not an end in itself but a means to help people is a myth political priests may use to mask their short-term, self-serving machinations from the long suffering public. When the government takes control of a society, it may be building itself up, but it also builds up a lot of aggravation and resentment. As agencies expand in size, productivity is reduced to the point that one might think waste has become an incentive. This is the point at which bureaucracies cease to solve problems and become problems themselves. While there is nothing quite so stupid and aggravating in public life as officials perversely persistent in pursuing a policy clearly in everyone's worst interest, the commitment of politicians to their favorite projects is a motivating force unto itself and makes government immune to reason and restraint. The short-term gain of power through corruption makes a mismanaged agency less ruly and more an end unto itself. This may make the

success of the press at its alleged job. (See the index for specific newspaper titles.)

Politics: Leaders

"Ins" temporarily stronger, but it also intensifies long-term resentment against them and fosters opposition to them.

The craftier politicians have found that, while stupidity may lead to unpopularity, popularity may lead to stupidity and that this is the most effective way to succeed in politics. If a politician really wants to be stupid, as so many seem to, he need not be too circumspect—all he has to do is find a popular cause. The more popular the cause, the less critical people will be about policies directed toward achieving the end: the more people want something, the less they will be concerned about how they get it. This gives stupidity full rein to flourish in the absence of skeptical criticism. Only after officials have persisted for a long time in contrived foolishness to the point that their actions become unpopular and finally unacceptable will a government to forced to do something intelligent. This is basically what happened with American involvement in Vietnam and is happening now in eastern Europe.

Generally in political organizations, the leader is a popular headman —the first among unequals. As a central reference point,[35] he may play a largely symbolic role in that, most of the time, people know what to do anyway.[36] Oddly enough, in our modern societies, traditional patterns of political behavior have been strengthened by the emphasis of the role of the "Leading man" as a symbol rather than as a doer. The American public, for example, forms lasting impressions from a President's incidental gestures as representative of the people but pays relatively little attention to what he does as chief of state.[37] More and more, when such leaders are chosen, they attain office because of their popular appeal rather than because they are effective administrators. In fact, the leader really does not lead anymore. He is just there, like an elected monarch, giving a general tone to society and providing a focal point for the reverence of those who believe in the system. He also provides the media with an object of attention, so that hundreds of photographers have someone to focus on and scores of reporters have someone to quote off the record. If any leading must be done, there is least friction if the people lead the headman where they want to go. On the other hand, the most effective leaders are those who can make people want to do what is necessary and make that appear to be right. Of course, stupidity thrives at its self-defeating best in the gray area between the appearance and actuality of necessity.

In terms of political organization, republics are particularly stupid, due to the temptation of representatives to give people what they want rather than what they need. (Fortunately, doctors do not prescribe medication according to this principle.) Elected officials, however, are seldom in a position even to consider what ought to be done[38] except in the neurotically paradoxical context of getting reelected. Further, the danger of gratifying the people is usually somewhat offset by the influence of special interest groups.[39] Their campaign contributions are a principle source of corruption among elected officials and make many of their acts appear to be as stupid to their constituents in the short run as they may prove to be embarrassing to the representatives themselves in the long run, if and when they are revealed. Not only does power corrupt, but it is eminently corruptible.

Governments not only administer stupid laws ineffectively but also provide a professional judiciary to apply them unjustly. There was a time when people were judged by trials of combat. There were also trials by water and fire.[40] These were all based on a belief that trials were moral confrontations. If a person was judged favorably, it was because he was right relative to another individual or neutral nature. Those who smile with derision at such judicial mechanisms might do well to take a good look at our modern jousting list—the court of law—where hired wits do battle[41] to determine the morality (guilt or innocence) of the person on trial. The hired guns—the lawyers—use all the tricks in the book to win "Their" case. At best, judges preside not to get the truth but to see that the game is played fairly, while occasionally, the rules of court obstruct any quest for the truth.[42] At worst, judges may intervene to interpret formalistic rules according to some preconceived notion of how the "Fair" game should end.

In all seats of political power, be they administrative, legislative or judicial, ceremony shapes the ways in which personalities interact to solve and create real and imaginary problems. The preoccupation with most political officials is with the rituals of government. As long as these assure the likelihood that those in power will retain their positions, the rituals are honored as sacred. The impact of decisions reached under such circumstances is usually secondary to the desirability of maintaining a modicum of decorum and giving speakers a chance to pronounce a few slogans for public consumption. The regulation of society is considered rather irrelevant and is indirectly affected only when conservatives become convinced the status quo must be further preserved and protected or reformers can convince political hacks it really is in their own best interests to apply some common ideal to reality.

One of the basic problems with which all community leaders must contend is that the ideals and ideas they are expected to use to solve existing problems are often simply common assumptions. This is particularly true in the field of economics—a domain in which beliefs and arguments over them have clearly become religious in nature. The general field of economics relates to the system of allocating productive goods and the land, tools and labor employed to produce them. The need for systems is a cul-

Economics: "Systems"

tural universal,[43] but one might legitimately inquire as to just how systematic the systems are. Capitalism really is not a system: it is economic anarchy. Socialism is too systematic: it stifles initiative with plans for state traction. Communism is economic democracy: it is collective stupidity, with each detracting according to his means.

Pure economic systems are not to be found except in the minds and tomes of economic theorists. In the real world, people need some way to organize their resources, equipment and labor so that goods can be produced and distributed.[44] The actual system used by a given society is an expression of its cultural ideology and is sanctioned by an economic schema which defines "Right and wrong" in quasireligious terms. The discrepancies between the ideal and real systems are due to the compromises people must make to function, however ineffectively, in a world of physical limitations, egos, selfishness and ineptitude. In fact, the theoretical systems might better be considered distractions which keep people from understanding what they are doing.

As unsystematic systems, economic disorganizations have ideological explanations which are neither reasonable nor accurate. Indeed, what devotees thereof have created for themselves is what they need—emotionally satisfying religious sanctifications. For example, Calvin Coolidge apparently thought the business of America was something holier than just business. He referred to the capitalist's factory in pre-Crash America as a "Temple", opined "The man who works there worships there"[45] and declared that "Advertising ministers to the spiritual side of trade".[46] It is hardly surprising that stupidity can play a very large role in economic life[47] when leaders who not only accept but even revere the establishment with religious fervor allow their beliefs to color their critical thinking.

For the sake of brevity, our analysis of economic systems will be arbitrarily limited to a consideration of the labor force. Stratified societies dominated by a strong political organization are often founded on forced labor systems.[48] However the coercion is structured—be it through slavery, serfdom or whatever, the emphasis is on political and social control rather than economic efficiency. Whatever is wasted (i.e., human labor) is considered expendable, and whenever a system considers its bottom strata expendable, its leaders are obliged to keep their followers as misinformed and credulous as possible.

In caste systems, work is performed by the members of all castes except the land owners. Actually, the land owners do a job of sorts: they decide the allocation of labor. Usually, the rule of thumb is that those lowest in the hierarchy do most of the work, and those highest do least. When it comes to distribution of the goods produced, the asymmetry remains but is, naturally, inverted.[49] Those low down get less; those high

105

Economics: Inequality

up get more. While it might seem unfair to sweaty laborers that the workers get the least out of the system, the priests justify distribution according to the worth of the people—inferior people get what they deserve, which is something less than what is received by superior people (meaning the priests and their elitist equals).[50] Such a system is aided by the stupidity (i.e., jaded education) of people accepting their fate and acquiescing in their own exploitation.

No matter what the system of labor organization, in agricultural communities, large families are advantageous in that there is always plenty of work to be done. However, as a society industrializes, the large family becomes a liability[51] rather than an asset. Thus, a cultural conflict develops as traditional values are strained by new working conditions and challenged by a different way of life. In such situations, stupidity is the big winner, with ignorance, poverty and despair following closely in about that order. More of these commodities are produced and distributed than can be imagined. Unlike the "Goods" of life, these "Bads" are doled out generously to those least in need of them. Seldom is the unstable base of such societies a serious concern to the leaders, who usually simply repress threats of change.

If there is one constant across all civilizations, it is the unequal distribution of wealth. The increased productivity of advanced societies never promotes equitable prosperity, as surpluses are drawn off to support those who organize most and produce least.[52] This inequality of wealth is so ubiquitous that the notion of economic equality must be one of those theoretical ideals which reformers find inapplicable to real humans. It seems that some people invariably lord it over others, so as in the caste system mentioned above, people generally share goods but not equally: Those responsible for dividing up the goods invariably give themselves more than they allot to the producers. Of course, all such systems are sanctified by priests, who are duly rewarded for their ideological support of the establishment. This arrangement is stupid for the workers while it lasts and stupid for the priests and their cronies when it fails. There is little consolation in knowing that any system which fails is likely to be replaced by one that is just as stupid, as a bunch of bandits replace a pack of thieves.

Along with poverty, another inescapable fact of civilization is collectivism. In most advanced societies, the larger productive goods—waterworks, roads, equipment used in public services, factories, etc.—are almost always collectively[e] owned either by private groups (corporations)

e Even in the self-styled capitalistic systems, there is a surprising degree of socialism—public ownership of utilities and transportation systems at the state and local levels.

or governments.[53] Bigness is inescapable and means that civilization is characterized by collective stupidity. Gone are the good old days when an individual could just go off and fall flat on his very own face. More and more, stupidity is organized for people who can merely select for which fools they will work and with which knaves they will invest their time, energy and money. In the business world, the small entrepreneur, who tries to maximize profits in response to the specifics of his economic conditions, has been replaced by the corporation man, who seeks promotion by responding less to external events and more to rules, regulations and policies generated internally by the company.[54] In the political domain, government is there doing its worst to see to it that each of us has the same chance to accept and conform to standards set by the Mediocracy. Further, as a tax payer, a person is working not for himself but for the government—the least responsible institution ever to evolve.

There is much more than irony in the fact that so many people are so willing to work so hard in their own worst interest. Such behavior is made all the more probable by the human capacity to believe in nonsense. People identify themselves so much with causes, institutions, ideologies and religions that they render themselves incapable of judging their own best or worst interests. It is sad enough if they believe that what is good for the system is good for them, but this belief tends to inhibit criticism. This gives leaders free rein to pursue their own self-aggrandizement. Labor unions provide some unfortunate examples of this phenomenon, as workers have eagerly lined up to be bamboozled by officials lavishly paid to price American workers out of the labor market.

It would be nice to think that the allocation of material rewards would provide all who contribute to the production of goods at least minimal means for subsistence. In primitive societies, rights of access to water, food and shelter are assumed and honored. A person can gather whatever is needed or wanted directly from nature and can share in the rewards of common efforts in rough proportion to his contribution to them. However, when existence depends on the ownership of land or on laboring for others, the issue of economic rights becomes both crucial and very arbitrary. Rights happen to be very circumstantial and incredibly alienable. Their existence is determined by people with a vested interest in seeing to it that workers get just enough to keep working. As we are seeing today in eastern Europe, rights turn out to be expressions of the numbers and organizational capacities of the disenfranchised and those sympathetic to their plight. Historically, in the case of the American labor movement, rights did not exist until workers brought them into being at the expense of owners' rights to control property. The waste to society of such conflicts of interest is the alternative to oppression of one group by another.

This, in turn, means that a certain amount of inefficiency is characteristic of culture, although the form will vary from one society to another.

Recognizing, much less dealing politically with such economic waste and inefficiency is complicated by the confusing number and nature of roles individuals can assume as their identification with different social groups shifts. Any human society is a welter of associations. The basic human social unit is the family, which is an association based on kinship. Beyond this, there are formal and informal associations designed to foster cooperation and restrain disruptive behavior[55] for the good of the dominant power group. Obviously, under certain conditions, a subgroup may find itself driven to disruptive behavior (as were trade unions in our recent past), but this is usually a last resort, when orderly means of attaining a group goal appear to be thwarted by the general society.

Not only are human societies assemblages of overlapping and sometimes contradictory associations, but they invariably have some form of class structure as well, with each class system supported by a formal ideology and set of rituals. The verbal doctrine emphasizes and the program of stereotyped behaviors reinforces the ideal virtues of the lower social orders, especially of those stupid enough to accept their inferior position and resigned to defer their rewards until later—like in their next life.[56] The presumably more eternal values of obedience and spiritual devotion are sanctimoniously contrasted by priests with the crass materialism of those who indulge in the luxuries made possible by the degrading practice of manipulating worldly power.

Classes become castes when they become rigidly defined to the point that membership is a birthright and intergroup mixing prohibited. Caste societies are not human universals, but they are common enough and represent extremes of the class system so that their intense stupidity warrants our attention. At all levels, caste position is ritualized so as to exaggerate awareness of separate group identity. There is usually little in the way of yearnings for upward mobility or improved status, as everyone's position is preordained. Along with established rituals, supernatural powers are at the disposal of the establishment and may be called upon by priests to punish anyone who transgresses the rules.[57] When religion is the establishment, critics may be motivated to proselytize, but ideological and social development is usually rigidly circumscribed. Thus, a caste system is the social structure typically found in a self-contained theocracy.

Even more rigid than designations of class or caste are those of race. Unfortunately for racists, there has been so much interbreeding among the human subspecies (races) that there is no genetic basis for making clear distinctions among them. Nevertheless, human groups are not only separated but invariably stratified by racial identity. All hierarchical rankings of race have only one thing in common: those passing judgment are always in the top group. When feasible, those in power will use racism to preserve their advantages,[58] but there are long-term losses to such a system in the protection afforded the inept of the dominant race and the suppression of the gifted and able of other groups. The sad thing about the long history of racism is that it is an important issue only to and because of those determined to make it one. In almost all matters of public importance, if decisions could magically be made on the basis of relevant criteria, race would be one of the last considerations in any culture.

Beyond consideration of caste or race, differentiation of individuals is a given of the human condition. Those who are most skilled or who possess some admired attribute are treated as important or socially valuable and are granted a larger share of available economic, social and political rewards.[59] This is discriminatory as well as universal in human culture.

However, the cognitive basis for much social stupidity is not discrimination based on ability but the human tendency to generalize behavior of differentiated members of a group into the form of a representative stereotype. This streamlines social decisions, as individual variation can be ignored and reactions keyed to specific characteristics deemed definitive for behavioral interaction. However, the loss to stereotyping is obvious: individuals are raised up or put down not because of their abilities but because they are lumped into a particular cultural/linguistic category.

Women, for example, have been universally and eternally victimized by stereotyping.[60] It is alleged that the female psyche has somehow been permanently shaped by the oft noted ability of women to have children. It may well be that there is something to this for mothers (who do usually tend to be female) who spend more than 24 hours a day in the presence of children. Anyone subjected to such stress and pressure might have to sacrifice something to reality, and it may be a bit of logic and sanity. Recent research indicates there are real differences between male and female brains, so there may well be a special brand of feminine stupidity. However, before we venture too far into the yet unchartered domain of comparative idiocy, let us indulge in an uncharacteristic bit of diplomacy and allow the possibility that the two sexes are, in their own aggravating ways, equally stupid.

Likewise, the down-trodden, the poor, the workers, all have been stereotypically regarded as social elements which somehow fail to fulfill the cultural ideal of success. At best, a culture will exploit those it has disenfranchised; at worst, it will ignore them. Throughout history, workers have been systematically fatigued, starved and forced to live in generally unhealthy conditions.[61] Anyone trapped in such conditions might indeed be better off were he too dull to criticize his own lot: ergo the basic undercurrent of tragedy in the human drama—that those most directly and hardest hit by social iniquities are almost blessed if they can accept their fate rather than become aware of their helplessness. It is a matter of record that many reform movements (i.e., abolition, mental health, etc.) derived considerable impetus from articulate, upper class ideologues who were morally outraged to the point of action by the appalling discrepancies between what society promised and provided.[62]

On the other hand, there are always some people who amass wealth and then use it, along with their superior political and social positions, to consolidate effective control over productive resources. They then further their interests by using their enhanced influence to gain yet more power.[63] This positive feedback system routinely creates social inequities which are compounded by laws passed and enforced, in the name of justice, to protect the special advantages and power of the few rather than to secure a minimum standard of decency for the many.[64] Differential access to privilege and power thus both produces and perpetuates social stratification, because the material prosperity of the upper class is usually created and maintained by the debasement of all others. Such a system may then go to excess as the mighty reinforce their own self-confirming, self-serving perceptions, attitudes and beliefs at the expense of objectivity.

Frequently, such ruling groups are also in charge of the theological establishment, so they control access not only to natural but supernatural resources as well. By using all the means available to them, leaders can assure themselves that the prevailing ideology sanctions their privileged status, economic influence and political rank. Not only do the established powers maintain the stratified system which supports them, but their position is further secured by popular belief in the system.[65] Modern societies have thus secularized religion while becoming religious about secular systems. All these factors can make the mighty self-assured to the point of complacent stupidity.

A major factor in determining the amount and nature of work performed in a society is the level and type of technology applied to the exploitation of its environmental resources. Basically, technology is that aspect of culture which encompasses the tools as well as the techniques people use in meeting their material needs.[66] It functions through time in its interrelations to other aspects of society, so its full significance can be appreciated only as means to maladapt a society not only to its environment but to itself as well.[67]

Regardless of the level of sophistication of its technology, when a group outstrips the carrying capacity of its environment, starvation will follow. This is a basic principle of life, and technology cannot alter it. Sophisticated devices and methods may expand the capacity of the environment to sustain a certain way of life, but when these new limits are quantitatively exceeded, the same predictable result is inevitable. In fact, without some guiding sense of the long-term impact of technoillogical exploitation of natural resources, technology serves only to build up a culture to a bigger and worse crash.

Just at the start of the Industrial Revolution, Thomas Malthus articulated the principle that starvation, disease and war have been, are and always will be the limiting factors on the growth of human populations.[68] It is a sad commentary on humanity that, although technological development has proceeded apace since that time, little in the last two centuries indicates that our political leaders are aware of the long-term dangers inherent in their shortsighted policies. We seem unable to reconcile the facts that we are both slaves to our cultural world and creatures of nature.

The chronic starvation in Ethiopia is a tragic example of the stupidity a simple culture can impose upon itself. There, agricultural techniques which sufficed for ages became ineffective as the environment changed. The problems of coping with extensive droughts were compounded by the contrived polices of the government to meet the crisis in a manner based on the Marxist ideology of Colonel Mengistu Haile-Mariam[69]—policies which proved to be at least as maladaptive as the traditional means for providing food. It is noteworthy that no one in a position of real authority did anything to promote birth control as a long-term policy for preventing future famines.[f] Presumably, famine acts as a Malthusian form of birth control since this matter is too important matter to be dealt with logically by informed, intelligent leaders.

Although the commitment of any civilization to its way of life may be irrational, it may also be regarded as quite efficient, if the same society provides the standard for measuring success. The hidden pitfall is not so much what that standard may be as what it is not—not what it includes but what it omits. In technologically advanced societies, the commission of machines to help people is clearly desirable, but the omission of people from the calculations of computer programmers is indicative of a cultured failure to perceive that people are not here to help machines. The social impact of technology and scientific ideology is commonly treated as an incidental spinoff from numerous, specific projects, each developed by single-minded engineers. However, the parts do not add up to a whole; they add up to a lot of parts. The material success of a technologically oriented society may impress those who revel in quantified analysis, but human and spiritual values have been sacrificed to the point that most

f President Mengistu resigned in May, 1991, but the disaster continues.

Art: Expression

of us cease even to wonder if life has any meaning beyond our self-constructed, self-destructive world. Today's overdeveloped nations insist on perceiving themselves more as thriving in their own technological present than withering in a spiritually and aesthetically sterile future.

Beyond the purely material and social dementions of the human condition, there is a universal artistic dimension to culture. Through techniques developed for the manipulation of the senses, people seek to express and communicate emotional experiences. Unfortunately, art is often judged to be stupid by many rational, articulate people who fail to appreciate it as essentially an emotional medium. Art serves to heighten and intensify feelings[70] by making them explicit, thereby making us self-consciously aware of who and what we are.

As a special creation, a work of art is both a part of and apart from reality. Through artistic expression, people affirm their potential to transcend and improve upon their immediate conditions. This creative impulse is undeniable, although its specific manifestations may be regarded as destructive by those who fear change. The greatest cultural contribution art can make is to promote a sense of faith in the human capacity to control change of superficial aspects of life so as to confirm or confront fundamentals. If the way people react to art is indicative of the way they feel about life, they will continue to embrace the idiotic as well as the barren in their historic attempt to both express and deny themselves.

Notes

1. Buchler, I. and Selby, H. 1968. **A Formal Study of Myth**. Monograph Series #1, Center for Intercultural Studies in Folklore and Oral History. University of Texas; Austin, TX.

2. Smith, R., Sarason, I. and Sarason, B. 1982. **Psychology: The Frontiers of Behavior**. Harper & Row; New York. 370.

3. Terman, L. 1906. **Genius and Stupidity**. Thesis; Clark University, Worcester, MA. [Reprint of a 1906 edition in 1975 by Arno Press; New York. 372.]

4. Pitkin, W. 1932. **A Short Introduction to the History of Human Stupidity**. Simon and Schuster; New York. 515.

5. **Ibid.** 501.

6. **Ibid.** 304.

7. Hammond, P. 1978. **An Introduction to Cultural and Social Anthropology**. 2nd ed. Macmillan; New York. 12.

8. **Ibid.** 318.

9. **Ibid.** 358.

10. Spiro, M. 1952. Ghosts, Ifaluk, and teleological functionalism. **American Anthropologist**, 54; 497-503.

11. Hammond. **op. cit.** 326.

12. Roszak, T. Mar/Apr 1993. **Sierra**, 78, #2, 59.

13. Bondi, H. 1979. Religion is a good thing. In **The Encyclopedia of Delusions** edited by R. Duncan and M. Weston-Smith. Wallaby; New York.

14. Wilson, E. 1975. **Sociobiology**. Harvard University Press; Cambridge, MA. 561.
15. Hammond. **op. cit.** 355.
16. **Ibid.** 321.
17. Arnold, T. 1937. **The Folklore of Capitalism**. Yale U. Press; New Haven, CT. 41.
18. Stevenson, C. 1938. Paraphrased in **Means of Ascent** by R. Caro. 1990. Vintage; New York. 165.
19. Hammond. **op. cit.** 353.
20. Bondi. **op. cit.** 206.
21. **Ibid.**
22. Robertson, W. 1976. **The Dispossessed Majority**. Howard Allen; Cape Canaveral, FL. 7(fn).
23. Hammond. **op. cit.** 318.
24. Jacobs, R. and Campbell, D. 1961. The perpetuation of an arbitrary tradition through several generations of a laboratory microculture. **J. Abnor. Soc. Psychology**, 62, 649-658.
25. Arnold. **op. cit.** 90.
26. Hammond. **op. cit.** 320.
27. Fried, M. (Ed.) 1969. **Readings in Anthropology**. Crowell; New York. Vol. 2, 615-616.
28. Hammond. **op. cit.** 343.
29. **Ibid.** 10.
30. Washburn, S. and Moore, R. 1973. **Ape into Man**. Little, Brown; Boston, MA.
31. Swinton, J. Quoted in Smith, P. 1984. **The Rise of Industrial America**. McGraw-Hill; New York. 379.
32. Tuchman, B. 1984. **The March of Folly**. Knopf; New York. 32.
33. Arnold. **op. cit.** 21.
34. Tuchman. **op. cit.** 33.
35. Redl, F. 1942. Group emotion and leadership. **Psychiatry**. 573-596.
35. Hammond. **op. cit.** 275.
37. Rowe, J. 1947. In a memorandum entitled **The Politics of 1948** allegedly prepared by Clark Clifford for President Truman. Cited in **The Best Years: 1945-1950** by J. Goulden. 1976. Atheneum; New York. 366-367.
38. Arnold. **op. cit.** 45.
39. Stockman, D. 1986. **The Triumph of Politics**. Harper & Row; New York. 33.
40. Mackay, C. 1852. **Extraordinary Popular Delusions and the Madness of Crowds**. 2nd ed. [Republished by Harmony Books; New York. 1980. 651-652.]
41. Morgan, E. 1935. In a review of **Trial Techniques** by Irving Goldstein. **Harvard Law Review**, 49, 1387-1389.
42. Morris, R. 1967. **Fair Trial**. Harper & Row; New York. xii.
43. Hammond. **op. cit.** 18.
44. **Ibid.** 104.
45. Coolidge, C. Quoted in **The Glory and the Dream** by William Manchester. 1973. Little, Brown; Boston, MA. 28.
46. Coolidge, C. Quoted in **American Heritage**. 1965: XVI, #5, 70.
47. Galbraith, J. June 20, 1994. Quoted in **USA Today** by Mark Memmott. 3B.
48. Hammond. **op. cit.** 129.
49. **Ibid.** 246.
50. Chamberlain, N. 1970. **Beyond Malthus**. Basic Books; New York. 16.
51. Hammond. **op. cit.** 128-129.

113

52. **Ibid.** 56.
53. **Ibid.** 116.
54. Galbraith, J. 1981. **A Life in Our Times.** Houghton Mifflin; Boston, MA. 350-351.
55. Hammond. **op. cit.** 220.
56. Pitt-Rivers, J. 1961. **The People of the Sierra.** U. of Chicago Press; Chicago, IL.
57. Hammond. **op. cit.** 246.
58. **Ibid.** 258.
59. **Ibid.** 242.
60. **Ibid.** 185.
61. Pitkin. **op. cit.** 142.
62. Hofstadter, R. 1963. **Anti-intellectualism in American Life.** Knopf; New York. 29.
63. Hammond. **op. cit.** 243.
64. **Ibid.** 62.
65. **Ibid.** 243.
66. Braudel, F. 1981. **The Structures of Everyday Life.** Harper & Row; New York. 334.
67. Hammond. **op. cit.** 34.
68. Malthus, T. 1798. **An Essay on the Principle of Population.** (Republished in 1959 by the University of Michigan Press; Ann Arbor, MI.)
69. **New York Times** (Large Type Weekly). Sept. 24, 1984. 4.
70. Hammond. **op. cit.** 22.

VI. A History of Western Stupidity

To the extent that Western Civilization is a distinctly identifiable historical adventure, its origins are discernable in and associated with the rise of ancient Greece. As Greek culture developed and flourished, it became clear to all that an excess of power led to a comparable amount of stupidity. After first presenting his vision of the philosopher-kings in **The Republic**, Plato had his doubts and concluded that laws were the only safeguard against abuses of power. Too much power concentrated anywhere is simply too dangerous, as it invariably leads to injustice. Arbitrary power[1] was recognized as an inducement to stupidity which in turn undermined the effectiveness of power. Stupidity could thus be seen as a check on excessive power, rendering it counter-productive as it became unjust.

Since we still revere Greek thought and honor Greek ideals, it is worth noting that these ideals were not of physical objects reduced to essence but archetypal models of theoretical ultimates which could not possibly be realized. Philosophers reveled in associating such idealized abstractions but always in static, non-algebraic modes of thought,[2] and in the purest philosophy of mathematics, the Greeks failed to develop any system of symbolic notation to express dynamic functions.[3]

As mathematical idealists, the Pythagoreans, for example, were in love with whole numbers. A veritable crisis in doctrine arose when the square root of two was found to be irrational.[4] This posed a threat to their schema, as it indicated that their mental world was somehow inaccurate, insufficient, incomplete and imperfect. Worse yet, it could not be made accurate, sufficient, complete and perfect by adaptation and/or expansion and still remain "Theirs". So, how did these great Greek mathematical philosophers handle this cognitive crisis? Pretty much as would anyone else: they suppressed knowledge of the square root of two.[5]

Likewise, they suppressed that other scourge of Pythagorean idealism —the dodecahedron. In this, they were so successful that hardly anyone now knows much less cares what a dodecahedron is. Nevertheless, anyone interested in Greek stupidity should note that Pythagoreans knew of five perfect solids—the tetrahedron, the cube, the octahedron, the icosahedron and the dodecahedron. The first four were conveniently associated with the four elements which constituted the Greek world—earth, air, fire and water. The fifth was regarded as a symbol of the quintessence of the other four,[6] thus presumably representing some unworldly, supernatural and perhaps even dangerous power.[7] Ordinary people were to be kept unaware of the dodecahedron as a matter of something like "Cognitive security". In fact, Pythagoreanism was popular until its practitioners were found to be dealing in this alarming and subversive subject, whence they were suppressed and some lynched, thus initiating the West's long and venerable tradition of persecuting intellectual heretics.[8]

Such actions were justified in the classical world by a schema which dealt with both ideals and ideas in terms of a desired moral end rather than accuracy and practicality.[9] Any object or observation might provide a starting point for a train of thought, but then a logical philosophy could be constructed based upon it without any particular concern for congruence with reality. Worse yet, a contrived system could be constructed for a particular moral purpose—i.e., to justify a particular desired policy—and many were and still are to this day.[10]

If Greeks were stupid in their philosophical ways, Romans were stupid in pragmatic, practical ways. Far from being thinkers, Romans were doers—short-range opportunists of the first order. Julius Caesar, for example, never had a long-range plan. His schema was to act to his immediate advantage, with his most brilliant stratagem being moment-to-moment scheming.[11] His assassination was the price he paid for his overwhelming success. He aroused resentment and jealousy in others in the way the Big Man on Campus might be hated for being so popular.

In its most characteristic and basic form, the Roman mind was dominated by a conservative, self-serving schema in which there was a conspicuous lack of imagination, creative fantasy and playfulness. Basically, the Romans really were not much fun to be around. The opportunity of the moment might be seized, but there was little creative in Roman culture. Its literature and art were wooden, and there emerged no genius in mathematics or science.[12] If the Romans had any genius at all, it was in applied intellect. For example, as engineers, they built to last, with some of their roads and aqueducts still in use today.

Romans fully expected their stand-pat, stagnant culture to last as long as their works in engineering. They deified "Law and order"—a defining component of the modern centurion's schema. They delighted in framing laws and profoundly loved systems. They defined the future in terms of the past and had no concept of progress.[13] They dominated for centuries and might have endured in fact as well as name for centuries more had they not, like Caesar, been so successful in their practical conquests and rigid in their devotion to themselves.

116

Rome

Some four hundred explanations have been suggested for the fall of the Roman Empire, so one more will not matter. It may well be that the Empire fell and for hundreds of years kept on falling because the Romans were stupid. More precisely, the decline and fall was due to socio-economic imprudence[14] compounded by a monumental measure of self-induced ignorance[15] and was a grand example of applied stupidity—the reciprocity of ignorance and misguided power.

The Empire struck out because the Romans were insensitive to the social aspects of trade and finance[16]—the twin underpinnings of their military juggernaut. They were simply unable to appreciate what they were doing to themselves and what kind of world they were creating. As their conquests spread, the lines of administration stretched to the point that even interpretation of dicta could not suffice to maintain both law and order. One of them had to go, so order was sacrificed for the sake of legal fictions, the image of invincibility and the fantasy of imperial propriety.

To put it simply, Rome could not survive its success. It became a case study of the neurotic paradox in action, with cravings for quick profits blinding those with naught but short-term gains on their minds to the social ills they were creating. Roman Senators and their cronies set the tone of legislators and their lackeys down through the ages as they skinned and fleeced their way through the lands surrounding the Mediterranean. Fertile land was tilled to the point of sterility, with nothing being done with fertilizers to rebuild it as the Chinese, at the very same time, were doing in their fields.[17] Nor did Romans condescend to help the impoverished peasants of the lands they overran and ruined.[18] Rome had no future because it had no concept of a future as anything but a continual adventure in exploitation.

Romans lived for the moment and thereby guaranteed that there would be, for them, no tomorrow. They enjoyed the good things in life—slavery, brutality and materialism. Consistent with their practical bent, their religions were blatantly commercial. Winning divine favor was considered a matter of paying value for value in an essentially economic religion, with the gods certainly owing the Romans something in return for the sacrifices made to them.[19] It was in this spiritual void that Christianity took root and flourished by appealing to the many have-nots, who had nothing material to sacrifice.

The political empire of the Romans was replaced by the spiritual empire of the Catholic church. For some thousand years, this institution defined the schema and life of Western Civilization. By any standard except the splitting of theological hairs, it was a time of cultural stagnation interrupted only when crusaders sallied forth to visit terror and destruction on the Holy Land.

The Crusades

As part of our common heritage of misunderstandings from the past, the term "Crusader" has survived as a designation of honor and virtue. This is rather incredible, considering that the original crusaders were little more than loosely organized mobs of cutthroats. Seldom in history have such vicious gangs of self-opinionated invaders robbed and slaughtered in such righteousness. If there is any lesson to be learned from the crusaders, it must be that the lowest acts of cruelty and violence can be motivated and hidden by the loftiest of ideals. Excesses are usually dangerous to everyone, and nothing goes to excess like religious zeal, since there is no internal check on power employed in a just cause.

One unanticipated boon of the Crusades for the Western world was the greater knowledge and awareness of peoples and cultures brought back by the brigands who returned, and this became a contributing factor to the outburst of secular enthusiasm for life which characterized the Renaissance. The fifteenth century saw a rebirth of interest in all dimensions of Western culture. Of particular interest to us was the renaissance in stupidity. No longer was idiotic irrelevance confined to scholastic arguments and monastic debates. A universe beckoned, and stupidity rushed out to fill the void. While, for the previous ten centuries, stupidity had been part of the exclusive domain of the Church, it suddenly was applied to any number of worldly pursuits.

Stupidity emanated like a burst of miasma from the stale closet of theology into the chaos and confusion of daily life. There was stupidity in exploration, stupidity in invention, stupidity in statecraft, medicine, art and war. Whereas until this age, only monks had been misinformed, Gutenberg's press made it possible for everyone to be misinformed. This was a tumultuous period when the zenith achieved in artistic expression was matched by the nadir attained in political morality. Whatever else it was, this was the period when a new religion of humanism and interest in worldly affairs challenged and to a degree supplanted the dogma of the Church and concern with the life hereafter.

As leaders of the Church, the Popes of this period (1470-1530) might be judged as unfortunate examples of Christian amorality. However, that would be to miss the point that they had eagerly embraced the secular norms of the age as standards for judging their behavior. They never did comprehend their successes according to their new standards designated them as failures to people who clung devoutly to the old. Their new schema of dedication to worldly achievement made them blind and deaf to the institutional dissonance and dissatisfaction their behavior engendered. As they plunged into the world, they became immune to the criticisms of those committed to the religion they were dragging into disrepute.[20]

118

Popes

It would have been bad enough had the secular spirit of the age merely glazed the Vatican in a superficial way. However, the venality, amorality and avarice of worldly power politics was carried to excess by the Renaissance Popes.[21] Sixtus IV (1471-1484) typified the new standard-bearer. He could not have been less interested in the internal health of the Church.[22] His great successes were all secular: he improved the city of Rome physically, invigorated the arts and made the papacy a powerful monarchy. On the other hand, his great failures were all moral: he conspired with assassins, blessed cannons and indulged in simony, nepotism and war[23]—all without shame.

The renaissance in papal stupidity was compounded by the self-serving nature of Vatican advisors, who were caught up in both the spirit of the age and the political character of their environment. As Alexander VI (1492-1503) observed, "The most grievous danger for any Pope lies in the fact that encompassed as he is by flatterers, he never hears the truth about his own person and ends by not wishing to hear it."[24] This danger is inherent in every political organization: if advisors are going to advise first and foremost to secure political favor, then everyone is going to lose one way or another, more or less, sooner or later. In fact, it is a basic, fundamental cause of stupidity common to every human organization.

One reason the Church was so unresponsive to complaints and ill-disposed to reform was that it had a long and venerable tradition of inciting and ignoring critics. More than a millennium of criticism had made it thick-skinned[25] and prone to dismiss calls for reform as part of the routine bother an established power had to expect from frustrated idealists.

By the early sixteenth century, serious dissatisfaction with and by the clergy had widened and deepened. This discontent was clearly expressed in every medium available both within and outside the Church.[26] Specifically, in 1511, Erasmus laid the ideological groundwork for Luther's impending attack with the publication of his biting satire **In Praise of Folly**. To everyone but those in power, an outbreak of dissent appeared both imminent and justified.

Had the Popes honored Catholic values, they would have prayed, studied and preached, and it was by the traditional standards of poverty, humility and chastity that their behavior was condemnable. However, by worldly standards, the Renaissance Popes achieved a degree of success by disregarding their vows and embracing stupidity. As Erasmus noted in his **Colloquies**, it would have been inconvenient for "Wisdom to descend upon them...It would lose them all that wealth and...all those possessions." He further noted that many pimps, bankers and others would have been thrown out of work.[27] These vested interests were strongly committed to the new morality, complemented the Popes' stupidity and proved to be the Protestants' greatest allies.

Not only had the standards of the Popes used for judging their own behavior shifted, but their rapacious pecuniary policies converted supporters into opponents. The emerging middle class became increasingly resentful of the insatiable demands of the papacy for more and more money to finance holy decadence,[28] so even by the new worldly standard of economics, the Church was a vexation. The break was successful, when it finally came, because princes and priests reinforced each other's concerns about the tax money being used in Rome to abuse the Bible. Like most successful sinners, the Popes made the institution they were allegedly serving pay for their indulgences: the Church they secularized lost half of its constituency to the Protestant secession.[29]

The specific abuse that caused the final break was the granting of indulgences. Although the faithful were offended by the general depravity of Rome and the reluctance of Popes to reform, the commercialization of spiritual grace was an insult as well as an expense which touched the devout in a very tangible way.[30] The money grubbing Church[31] had prostituted itself[a] to the point that the sale[b] of future indulgences actually encouraged sin,[32] and this is what the Protestants were protesting.

Abuse of the Church by its officials was to continue ever after, but 1517 was still a turning point in history: the Church simply failed to turn. This was the year when Martin Luther nailed the clergy to the Church door. As an agent of the Reformation, Luther was inspired by the idea that the Church should live up to itself. It was this peculiar notion which led him to become the greatest whistle blower in history.

Luther's official antagonist, Pope Leo X, was the man on the spot at this rather dramatic moment, and he did not have a clue as to what was going on. If he had, he would not have known what it meant, being insulated to the point of being unaware of the issues in dispute and thus comprehending nether the specific protests nor that the general condition of the Church had been deteriorating for the previous fifty years.[33] Even if he had known what was going on, he would not have known what to do.

Once the protests became public and widespread, not even his Loftiness could feign ignorance of the revolt which crashed upon the Church.

---

a Although much reformed, the Catholic Church remains today the world's largest corporation—shaming the most gigantic multinational conglomerates into pettiness as it saps the meager financial resources of the submerging nations of the Third World.

b Technically, they were not sold—they were granted, with the grantee just happening to make the Church a gift scaled to the scope of the indulgence and his own financial situation.

Protestants

In 1518, when asked to vote a tax for a crusade against the Turks, the Diet of Augsburg replied that the real enemy of Christendom was "The hell-hound in Rome".[34] The popular feeling was that the proper concern of the Church was neither art nor war but the spiritual needs of the faithful. Just as Christianity had developed to fill a spiritual void in the Roman Empire, so did the Protestant movement develop in response to the spiritual vortex created by the internal corruption of the Catholic empire. Thus, it was not so much a response to a failing of the Christian schema as it was a reaction to its replacement by a secular ethic.

The Popes, by their very success according to their new standards, alienated those faithful to the old morality while simultaneously fostering hostility among the princes, who became increasingly jealous of the prosperity and influence of the Church. In this context, the conservative nature of the Protestant movement is worth noting. In an ideological sense, Protestants rejected the worldly Popes and returned to the scriptures to find meaning in their faith and lives. In this way, they were typical of many revolutionaries who break away from establishments which have betrayed ideals and been corrupted by power. As it turned out, Protestants were actually interested as much in the economic gains to be made by disemboweling the Church as in doctrine. However, it was not squabbling over riches but theological disputes reflecting doctrinal differences which riddled the Protestant movement from its inception and shattered any chance it might have had at unity and strength.[35]

In the emerging modern world, the power of belief in oneself as a major source of stupidity was personified in Philip II of Spain. No failure of his regal policy could shake his faith in its essential excellence.[36] He firmly believed that, as king, he could do no wrong, since he was convinced that all his labors were for the service of God.[37] His selection of the Duke of Medina-Sidonia as Admiral of the Armada was done against the Duke's protestations of his own ill-health, inexperience and lack of qualifications.[38] Philip disregarded these protests and, in 1588, the fleet suffered the disaster he courted. For his role in the debacle, the Duke was promoted to rank of Supreme Commander in Politics and War by his persistent, headstrong king.

George III of England was only slightly more reasonable. As his tutor Lord Waldegrave put it, he would seldom do wrong "Except when he mistakes wrong for right". When this happens, the good Lord continued, "It will be difficult to undeceive him because his is uncommonly indolent and has strong prejudices."[39] Poorly educated and resolute to the point of obstinacy,[40] he was a menace to his own empire even when he was sane. Of course, as a threat to the system, he was aided by his ministers, most of whom were both unfit for office and corrupt.

Most of them were unfit because they were elitists trying to maintain traditional roles in a changing world,[41] and in this sense, the King epitomized the plight of the ruling class. A determination to conserve old ways in the face of new conditions made official behavior increasingly irrelevant if not counter-productive,[42] so the government consistently converted problems into crises, thereby undercutting its authority and prestige.

It is still difficult to evaluate British colonial policy for the period from 1763 to 1776, as it is not yet clear what it was or even if there was one. There may have been none; there may have been many. If there was one, it was a policy of deliberate and systematic stupidity, but Edmund Burke could not find any.[43] Although the net effect of governmental action was clearly self-defeating, he considered that to be the result of haphazard, individual decisions. There certainly was no colonial policy set out on paper. Nevertheless, there seemed to be some underlying principle at work, for no matter what the specifics of the situation, officials were consistent in their ability to take any colonial situation and make it worse.

If policy at the time was unclear, action was confused. Official British behavior toward the colonies was weak, contradictory, irresolute and unconstitutional. The government's record was one of backing and filling, passing and repealing acts, threatening and submitting.[44] The only constant was that everything the British did turned out to be wrong. Not once did they do something right or just happen to stumble onto anything sensible by sheer accident.[45]

In the long litany of British blunders which transformed loyal colonists into Americans, the Stamp Act exemplifies the absurdity of official ineptitude. This was a case where the law was, fortunately for the government, ineffective. As it was, it cost those who created it, supported it and tried to enforce it political points. However, had it been successful, it would have cost the British one or two million pounds a years in lost trade to collect about £75,000 in taxes.[46] This was but typical of the way common sense was sacrificed to political principle. The tax on tea, which led to the Boston Tea Party, was another example. It would not even pay to collect itself,[47] but it was retained, apparently, just to demonstrate how perversely stupid the British could be.

In retrospect, it appears that there was indeed a British colonial policy during this era. It was an irrational, subconscious assertion of the nobility's right to suppress the rising commercial interests in England. To the extent that this policy damaged the merchants, it suited the landed gentry, which was simply doing its worst to prevent England from obtaining an empire. Fortunately for England, the nobles were rather studied in their supercilious mismanagement of affairs. As an expression of classism, colonial policy was an attempt by aristocrats to shoot Britain in the purse, and they missed. Even without the United States, the Empire developed and flourished to degrees unimaginable had Parliamentary mismanagement continued.

When armed rebellion broke out, the government persisted in its efforts to lose the colonies and added an idiosyncratic touch to routine idiocy when brothers Vice-Admiral Richard and General William Howe were assigned the contradictory roles of being a military commanders and peace commissioners. Just how they were to reconcile these was never made clear to anyone—especially to them, and they never really succeeded in either. This double failure may have been, to some degree, deliberate because the Howes were basically sympathetic to the American cause, since older brother Lord George Augustus Howe had fought alongside New England troops until his death at Ticonderoga in 1758. In addition, the Howes were opposition Whigs and reluctant to win a victory which would rebound to the credit of the Tory government. It was probably this personal sympathy for the rebels and political hostility toward the government which led peace commissioners Richard and William Howe to allow General Washington's army to escape from sure destruction time after time in the early stages of the war[c].[48]

In its battle for independence, America's best ally was not the French Navy but the British government's casual approach to the war. The classic case of this was Lord Germain's failure to coordinate General Howe's 1777 campaign, which ended up in Philadelphia, with that of General Burgoyne, which ended up in the dumper at Saratoga. The order directing Howe north from New York simply reached him too late. Although difficulty in communication is common in human affairs, most people make an extra effort to get their messages through when important matters are involved. Perhaps Lord Germain could not condescend to take mere colonists seriously, so a second secretary was left to write General Howe.[49] The letter missed the boat, and Burgoyne was stranded.

It cost the British about £100 million to lose the colonies,[50] and whatever the cause, it was not ignorance. The ministry had known of colonial discontent and the futility of their own policies. These were matters which were routinely debated in Parliament and occasionally caused riots in the streets of London. The ruling majority stuck to its schema of repressing emerging commercial interests with policies which grew increasingly inept and ineffective. The situation deteriorated into a vicious cycle with each failure engendering more colonial animosity which, in turn, called

---

c Likewise, early in 1776 Sir Guy Carleton trapped the American troops who invaded Canada but deliberately allowed them to escape, believing that magnanimity was the best policy.

forth sterner measures of futile repression. Until it was too late to save the American colonies, the government would not modify its superior attitude toward the colonists[51] nor toward the merchants upon whom the British Empire would be built.

The endemic reluctance to benefit from experience evinced itself in an early form of French stupidity when the fourteenth-century Valois monarchs repeatedly devalued their currency whenever they were desperate for cash. That this policy wrecked the economy and angered the people was lost on the leaders until finally their persistence in this aggravating practice provoked a rebellion.[52] This was but another case of insulated rulers, convinced they were right, bringing ruin upon themselves.

With the Bourbons, French stupidity burst into true brilliance. As the consummate monarch, Louis XIV certainly consummated his country with his ceaseless wars, and in his way, he contributed more than anyone else to the collapse of his way of life.[53] As an absolutely self-centered ruler, he allowed neither good sense nor reasonable compromise to restrain his unlimited power as he prepared France for the deluge. National unity was his grand objective, but in a land weakened and impoverished by his insatiable pursuit of power and wealth, his legacy was one of bitterness and dissent.[54]

Along with adventurous militarism, Louis was afflicted by the disease of divine mission which had claimed Philip II a century earlier. He suffered the usual symptoms of conceiving himself to be an instrument of God's will and convincing himself that his own were the Almighty's ways of bringing holiness to the world.[55] His single stupidest act was also his most popular: the revocation of the Edict of Nantes in 1685 converted his country from a land of toleration into one of persecution as the Catholic multitudes set themselves upon the Huguenot minority.[56]

The long-term effects of the revocation were clearly negative, but they paled when compared to the results of centuries of the asymmetric distributing goods and power in France. The concentration of material wealth and coercive power lay in the hands of the landed aristocracy. Like their British counterparts, who were doing their stodgy best to abort the Empire, the French nobles in the eighteenth century were intent on creating a revolution by manipulating their power to their own short-term advantage. Caught up in the neurotic paradox, they lived in luxury while the supporting peasants were allocated just enough to sustain their support.[57] While it lasted, it was a system of injustice supporting power,[d] with producers having nothing to say about the distribution of their products and

---

d as in eastern Europe 200 years later!

distributors passing judgment on themselves and their system. The wonder is not that there was a revolution but that it was so long in coming. In order to foment a revolution, the ruling class must fail to distribute goods according to the demands of the people. Thus, the trick is to control the demands. When demands increase and the supply system remains constant, a band of revolutionaries appears promising to satisfy those demands.[58] In the case of eighteenth century France, the aristocracy really did not have to do anything new or different to precipitate the revolution. Accumulated grievances simply built up to the breaking point so that once they were given the opportunity for expression (as they were with the summoning of the States General in May of 1789), revolution burst upon the land. It was the stupid failure of the rigid French establishment to adjust and respond to the conditions it created that caused the revolution.

The French Revolution was archetypical in that the anarchy and chaos of misapplied ideals brought on a reversion to autocracy as soon as an able administrator could assert himself. Although the revolutionaries defeated both their foreign and domestic foes, they could not control themselves.[59] (This factor of effective self-control is ever missing in the human equation.) Napoleon seized power after the desire and need for order became popularized by the excesses and abuses of freedom.

Napoleon's career serves as an example of the positive correlation of power and stupidity. As his power grew, his judgment weakened.[60] In this respect, he appears very human, as people use their wits to gain power and then use their power and lose their wits. Although one might assume that those in power would need their wits more than others, and indeed they may, the mighty seldom seem to have even common sense, much less uncommon wisdom. It may well be that stupidity is power's way of moving on. As it corrupts judgment, stupidity encourages others to become powerful, thus permitting the expression of new combinations of developing trends.

Actually, Napoleon's rise and demise serve as a lesson for all students of Western Civilization. He was thoroughly modern in that he was totally amoral and as great as anyone could be without being good. He was extremely efficient up to and even including the point that he destroyed himself through arrogance and overextension. (There is a peculiar irony in the ability of humans to be so effective at self-destruction.) Along the way, Napoleon brought organization to chaos and occasionally brought worthy ideals to life: for example, he selected officials according to their intelligence, energy, industry and obedience[61] rather than their ancestry, religion or other criteria unrelated to job performance. Although he was very efficient at achieving his ends, his basic problem was that there was no self-imposed end to his ends. His urge for self-aggrandizement was insatiable, and it motivated him to both succeed and fail. He could not perceive that the pursuit of his own best interest came to be in his own worst interest because there was no greater purpose controlling his development and directing his behavior. He personified action for its own sake and burned himself out proving that his power had meaning only if it could be used to gain more power.

That he attained so much power was partly because his mind was logical, mathematical and retentive and partly because he was unscrupulous and insensitive to misery and suffering. He was a careful, precise planner whose fatal error was one any good fighter might have made—he could not anticipate that the Russians would not give him a decisive battle in 1812.[62] He could not consider this possibility because he made the typically human mistake of judging others by his own values, and "Not fighting" was not an element in his own schema.

History, usually so sparing with second chances, was generous[e] to the Bourbons, but they proved totally unequal to their opportunities. Their attitudes and behavior warranted and elicited the condemning comment that they had "Learned nothing and forgotten nothing".[63] They attempted in a hopeless way to turn the clock back and live by the schema that had once produced a revolution, and again, they brought themselves down as they failed in their efforts to regain the property and privileges of the old regime. The more trenchant observation was that they had "Learned nothing and forgotten everything".

Had doctors learned how to forget their limiting attitudes in the nineteenth century, a once heretical idea would not have become an orthodox dogma. In the late 1840's, the germ theory of disease was very much at odds with popular theories that illness was an expression of God's wrath against a sinner and/or caused by the breathing of bad air. The only thing poisoned by bad air was objectivity, which hardly could thrive in such an anti-intellectual atmosphere. When Dr. Ignaz Semmelweis briefly introduced sanitary measures in a maternity hospital in Vienna, he was greeted with vituperous denunciations. Until he insisted that doctors wash their hands between performing autopsies and examining patients, mortality rates stood at 18%. Within a month they dropped to 3% and a month later to below 2%.[64]

A year of success by Dr. Semmelweis was too much for his critics. His contract was not renewed, so the good doctor went to Budapest to re-

---

e Actually, the Bourbons had three chances. Their second came when Napoleon was exiled to Elba. They fled upon his return and were restored again after Waterloo. (The Stuarts also had a second chance in seventeenth century England but blew it.)

The Russian Revolution

peat his performance with the same conclusive results. He then authored a book codifying his methods and analyzing his data statistically. Both book and author were roundly ignored, rejected and disdained. Ten years of Hungarian sarcasm were all he could endure. His mind snapped, and he died in a mental institution.[65]

Despite Dr. Semmelweis's work, in 1880, it was still possible to debate the validity of the germ theory as a functional explanation of disease. However, during the next twenty years, the work of Lister, Koch and Pasteur silenced such debate and established the germ theory as the explanation for cause of disease.[66] Unfortunately, there is something singular about the human mind, in that an explanation for a phenomenon usually cannot be accepted as just that but comes to be regarded as the explanation for it. In this case, once the germ theory was established, it served to block recognition that mosquitoes could carry and spread malaria (meaning "Bad air") and yellow fever.[67] Fortunately for untold millions, Drs. Ronald Ross and Colonel William Gorgas learned their medicine far from the established medical schools[68]—centers not of higher learning but of higher orthodoxy. Once again, fact battled fancy, as heretics had to demonstrate time and time again that mosquitoes, not filth, conveyed these two dread diseases.[69] By 1900, the formerly unorthodox germ theory had become enshrined as the bastion of medical belief, so it was only with phenomenal persistence that Dr. Ross was able to convince his colleagues that more than one theory might be right[70] and Dr. Gorgas to show how the spread of the diseases could be controlled.[71]

One of the common marvels of the human mind is its effectiveness in preventing people from recognizing facts which fail to conform to conventional ideology. As something of a counterpoise, the liberal tradition permits all ideas to flourish so that the one that best fits the facts may finally prevail. However, any ideal can be misapplied, and this one certainly was when the tolerance of liberals eased the way of the Communists to power in Russia in 1917 to the long-term detriment of liberalism there and elsewhere.[72] Under the Tsars, the liberals convinced everyone including themselves that living conditions were so terrible that they could not possibly get any worse, but the Communists set out to prove them wrong. At first, liberals blamed Revolutionary excesses on the civil war and post-War allied blockade:[73] too late, they learned that one of the Communists' chronically favorite excesses is the suppression of liberalism.

This stupidity of Russian liberalism was personified in Alexander Kerensky. In all of history, it is impossible to find so consistent a record of well-intended blunders as his.[74] His pitiful attempt to lead a democratic Russian state put him in the class of Woodrow Wilson as one of the great misplaced idealists in an age of misplaced idealism.[75]

127

Lenin

By way of contrast, it is difficult to find in all of history so thorough a repudiation of liberalism as was personified by Lenin, who swept the feeble Kerensky off the political stage.[76] Lenin considered ruthlessness the greatest virtue, and once convinced of his course of action, he despised debate. He proved that fanatics need not necessarily be stupid,[77] if a crisis does in fact call for firm, decisive action. The stupidity of fanatics is that they so routinely foment crises so as to justify and perpetuate their fanaticism.

If there is a single, simple lesson to be learned from the career of Lenin, it is that the clever use of slogans is paramount, as slogans shape the perceptions people have of experiences and thus control comprehension of what is happening. "All the land to the people" was the cry of the Bolsheviks before the revolution, although by 1916, 89% of the total cultivated land and 94% of the livestock was owned by the peasants. "All land from the people" would have been an appropriate slogan when, in 1929, Stalin stole the land back from the peasants and restored them to serfdom.[78] Not only was this an outrage, but it was incredibly stupid, because collectivization is simply not an efficient way to organize agriculture. However, that is what Communist ideology called for, and, as it also passed with Stalin's penchant for power, that is what was done.

Until well after World War II, Russia was, by any standard, much worse off under Communism than it had been under the Tsars. Nevertheless, the myth persists that everything improved directly after the revolution. This attests to the power of propaganda in the formation of perceptions and the structuring of comprehension. Of course, the Communists in Russia must now be accorded a kind of brutal success. At the cost of cruelty and tyranny that would have shamed the Tsars, Russians have come to enjoy a material standard of living higher than ever before.[79]

Although Communist ideologies are expressly nontheistic, they are rational expressions of an underlying religion which, through stupefication, promotes cohesion and inhibits criticism. These ideologies include strong elements of ritual and provide detailed guides to correct action. Belief in the edifying effect of a pilgrimage to Lenin's tomb reinforces veneration for him. Similarly, sing-song incantations of maxims from Mao's Little Red Book once served to honor him. All such systems use slogans and symbols to reinforce belief, build social cohesion by providing the devout with an exalted sense of righteousness[80] and inhibit comprehension and criticism of what is actually happening. In the guise of explanations, ideologies serve not only to codify behavior but to also to unify spirits and motivate people. Of course, as we have seen recently in China and eastern Europe, even totalitarian ideologies are not total in their control of

World War I

information: some knowledge may seep in and undercut all the determined opposition of ideologues to change and improvement.

The Russian Revolution was played out against the setting of World War I, and if there ever was a event which deserves its own chapter in a book on stupidity, that war is it. (However, in the interest of brevity, we will have to content ourselves here with a few selected lowlights.) It was a grand fiasco, with all sides bent on matching each other blunder for blunder—a war in which sanity was lost in the midst of millions of madmen adoring their own madness[81] and fairly reveling in their own stupidity. The British would muddle through; elan would carry the French to victory; German arrogance would prevail; Russian peasants would serve the Tsar as cannon fodder—and it went on for years. It was a world in which pointing out the obvious could be considered an act of treason, but for every whistle blower who noted that something was amiss and asserted that the war was not working, there were millions who could not hear the whistles for all the cheering at parades and shouting of propaganda.

Even before the war, the French made an incredible strategic error by repeatedly ignoring warnings from Military Intelligence about the German Schlieffen plan to sweep through Belgium and then hang a left toward Paris.[82] Fortunately, for the French, the German High Command came to their rescue. Faulty execution of the plan prevented the Germans from capitalizing on the French collapse.[83] With stupidity so evenly balanced on both sides, the war quickly became a stalemate.

For sheer tactical idiocy, however, nothing could match that of the generals who clung to their "Attack" schema long after it had been rendered clearly obsolete by modern weaponry.[f] Time after time, wave after wave of troops proved that direct frontal assault was a futile exercise in carnage. Everyone knew it but those in command. It took a few years and millions of casualties for this idea to trickle upward in a convincing fashion to those who found explanations for failure everywhere but in their own planning. In fact, it probably never would have made it on its own but was carried along with field officers as they gradually were promoted to staff officers with the passage of time and then could make their views known to some practical effect.

In a war of black ribbon blunders, few campaigns can match the disaster at Gallipoli, and among the debacles there, none compares in stupidity to an advance made by the Allies at Anzac Bay on Aug. 6, 1915. A col-

---

f Actually, this lesson should have been learned fifty years earlier in the American Civil War. Even by then, the advantage had shifted from the attacker's bayonet to the defender's rifle, but no one except the soldiers seemed to notice.

129

umn moved to within a quarter of a mile of the ridge with only twenty Turks ahead of them. They could have easily taken the high ground and turned the entire campaign into a glorious triumph. Turkey would have then been knocked out of the war. Bulgaria would then not have joined the Axis powers. Austria would have been vulnerable, Germany isolated and the war over. So, what did the troops in the column do? They stopped for breakfast![84]

The only thing that could possibly have been any stupider would have been if they had stopped for tea! This was but one example of the general British inability to comprehend the importance of time in affairs of action. Again and again, throughout the war, simple delays of minutes and hours spelled the difference between easy victory and disastrous defeat. The British knew the war was not a cricket match but nevertheless conducted their efforts with a casual indifference to time born of leisurely bowling when ready; they never could quite grasp the notion that at a given moment fifty men might accomplish what thousands could not do an hour later. As for the troops breakfasting at Gallipoli, when they were finished, they were finished. The Turks had reinforced the ridge, so the well-fed column traipsed back down the hill for lunch.

Fortunately for the Allies, the German Admiralty was there to save them. In September of 1915, Admiral Alfred von Tirpitz was ousted from control of the German Navy for protesting the restriction of submarine warfare. He called for the sinking of every enemy ship afloat and every neutral vessel in the war zone. This was, of course, the policy adopted early in 1917, so he was dismissed for calling for the right policy at the wrong time. His replacement, Admiral von Capelle, rejected, in 1916, a proposal that the shipyards increase submarine production by a factor of five. His rationale must rate as one of the stupidest remarks ever made—"Nobody would know what to do with so many U-boats after the war"[85] —and it probably sounds even worse in German.[g]

Aside from the human suffering created by the war, it also was a colossal economic disaster for Europe. Never has there been so crushing a refutation of Marx's theory of economic determinism. The war impoverished and destroyed people, rulers and states. It cost thirty-three times all the gold money in the world at the time. Almost all of this was devoted

---

g Apparently, the German military failed to learn anything from this event, as the second stupidest remark might be that made by the Berlin Air Ministry in 1940, when postponement of work on all planes that would not be operational in two years was ordered because "Such types will not be wanted after the war". Likewise (and apparently for the same reason), in the spring of 1942, Hitler canceled work on all new weapons systems—including the atom bomb—which would not be operational in six weeks.

Appeasement

to the art and science of destruction. If Marx had been right and economic motives ruled, there certainly would have been no war.[86]

If the magnitude of stupidity induced is any measure of motivation, fear must be, unfortunately, a more powerful motivator than profit. Like so many emotions, fear is not so much a blinder as a fixator, in that the paranoid fixes on one feature of a situation while dissociating from and forgetting the relevance of other factors. The French policy toward Germany after World War I was a classic example of fear cum stupidity.[87] The French fear of Germany contributed to the creation of a "Frankundstein" monster via the terms of the Versailles Treaty which not only failed to bury German militarism but provided a basis for propagandistic rationalizations which Adolf Hitler used to ease his way to power.[88]

Not only did the Treaty and the world-wide economic depression of the early 1930's play into Hitler's hands, but he was able to exploit given conditions because he well knew the limitations of ethics, objectivity and accuracy. He knew that truth was useless for capturing crowds, so he was not particularly interested in it.[89] What he was interested in was power, and he knew that to get it, he had to tell the Germans what they wanted to hear (which happened to be what he believed anyway). He provided them with something in which and someone in whom they could believe. That the basis for his schema was self-hatred[90] and nonsense made it no less appealing to a people who felt betrayed and humiliated. He provided Germany with a way out of the miserable aftermath of World War I, and only too late did it become clear to the devout that the way out was a way down to a cultural carnage that would have shamed the Devil himself.

Before the war, the British attempt to appease Hitler was both a sad and classic example of groupthink. More specifically, it was a case of an anti-war group contributing unintentionally to the outbreak of war by basing policies on their own wishful thinking. In 1938, the Chamberlain government had absolutely no interest in information that challenged their naive assumptions about Hitler's peaceful intentions. In acts unprecedented in the annals of diplomacy, German generals sent three messages to the British urging a firm stand against Hitler,[91] but the British ambassador to Germany, Neville Henderson, played "Mindguard" and advised ignoring them. Basically, His Majesty's Government insisted on perceiving Hitler as a nationalist who would combat Communism.[92] Official views of events were so totally askew that the Czechs were castigated for threatening peace simply because they did not want to give their country away to Hitler at the Munich Peace Conference. To the credit of the Foreign Office, there were critics of Chamberlain's policy, but they were ignored in the Cabinet's inflexible pursuit of folly.[93]

Pearl Harbor

When war did come, some of the revelations it brought with it were shocking to the point of enlightenment. For example, it was quickly discovered that Singapore was a pregnable fortress, the fall of which was made all the more likely by the belief that it was invulnerable. It might indeed have been impregnable had the Japanese attacked from the sea as expected. However, being at war, the Imperial Army was hardly disposed to cooperate with its enemies, so it invaded overland instead. Singapore found itself added to the undistinguished list of presumably impregnable fortresses which, like the Maginot Line, were invulnerable to everything but imagination, maneuver and attack.[94]

Those three elements mixed with fatal overdoses of wishful thinking and complacent preconceptions on the part of those responsible for defense provide an explanation for the debacle at Pearl Harbor.[95] Again, groupthink played a crucial role in the realization of the unthinkable,[96] with warnings being repeatedly ignored if they contradicted the popular belief that "It couldn't happen here".[97] Thus, in March, 1941, when two aviation officers presented a paper concluding that an attack at dawn on Pearl Harbor launched from Japanese aircraft carriers could achieve a complete surprise, it was considered and dismissed because the commanders at Pearl believed the Japanese just would not take that chance.[98]

Washington did not help clarify matters: all of their warnings were ambiguous. Still, it is a commander's job to protect his base, so in the event of ambiguity, prudence would suggest caution. The basic mistake base commander Admiral Husband Kimmel made was in assuming an attack would not occur at Pearl Harbor. It is only fair to mention that the ambiguous warnings were received amidst background "Noise" of many competing and irrelevant signals. The failure to heed the warnings, such as they were,[h] was due to the tendency of people to note and give credence to data that support their expectations, as analysts are generally inclined to select interpretations of data or messages which confirm prevailing hypotheses.[99] In this particular case, both perceptions and interpretations were shaped by the self-confirming schema that the Japanese would attack somewhere else—probably thousands of miles west of Hawaii.[100]

On December 7th, in the complacent state of presumed invulnerability,[101] two more warnings were missed. The incoming planes were detect-

h New research strongly suggests that Washington deliberately withheld information from the base commanders because President Roosevelt wanted an incident which would get us into the war. Thus, Admiral Kimmel may have been a victim not only of Japanese aggression but of political duplicity on the part of his Commander-in-Chief. It is indeed a sad commentary to note that one hopes this was a case of just stupidity, because if it wasn't, it was one of Presidential treachery of the worst order.

ed on radar and reported to army headquarters where they were misidentified as an expected flight of B-17's from the mainland due in at about that time.[102] Once again, we find data interpreted according to expectation if convenient. No one attempted to confirm that the planes spotted were in fact the expected bombers: it was just assumed they were, and that ended that. Also, a destroyer sighted and attacked a midget submarine trying to sneak into the harbor.[103] This action was reported to naval headquarters where the sub was dismissed as a false sighting,[104] of which there had been some before.

The contribution of groupthink to the disaster at Pearl Harbor was that it inhibited anyone from breaking ranks and asserting that the base was vulnerable. That would have been contrary to group norms and probably would have been a wasted gesture anyway. Usually, people do not contemplate scenarios that contradict group assumptions. The resultant communal mindset may boost morale, but the false sense of security provided is produced by distorting perception for the sake of the pleasing image.[105]

As for the Japanese, they accepted the risk of attack out of necessity. The Empire had to expand or die, as the leaders had become prisoners of their own ambitions. Nevertheless, in a war of miscalculations, the attack on Pearl Harbor ranks as one of the worst. It was one of the few things that could have galvanized Americans into a united war effort, but this point probably was wasted on the Japanese, who misjudged America by their own imperial standards and assumed that Roosevelt could lead the country into war whenever he wanted. They did not realize they were doing the one thing that would bring an expanded war upon themselves.[106]

As it turned out, Pearl Harbor was only the most striking example of the Allied propensity to ignore warnings during World War II. Before the battle for the bridge at Arnhem in September, 1944, the British were clearly warned by the Dutch underground that the paratroopers would be dropping right onto German tanks.[107] Unfortunately, General Montgomery had a plan, and since the panzers were not in it, a compromise had to be found, and it was: it was blithely assumed the tanks were out of gas, and the debacle went off on schedule.

Similar warnings were given the Allies before the Battle of the Bulge a few months later when refugees told of masses of German troops concentrated just out of sight of our armies. However, these reports were dismissed rather than checked out, and other reports of a coming offensive filled intelligence files but were given scant attention.[108] Fortunately, the GI's had learned something from their recent experience and in their jaunty way made an explicit point of winning the battle before Monty could come up with a plan to save them.

The Bay of Pigs

It should not be concluded that part of an officer's training is an extended course on "Warnings: How to Ignore Them". Major General John Lucas proved this in a backhanded way as commander of the American landing at Anzio in January, 1944. This was an unfortunate example of an army fighting the previous battle. General Lucas had been at Salerno, where a divided Allied force had nearly been pushed back into the sea,[109] so despite the total lack of confirming evidence and in the face of reports of minimal opposition, he remained convinced that the Germans were nearby in force just waiting to pounce as soon as he moved inland. It became a self-realizing delusion, since the General's insistence on heeding warnings which did not exist, his desire to avoid another Gallipoli and a conservative interpretation of his orders gave the Germans time to trap his troops on the beach.[110] Rome's liberation, which should have taken five hours, took five months instead.

In the treasure chest of American stupidity, the Bay of Pigs invasion is justly stashed away in the bottom drawer. As the classic example of groupthink, the decision to attack Cuba was pure, clear, crystalline, ideal, quality stupidity. In a culture given to bigger and better stupidity, Vietnam and Watergate have since eclipsed the Bay of Pigs in the American popular mind, but for the connoisseur of Presidential blunders, this little gem has lost none of its luster over time. We were all most fortunate that the stakes in this disgraceful misadventure were so limited.

The sad thing is that, based on the information given him, President Kennedy was really justified in ordering the invasion.[111] The fault was not in his decision as such but in the data presented to him and the climate in which discussions were conducted. It is important to note that his advisors were all shrewd, astute and as capable as anyone of objective and rational analysis. Nevertheless, collectively, they led themselves into an unmitigated debacle.[112] The whole proved to be considerably worse than any individual part.

Although the data presented to the President may have indicated the advisability of invasion, he certainly did not get a balanced picture of the situation. The information provided was that selected by the CIA, which chose to ignore reports of Cuba's military strength by experts in both the State Department and the British intelligence.[113] The basic problem was that the leaders of the CIA, Director Allen Dulles and Deputy Director Richard Bissel, had become emotionally involved with the plan to the detriment of their ability to judge it.[114] Not only did they cull out data conflicting with their commitment to disaster, but they limited consideration of the plan to a small number of people so that it would not be too harshly or thoroughly (i.e., fairly) scrutinized and criticized. They were so much in love with their plan that they could not be objective about it and did not want anyone else to be objective about it either. When the time came, they did not so much present it as sell it to the White House.[115]

Among the President's advisors, groupthink took over as members of the in-group became cohesive and suppressed deviations from the prevailing belief of the team in the plan. The goal shifted from hammering out an effective plan to that of obtaining group consensus. When Arthur M. Schlesinger, Jr. expressed opposition to the plan to Robert Kennedy only days before the invasion, Bobby's response was that it was too late for opposition.[116] There is a time to debate, a time to decide and a time to do. The questions then arise: when is it too late to oppose a faulty plan? When is it too late to correct a mistake? When is it better to go with a decision than to improve it or scrap it? Is it more important for people to be together than for them to know they are going down together?

To his credit, Undersecretary of State Chester Bowles was one of the few members of the State Department who was critical of the invasion plan.[117] It is a sad commentary on people and the political process that he was the first to be fired after the fiasco—that is, getting canned was his reward for being right when everyone else was wrong.[118] On the other hand, Dean Rusk, who had suppressed Bowles' doubts, was retained as Secretary of State because he was so nice.[119]

Although the Bay of Pigs invasion was as close to an ideal case of stupidity as we should ever hope to see, it hardly compares in size and scope to the debacle in Vietnam. American policies and actions there are now generally recognized as having been quite stupid, but the whos, hows and whys remain as debatable as ever and probably never will be completely clear. American involvement in Vietnam was a case of compound stupidity, with ignored warnings interlaced with wishful groupthink. The escalation of the mid-1960's was pursued in the face of strong warnings from practically everyone who was concerned and powerless, but naturally, these were totally lost on those in positions of irresponsibility. Again, we find conscientious statesmen ignoring both experts and everyone else voicing concern over the military, political and moral consequences of deliberately planned idiocy.[120] Within the American political community, criticism could usually be stilled quite easily because no one wanted to be the one responsible for losing Vietnam to Communism.[121] The fact that we never had it to lose was one of those relevancies lost on the mighty.

Nevertheless, in the cause of retaining what it never had, the American government was determined to be misled by misinterpreting events in Vietnam. The cause of the war was that Americans were thought they were fighting Communism while the Vietnamese were fighting colonialism. From 1945 onward, we consistently misconstrued all evidence of nationalism and the fervor for an independent Vietnam.[122] This did not mean

135

we ignored facts so much as we failed to perceive them in their relevant context. We insisted on perceiving events in Vietnam in a global context of a Communist conspiracy to rule the world.

This misperception was facilitated by the self-serving invention of labels to justify our sacrilegious, self-defeating cause. The "Commitment" to the "Vital interest" of "National security" became a positive feedback system which took on a life of its own as those in power came to believe in and become imprisoned by their own rhetoric.[123] As it turned out, all the power committed to Vietnam in the name of "National interest" worked against us. In fact, in terms of American interest, the war was clearly a self-generated blunder, as we had no[i] perceivable interest in the area at any time.[124]

As our leaders came to believe increasingly in their own clichés about American policy toward Vietnam in the late '60's, phoney, invalid optimism was replaced by genuine, invalid optimism.[125] Consequently, during the Johnson years, there was an abundance of unrealistic planning due to overambition, overoptimism and overignorance[126] in the Oval Office. As always, the key to stupidity lay in the discrepancy between what was believed and what was happening, and not only was the official government schema out of sync with Vietnamese reality, but it was systematically programmed to endure unaffected by events in Southeast Asia, which thus remained beyond American comprehension.[127]

As the Vietnam debacle developed during this era, the Johnson administration turned inward, consulting more and more with military priests, who had learned the lesson at Munich (i.e., that appeasement does not deter an aggressor) too well[128] and were determined to apply it where it did not fit. To such people, there was invariably only one solution to any problem—escalation.[129] This escalation became a perfect example of a positive feedback mechanism going to uncontrollable excess, as there was no mechanism within the government which could check policies accepted without reservation by those devoted to the incestuous administration. Fortunately, the war was very much debated by citizens who found the more they questioned and learned, the less they understood. A gnawing doubt became a growing awareness of the fundamental absurdity of our

---

i There is a ghostly possibility that our involvement stemmed from an interest in oil in the Spratly Islands located 300 miles east of Vietnam in the South China Sea. Red China and Vietnam both claimed the area (and still do), and in the best Cold War tradition, we may have wanted to thwart Chinese interests in the area while promoting our own by maintaining a friendly regime in Saigon. If this indeed was our "National interest" in the area, it was perceivable as such only to the oil industry and Washington loopers and was kept well hidden from the public.

involvement, and then gradually the realization spread that the establishment was out of its mind.[130] It was America's good fortune that the insanity of its leaders could be checked by the common sense of a few million skeptics.

Leaders do not usually appreciate this built-in restriction on their power to wreck the system, and Richard M. Nixon was one who became increasingly vexed as the descent of his administration to new depths of political morality was made evident by the media and then finally halted by public outrage and Congressional power. The irony of the Watergate fiasco was that Nixon ran on a "Law and order" platform in 1968, but four years later, his campaign was characterized by burglary, bribery, forgery, perjury and obstruction of justice.[131] Even this litany of crimes would have come to naught politically had executive sessions in the Oval Office not been taped and the tapes retained. It was the combination of these incredibly stupid blunders with the crimes themselves which led to the President's resignation.

As might be expected, groupthink played a major role in this debacle, and members of the White House staff did indeed share the overoptimism and sense of invulnerability common to groupthinkers living in an unreal world[132] defined by their own separate, narrow, closed standard of immorality.[133] As usual, when people are absolutely devoted to their plan, cause and themselves, warnings of impending disaster were ignored.[134]

This failure to heed warnings was due to both the nature of the Nixonian schema and the tenacity with which it was held by loyal staff members. The schema itself was basically one of methodology—specifically, that any creepy means could be employed to maintain the image of the hollow administration. This was the subconscious guide for strategy and behavior which was shared by the Nixon staff and which led them to perceive the Watergate scandal as a public relations problem. In doing so, they were at least consistent: they perceived everything as a public relations problem.[135]

The impact of this schema's limitations was compounded by the persistence of the President's staff in adhering to it despite its obvious drawbacks. At every stage of the Watergate morass, there was a consistent failure of those involved to face irrefutable facts even when they were known to be irrefutable.[136] With all signs indicating failure, loyal staff members carried on very much as usual and so validated the signs.

If there is a lesson to learn from this pocket review of history, it must be that stupidity flourishes with ageless consistency. It is sad to note that it is as common in modern America as it has ever been anywhere.

Notes

1. Plato. ca. 355 B.C. **Laws, III.** (Harvard University Press; Cambridge, MA. 1967).
2. Dantzig, T. 1930. **Number, The Language of Science.** New York. 80.
3. Spengler, O. 1918. **The Decline of the West.** Edited by H. Werner. 1962. Modern Library; New York. 55.
4. Sambursky, S. 1956. **The Physical World of the Greeks.** Routledge & Kegan Paul; London. 34.
5. Sagan, C. 1980. **Cosmos.** Random House; New York. 185.
6. Spengler. **op. cit.** 48fn(#3).
7. Sagan, C. **op. cit.** 184.
8. Spengler. **op. cit.** 48fn(#3).
9. Taine, H. 1876. **L'Ancine Régime.** Paris. 262.
10. Russell, B. 1945. **A History of Western Philosophy.** Simon and Schuster; New York. 78.
11. Pitkin, W. 1932. **A Short Introduction to the History of Human Stupidity.** Simon and Schuster. New York. 390.
12. **Ibid.** 387.
13. **Ibid.**
14. Jones, A. 1964. **The Latter Roman Empire.** University of Oklahoma Press; Norman, OK.
15. Pitkin. **op. cit.** 392.
16. **Ibid.**
17. **Ibid.** 390.
18. **Ibid.** 391
19. **Ibid.** 390.
20. Tuchman, B. 1984. **The March of Folly.** Knopf; New York. 125.
21. **Ibid.** 52.
22. **Ibid.** 64.
23. Durant, W. 1953. **The Renaissance.** Simon and Schuster; New York. 398-399.
24. Jedin, H. 1957. **A History of the Council of Trent.** London. Vol. I, 126.
25. Tuchman. **op. cit.** 64.
26. Hughes, P. 1947. **A History of the Church.** New York. Vol. III, 491.
27. Erasmus, D. 1516. **Colloquies.** (University of Chicago Press; Chicago, IL. 1965.)
28. Tuchman. **op. cit.** 111.
29. **Ibid.** 52.
30. **Ibid.** 113.
31. Colet, J. 1513. In **Renaissance Europe: 1480-1520** by J. Hale. 1971. Berkeley. 232.
32. Shaff, D. 1910. **History of the Christian Church.** Grand Rapids, MI. Vol. 6, 766.
33. Tuchman. **op. cit.** 115.
34. Dickens, A. 1966. **Reformation and Society in Sixteenth Century Europe.** New York. 23.
35. Tuchman. **op. cit.** 119.
36. **The Encyclopedia Britannica.** 1930. 14th ed. London.
37. Pitkin. **op. cit.** 254.
38. Fronde, J. 1892. **Spanish Story of the Armada.** New York.

39. Waldegrave, J. Quoted in **King George III** by J. Brooke. 1972. New York.

40. Durant, W. and A. 1967. **Rousseau and Revolution.** Simon and Schuster; New York. 687-688.

41. Churchill, W. 1957. **The Age of Revolution.** Bantam; New York. 108.

42. Plumb, J. June, 1960. Our Last King. **American Heritage**; XI, #4, 95-96.

43. Burke, E. Apr. 4, 1774. A speech in **Parliamentary History of England** edited by T. Hansard. XVII.

44. Tuchman. **op. cit.** 201.

45. Meredith, W. 1770. In Hansard. **op. cit.** XVI, 872-873.

46. Chesterfield, P. 1766. In **Letters** edited by Bonamy Dobrée. 1932. London. VI, #2410.

47. Meredith. **op. cit.**

48. Fleming, T. Feb. 1964. The Enigma of General Howe. **American Heritage**; XV, #2, 11ff. Fleming, T. 1975. **1776: Year of Illusions.** Norton; New York. 245.

49. Valentine, A. 1962. **Lord George Germain.** Oxford.

50. Tuchman. **op. cit.** 228.

51. **Ibid.** 229.

52. **Ibid.** 7-8.

53. **Ibid.** 19.

54. **Ibid.** 23.

55. Treasure, G. 1966. **Seventeenth Century France.** New York. 368.

56. Tuchman. **op. cit.** 19.

57. Hammond, P. 1978. **An Introduction to Cultural and Social Anthropology.** 2nd ed. Macmillan; New York. 159.

58. Arnold, T. 1937. **The Folklore of Capitalism.** Yale U. Press; New Haven, CT. 38.

59. Tuchman. **op. cit.** 6.

60. Pitkin. **op. cit.** 284.

61. Tuchman. **op. cit.** 6.

62. Pitkin. **op. cit.** 282.

63. Talleyrand-Perigord, C. 1796. In a letter of Mallet du Pan from **Chevalliar de Panat.**

64. McMillen, S. 1968. **None of These Diseases.** Fleming H. Revell Co.; Old Tappan, NJ.

65. **Ibid.**

66. McCullough, D. 1977. **The Path Between the Seas.** Simon and Schuster; New York. 410-411.

67. **Ibid.** 442.

68. **Ibid.** 410.

69. **Ibid.** 414.

70. **Ibid.** 410.

71. **Ibid.** 415.

72. Welch, C. 1979. Broken eggs, but no omelette: Russia before the revolution. In **The Encyclopedia of Delusions** edited by R. Duncan and M. Weston-Smith. Wallaby; New York. 59.

73. Wolfe, B. Feb. 1960. The Harvard Man in the Kremlin Wall. **American Heritage**; XI, #2, 102.

74. Pitkin. **op. cit.** 239.

75. Reinsch, P. 1905. The negro race and European civilization. **American J. Sociology,** 11, 148. (This is really a negative reference because the author's point was that the nineteenth century error of imposing institutions where they did not belong had not been committed in the twentieth century—which was all of four years old at the time. However, that

is exactly what was done after World War I, when the victorious powers insisted the former monarchal Germany become an economically devastated republic.)

76. Van Doren, C. 1991. **A History of Knowledge**. Ballantine; New York. 261.

77. Pitkin. **op. cit**. 240

78. Welch. **op. cit**. 53.

79. Tuchman. **op. cit**. 6.

80. Hammond. **op. cit**. 334-335.

81. Céline, L. In **The American Heritage History of the 1920's and 1930's**. 1970. New York. 13.

82. Tuchman, B. 1962. **The Guns of August**. Bantam; New York. 61.

83. **Ibid**. 243.

84. Taylor, A. 1963. **The First World War**. Putnam; New York. 95.

85. Pitkin. **op. cit**. 489.

86. **Ibid**. 476-477.

87. **Ibid**. 293.

88. Thomson, D. 1962. **Europe Since Napoleon**. Longmans; London. 571.

89. Szasz, T. 1979. The lying truths of psychiatry. In Duncan and Weston-Smith. **op. cit**. 140.

90. Waite, R. 1971. Adolf Hitler's guilt feelings: a problem in history and psychology. **J. Interdisciplinary History**, 1, #2, 229-249.

91. Shirer, W. 1959. **The Rise and Fall of the Third Reich**. Simon and Schuster; New York. 380-381.

92. Janis, I. 1982. **Groupthink**. Houghton Mifflin; Boston, MA. 190-191.

93. **Ibid**. 187-188.

94. Wohlstetter, R. 1962. **Pearl Harbor: Warning and Decision**. Stanford University Press; Stanford, CA. 397-398.

95. O'Toole, G. 1991. **Honorable Treachery**. Atlantic Monthly Press; New York. 382.

96. Janis. **op. cit**. 72-73.

97. Earle, J. 1946. **Hearing before the Joint Committee on the Investigation of the Pearl Harbor Attack**. 79th Congress. U. S. Government Printing Office; Washington, D.C. Part 26, 412.

98. **Ibid**.

99. Wohlstetter. **op. cit**. 392-393.

100. Janis. **op. cit**. 81.

101. Morison, S. 1950. The rising sun in the Pacific: 1931-April, 1942. **History of United States Naval Operations in World War II**. Vol. 3. Little, Brown; Boston, MA. 138.

102. Wohlstetter. **op. cit**. 68.

103. Prange, G. 1981. **At Dawn We Slept**. Penguin; New York. 495-496.

104. Wohlstetter. **op. cit**. 16-17.

105. Janis. **op. cit**. 88-89.

106. Tuchman. 1984. **op. cit**. 31.

107. Ryan, C. 1974. **A Bridge Too Far**. Simon and Schuster; New York.

108. Payne, R. 1973. **The Life and Death of Adolf Hitler**. Praeger; New York. 524.

109. Wallace, R. 1981. **The Italian Campaign**. Time-Life Books; Alexandria, VA. Chap. 2.

110. **Ibid**. pp. 130-132.

111. Kennedy, R. June 1, 1961. In a memorandum quoted in **Robert Kennedy and His Times** by A. Schlesinger, Jr. 1978. Ballantine Books; New York. 477. (Bobby may have

been trying to cover for his brother and the team, but it appears those making the decisions were indeed given partial and biased information.)

112. Janis. **op. cit.** 19.
113. **Ibid.** 23.
114. Hilsman, R. 1967. **To Move a Nation.** Doubleday; New York. 31.
115. Janis. **op. cit.** 46.
116. **Ibid.** 40.
117. Schlesinger, Jr., A. 1965. **A Thousand Days.** Houghton Mifflin; Boston, MA. 250.
118. Janis. **op. cit.** 44.
119. Schlesinger. 1965. **op. cit.** 438.
120. Janis. **op. cit.** 44.
121. Ellsberg, D. 1971. The quagmire myth and the stalemate machine. In the spring issue of **Public Policy.** 246.
122. Tuchman. 1984. **op. cit.** 376.
123. **Ibid.** 374.
124. Ridgway, General M. July, 1971. Indochina: disengaging. **Foreign Affairs.**
125. Ellsberg. **op. cit.** 262.
126. White, T. 1969. **The Making of the President 1968.** Atheneum; New York. 16-19.
127. Janis. **op. cit.** 129.
128. Hargreaves, R. 1973. **Superpower: A Portrait of America in the 1970's.** St. Martin's; New York. 339.
129. Thomson, J. April, 1968. How could Vietnam happen? An autopsy. **The Atlantic Monthly.**
130. McNaughton, J. 1967. A memorandum for the President in the **Pentagon Papers: History of United States Decision Making on Vietnam.** Senator Gravel edition. 4 Vols. and Index Vol. Boston, MA. 1971-1972. Vol. IV, 478.
131. Tuchman. 1984. **op. cit.** 370.
132. Magruder, J. July 26, 1973. From an interview with Charles Wheeler in **Listener.**
133. Sloan, H. May 18, 1973. From an interview in **The New York Times.**
134. Janis. **op. cit.** 220.
135. Nixon, R. 1978. **R.N.: The Memoirs of Richard Nixon.** Grosset & Dunlap; New York. 773.
136. Haldeman, H. (with J. DiMona) 1978. **The Ends of Power.** Dell; New York. 62.

VII. Modern American Stupidity

Stupidity has been a component of Americana ever since the first explorers stumbled onto the New World. In fact, the most surprising thing about America's discovery is not the usual "When" and "By whom" but the "How often" explorers had to learn of it for themselves. No other land has been discovered so often, and if all claims in this matter are valid, it was first discovered by the Irish, Romans, Phoenicians, Egyptians, Libyans, Norsemen, Welsh, Scots, Venetians and Portuguese.[1]

Of Columbus, it might be said he was the last to discover America. He is honored as **the** discoverer because he had the good fortune to make his discovery when his supporting culture was cognitively prepared to appreciate it and technologically developed enough to exploit it. However, he had no inkling of what he had found nor even where he was when he set foot in the New World.[a] He had started out for east Asia and just happened to bump into America because it was in the way. Since he had no idea what the Orient was like, he assumed he had achieved his goal and died without knowing he had accomplished more as a failure than do most "Successful" explorers.

After Columbus had shown the way, the Old World was ready and eager to follow his lead to where ever it was he had gone. The horizons and opportunities for stupidity now widened and broadened, and new forms of idiocy burst out of the traditional molds of misbehavior. Stupidity was no longer confined to the stodgy constraints of restrictive patterns of thought and action but became brash, reckless and inventive in a world in which imagination seemed the only limitation on possible blunders.

Despite this, generally speaking, those who settled the New World could not miss. Once a colony was established, the land was so rich that it did not matter what system or non-system of government, economy or society developed: nature was so generous that any would succeed.

The nineteenth century saw the end of the Golden Age of individual stupidity. In the 1800's, people went out on their own, made their own

---

a A modern Columbus might have blasted off for Mars and landed on the moon simply because it got in the way. After four round trips, he would still believe he had been to Mars.

Pluralism

mistakes, paid for them themselves on the spot and learned as little as possible from the experience. But, gone now are the good old days when a person could go out and fail on his own at his own pace. Now he must join a firm which is overcharging its customers or work for the government, which is, true to the spirit of democracy, ripping off the people. Stupidity is now cultivated, developed and promoted by the calculating professional. It has become organized, streamlined, modernized, and incorporated. Mismanagement is now computerized so that errors which used to take weeks to unfold can be perpetrated in seconds. In a world in which stupidity has reached such bewildering bureaucratic complexity, Americans are justifiably confused and searching for something in which they can still believe.

The composite American today entertains a number of religious beliefs all of which predominated at one time or other and still comprise a significant part of his cultural heritage and national identity. The general American is sort of Christian in belief and/or behavior. Politically, he believes in democracy, although the Constitution guarantees and surprisingly provides a republican form of government. Economically, he is a devout capitalist, even if private enterprise has been pushed to the fringe by the systematic organization, ownership and control that government and big business fascistically[2] exercise upon each other. Finally, he is socially egalitarian, at least within his own peer group. If there are contradictions in the expressions of these belief systems as they shape daily life, they are happily lost on most of us. First and last, we are pragmatists ill disposed to let beliefs disrupt the market place of life.

Not only is American stupidity thus fragmented, due to the lack of a unified belief system, but we lack a basic knowledge about ourselves for exactly the same reason. In fact, if there is one subject upon which we are invincibly ignorant, it is America,[3] and this self-unconsciousness is traceable to the multi-schemas which provide several ready-made explanations for anything. This is one of the distinctive features of American culture: we do not have "An" answer for or "The" solution to a given question or problem. We have a variety of answers and solutions from which we can pick the one which is most appealing if not most relevant.

The pluralism of American society has not only made tolerance a necessity but has given American stupidity its anarchistic flavor. Each immigrant strain has made its contribution to the caldron of idiocy and made diversity our greatest weakness. The sloth of Hispanics contrasts with the arrogance of Germans. The self-righteous prudery of the English clashes with the emotional abandon of Africans. Each detracts in its own way from the self-confidence of the nation as every failing and drawback of the world's jetsam and flotsam has drifted to our shores and become part of our kaleidoscope schema.

Naturally, we like to make the most of the noble purity of our ancestors. We see them as moral zealots struggling for justice and freedom against religious tyranny and political oppression. However, not since the Crusades could one find a more opinionated band of bigots than the early colonists, who had no fundamental objection to despotism, so long as they were the despots imposing their oppressive views and values on others. Added to these dictatorial bigots were successive waves of klutzes, deadbeats and malcontents—the scum from all the slums of Europe. Throw in Africans dumb enough to get caught by slavers, Orientals shrewd enough to work forever for a pittance and some Indians who acquiesced in the longest-running real estate swindle of all time and you have the makings of the social handicap of which we are so proud. Stir a little and heat a lot, and you have a model of our faltering, sweltering pot society.

Although we do not brag about it, America was peopled by failures. Our ancestors came here because they were or anticipated being failures in the old country. Upon arrival, they failed in farming, mining, business and battles. Crackpots invented ships that would sink, shovels that would not dig and boilers that would explode. Builders constructed firetraps that were unsafe an any height. As development progressed, slums arose in the cities while in the country, land was cleared so that the topsoil could erode faster. Railroads to nowhere were constructed, with promoters then misleading the unwary into settling along the wrong-of-way so that they could be more easily exploited later on.

Thus, American stupidity cannot be truly appreciated as a stagnant, torpid force but must be perceived in the dynamic context of a linguistic current ever at odds with the realities of life. Much as our national character, composition and goals have changed throughout the life of the nation, so has our native stupidity devolved so that we might always have difficulty recognizing ourselves and meeting our challenges. To illustrate the point, we need only note that the patriotic rhetoric of 1776 was mostly about "Liberty". A bell was cast and promptly cracked to symbolize our qualified commitment to this ideal. Two hundred years ago, slave owners fought for their own liberty, and now the word is all but forgotten. The current watchword is "Equality", and the government conceived in liberty has been pushing equality[b] on the country for more than a generation. In both cases, the catchwords motivated radicals and obscured

---

b The deterioration of American ideals is indicated by the fact that no one has even suggested casting an "Equality bell" or erecting a "Statue of equality".

the reality that as pure ideals, they were basically inapplicable in a healthy society. Still, as a people divided by a common language, we can be as stupid as any and will no doubt continue to wrap ourselves in the illusions of misleading labels.

The importance of a word in maintaining an illusion was made vividly clear in 1902, when President Roosevelt was trying to appoint a commission to settle a coal strike. The mine owners refused to accept anyone on the commission who was designated as a union man. It was perfectly acceptable for a union man to be on the commission, but he had to be called something else (i.e., "An eminent sociologist").[4] Until this subtlety was realized by the President, language really was a stumbling block. Terminology prevented a resolution of the crisis so long as seating a "Union man" was perceived as granting Labor's right to representation.

Actually, twentieth century America is a concoction of misperceptions. In the early 1930's, for example, Americans did not perceive business organizations as "Governing bodies". Giant corporations were perceived as eminently successful rugged individuals. Another part of American fiction was that the nominal government in Washington had some kind of power to control events. However, in the daily life of the average citizen, a private organization determined when to get up in the morning, what to eat, what to wear, what working conditions would be and how leisure time would be spent.[5] Today, the government at least attempts to govern. However ineffective it may be, the bureaucracy belatedly asserted itself and tries to regulate the special interests which control it and us.

The big change in thinking which occurred during the 1930's was that the "People" were mixed into the Government=Business equation. All the regulations which had been cultivated by the business community to harness government to the promotion and development of corporations[6] were converted into mechanisms of government regulation over the industrial complex. The change occurred for the best of reasons—it had to. The business community had been granted the license to run itself and the country into the ground and had proceeded to do so.

Had necessity not been quite so compelling at the time, Americans would have been more reluctant than they were to convert from worshipping business to worshipping government. Rituals and jargon all favored the status morbus. The only problem was pragmatic—the system did not work. Of course, nothing the befuddled New Dealers did for eight years worked very effectively either until World War II bailed the country out of the Depression.

In a general and abstract sense, the New Deal amounted to an admission that the old beliefs in capitalism and the mechanisms by which business controlled politics worked to everyone's worst interest. The new

The Depression

emerging schema was based on belief in legislation designed to help people by limiting business. Unfortunately, the pragmatic result was not government by law but by organization. Although the underlying principles upon which government is based may be theoretically sound, human organizations are prone to take on self-serving lives of their own. Hence, the efforts to realize our ideals by legislating control have strangled business with fascistic regulations.[7]

If the preoccupation here with systems and principles seems out of place, it nevertheless reflects the prevailing attitude of those who lived through the American Reformation of the 1930's. During the Depression, people who had gone bankrupt commonly spent their working lives trying to pay off their creditors. Few groups received or even sought[c] handouts from the government. Mostly, they were seeking explanations—new ideologies (Socialism, Communism, Etcism) to replace the ragged individualism created by capitalism. The point is that very few people with any articulate political force actually demanded bread[8] instead of the political circuses of the New Deal.

In one of the few intellectual ironies of the 1930's, while the people were looking for reassuring answers to theoretical questions, their leader was searching for practical solutions to real problems. As an inveterate non-ideologue, President Roosevelt was a pragmatic empiricist committed to trying one thing after another in a hit and miss fashion until he found something that worked.[9] Despite the lack of systematics, the government's perceptible slide toward a fascistically controlled superstate was greeted by conservatives with much righteous hand wringing and expressions of concern about the downfall of laissez faire capitalism, the destruction of individual initiative and the ruin of national character. How anyone could have missed the subtlety that capitalism was already down and out can be attributed only to the incredible power of the "Laissez unfair" schema to prevent awareness of the most obvious facts of life.

On the other hand, Americans redefined themselves and turned in the tarnished idol of the brazen individual seeking opportunity for that of the cautious conformist seeking security.[10] The resultant welfare programs may have been a boon to civil service bureaucracies, but recipients of the dole, for some unexpected reason, seem to have lost a general sense of social responsibility. As irresponsibility was not the intended goal but an undesired side effect of the welfare state, it was unanticipated by those who approved and those who administer the programs. The subtlety that

---

c The World War I veterans who staged their Bonus March in Washington were exceptional in this regard.

Advertising

people given the means for subsistence tend to lose respect for everything including themselves was lost on everyone. However, after fifty years of experience with dependence on the dole, we are beginning to realize that the quest for economic security has indeed undermined our sense of individual responsibility. Basic physical security in our cities is subject to the irresponsible whims of vandals and hooligans showing their disrespect for property and their resentment for those who own it.

Not only have we redefined ourselves, but we are continually in the process of redefining if not flat outright abusing our language.[11] Is there not something inherently unsettling about a President referring to a nuclear missile as a "Peacekeeper"? Equally odd was Secretary of Defense Caspar Weinberger's reference to the Marines' withdrawal from Lebanon in 1984 as "Redeployment"[12] after the nuisance of their presence made them a threat to no one but themselves. One wonders if a person who confuses retreat with redeployment should be in charge of "Peacekeepers". After all, what would happen it he were to "Evaluate" one of them?

In a lighter vein, the Attorney General of New York in 1977 put a halt to an advertisement for the sale of "Grass". The ad read: Marijuana cannot be sold through the mail but "grass" can... People were sending in money and getting exactly what was promised—lawn cuttings. Now, that is not the funny part. The funny part is that the ad was stopped because it was considered false advertising,[13] although it probably was one of the most honest ads ever placed. It could not have been stopped for being misleading (creating a false image), because that is what creative advertising is all about. It should have been stopped on the grounds of honest advertising because in a world of phonies and scams, nothing is so disturbing and disruptive as accuracy and honesty.

For sheer tomfoolery, however, nothing matches the advertisers' code which prohibits showing people drinking alcoholic beverages. People are shown having a wonderful time pouring beer or wine into their glasses. They sniff. They smile. Suddenly, a moose is running through a forest. Then the glasses are half empty and the people are beaming delightedly. This is obviously a childish compromise for advertisers who want to promote sales of these products (and distilled spirits as well) without being responsible for their consumption.

As amusing and innocent as this example may be, there is a sinister side to the deliberate control and manipulation of information by the media. In totalitarian states, the government uses mind control to maintain belief in the leaders. In America, the media are businesses committed to maintaining belief in the sponsors. Information which is acceptable to advertisers is presented in a manner calculated to make money by increasing circulation or ratings. If this tends to make material superficial, it is because the people will tune out anything which turns them off.

Actually, the history of modern communications in general has been a story of developing the ability to mislead more and more people faster and faster. Television, especially, can convey all kinds of false impressions, most of them carefully contrived to keep the viewer tuned in for further misinformation. Usually just enough harsh reality filters through to make some prudes scream "Bad taste" but not so much that the public would be viscerally revolted by the disaster of the day on the news or the violent climax of a movie.

The media's compromise of keeping the public semi-informed is challenged every four years when pollsters make projections of the Presidential elections. In 1980, they forecast a tight race even though they knew days before the election that Reagan would win handily. Their rationale for misrepresenting their findings was that they did not want to cause a landslide for the Republicans. One must wonder just exactly what they were doing or what they were supposed to be doing. If it was going to be a big win for Reagan, was there something wrong with saying so? Were they making data available to the public? Were they misleading the public? Presenting or hiding results? Just what criteria are used to determine what the public will be told? Election night returns and network projections of winners now present problems of national importance, and the public will be informed as to what is happening when the media feel the time is right.

The more responsible media tend to be very self-conscious about the effects their news and other fictional stories will have on the public. In fact, they tend to present material for the sake of desired effect rather than simply because it is relevant and important. The initial skyjacking stories, for example, seemed to induce more skyjacking.[14] This presented news editors with a dilemma. Reporting the news in a straightforward fashion put people in jeopardy. It simply would not do for the TV networks to inform the public about skyjackings so that the people could decide what should be done about them. The bottom line is that part of the role of the media is to keep citizens in a democratic society uninformed and misinformed.

It is in the vested interest of the monied powers in America that the public be informed just enough to conform, that beliefs in the system are confirmed[15] and that criticism is trivialized. Basically, the leaders need stupid followers. They do not want intelligent, informed, concerned citizens who are well qualified to criticize the imbalance of power in society. Stability is best assured by a pliant and compliant public, and this is exactly what the educational institutions produce and the media maintain.

Politics

This point is dramatically demonstrated during political campaigns. Increasingly, elections are decided by 30-second spot ads aimed more at the gut than the mind[16]—commercial techniques of image-making which pervert the process into, at best, a popularity contest. Negative campaigning against the opponent aside, the fundamental idiocy of electioneering is that it is largely unrelated to the qualifications and abilities an official needs for performing his duties once elected.[17] That is, a candidate may be chosen on the strength of attributes irrelevant to job performance. An administrator has to be organized and make decisions, yet he might be elected because of a winning smile.[d] It is apparently too much to expect that our political leaders might be selected for job-related skills. Increasingly, the ability to look and act the part is eclipsing the ability to play the role as a qualification for attaining office, so we can only hope that the system will somehow be able to produce some worthy leaders as, miraculously, it has in the past.[18]

The pragmatic compromise which American political institutions have found expedient to make is one of trading off logical consistency for responsiveness to popular demands. It is much more important that governments and parties be sensitive to the general public or their own members than that they adhere to set policies and eternal principles.[19] American "Democracy" has been redefined and adapted to a republic. The people make essentially no decisions except to choose representatives to play "Let's Make a Deal" with the lobbyists for special interest groups. In the new sense of the term, a "Democracy" is a political system which cultivates good relations with its people. Thus, America maintains the semblance of a democratic tradition, in that the people are periodically consulted and occasionally considered even while being deliberately misinformed[20] by "Ins" determined to get reelected.

Hence, the basic myth about American government—the belief that it is working for the people. This is the root cause of much political stupidity. Two hundred years ago, this notion might have been amusing, but reality has long since supplied ample, dispelling evidence that, in fact, the people are working for the government. The average American works for four solid months—one out of every three working days—for the government. That much of his labor goes for taxes. This the average American boob does despite the growing realization most governmental agencies are working for themselves rather than the poor tax payer. Cabinet members

---

d Actually, this may simply be the American version of a common political problem—that the skills necessary to get power may be different from those needed for its proper use. For example, revolutionaries may be well suited to depose a corrupt regime but may not be well endowed with the abilities needed to run a government themselves.

149

use issues as levers to aid them as they jockey for position in the "Power Stakes". Congressmen logroll to their mutual advantage and the detriment of everyone else. Boondoggle begets boondoggle, and governmental stupidity becomes a mixture of departmental ineptitude compounded by the noise and friction of competitive haggling among the many bureaucratic agencies.

Whether this is really stupid or not depends upon one's perspective. However, in politics, it is power which defines perspectives. As a repository of power, government is clearly a means which has become an end in itself. Although the original idea was that the government was to be there to help the people realize themselves, it has indulged in a tradition of making and interpreting its own laws in self-serving ways. Government has emerged supreme. It is strangling the people it was designed to serve and who continually struggle to support it. One is hardly surprised that faith in the political system has been eroded: the surprise is that there is any left at all.

Generally, the religious fervor that was once inspired by democratic terminology has been badly compromised by pragmatism: "Liberty" is hardly worth killing for these days and certainly not worth dying for. If democratic slogans have ceased to be accepted as inspiring truths, now that we have endured over a century of hacks running the political machines,[21] there is some consolation in knowing that bribery and corruption have become more refined and discreet. Aside from the Nixonians (who were justly punished as warnings to others not to get caught), we now have a higher class of political crooks. They are slicker, subtler and more sophisticated than before and quite capable of providing the modern public with both the image and reality expected and needed.

Stupidity becomes apparent, however, whenever the discrepancy between image and reality bends or stretches credulity beyond the breaking point. For example, for years the federal government indulged in a Soil Bank program, paying farmers to reduce food production[22] while people all over the world and even in this country and were starving to death. Why that same money was not paid to farmers to grow food which then could have been distributed (along with contraceptives) to the impoverished needy has never been explained. It need be explained only if people realize how stupid it was for a government to prevent food production in a world of famine and an era when America was presenting itself to the world as a national embodiment of Christian ideals and compassion.

Slightly more idiotic than the Soil Bank program are the contradictory policies in Washington toward tobacco. This is a substance recognized as a poison by everyone but those controlled by it. Yet, because of the political clout of the tobacco states on Congressional committees, the government supports the price of tobacco. Then it taxes cigarettes and assures us they menace our health. Just why tobacco farmers cannot grow food, which would help people live, is more a matter of money than morals. An obvious victim of political morality was the Constitutional mandate that the government promote the general welfare of the people. Perhaps we should all be grateful that the cyanide industry is not powerful enough to enlist government support for its product.

Even stupider than the government's policies toward tobacco is its policy toward drugs. Twenty years and $70 billion after the War on Drugs began, American society is still inundated by cocaine and heroin.[23] Increasingly, it is becoming obvious that we will never lick the drug problem as long as we deal with it as criminal behavior. There is simply too much money available to corrupt any efforts to put an end to drug dealing. **The only way to win the war on drugs is to legalize their use and deal with the whole matter as a problem of health.** Users could then go to physicians, enroll in rehabilitation programs and get prescriptions for their needs which could be filled at prices so low[e] that the drug cartels could not compete. Until we adopt such a strategy, the drug problem will remain no matter how much money the government throws at it. When we legalize drugs and let the medical establishment monitor and control their use, the problem will disappear. Of course, the main stumbling block to adopting this kind of policy is primarily psychological—we would have to change our drug-related schema so that we would perceive the addict not as a criminal but as a sick person who needs and deserves professional help in finding a cure.

It is rather sad to note that nothing makes government look stupider than an accurate, objective recitation of official acts and policies. Much as people need to believe in the system, they find it difficult to worship an organization which insults their fading mental sensibilities as it pours their tax dollars down one bottomless rat hole after another. Our current crusade to represent the "Underprivileged person" as a cause célèbre[f] in our political conscience is a case in point. Helping people help themselves is one thing, but the goal of making everyone equally privileged is so asinine that only a democratic government could embrace and only a totalitarian government could achieve it. While handouts and doles are worthy short-term, emergency measures, they have now become standards in a

e Profits from (or taxes on) even these low prices could be used to fund the rehab programs and maybe pay off the national debt.

f Past crusades focused on the freed slave, the reformed drunkard, the ennobled worker, the emancipated woman and "Our most precious resource"—the child.

culture which accepts emergency conditions as normal. Government is promoted but the establishment of effective, long-term solutions to our social problems is actually thwarted by the institution of such desperate programs, which foster not human development but human dependence on self-perpetuating, self-defeating bureaucratic agencies.

The functional guiding principle of crafty administrating is really quite simple—offend as few significant people as possible while placating as many as possible. Thus, when a decision is made by a civil servant, the prime concern is the satisfaction of the noisiest and most influential pressure group. Other factors which also enter into the decision-making process are (in order of importance); 1.) advancement of the decider up the pecking order, 2.) thwarting interdepartmental rivals, and 3.) facts relevant to the particular problem at hand.[24] If public interests happen to be served by such officials, that is only because they happen to fall in line with these criteria deemed crucial by those laboring in the context of the bureaucracy.

In public service, employees and officials routinely find that institutional stupidity in its many forms makes their jobs (i.e., helping people) all the more difficult. Organizational guidelines take on lives of their own and inhibit even the well-intentioned workers from accomplishing their appointed tasks. Hospital personnel spend as much time filling out forms as tending to patients. School teachers spend one or two class periods a day administrating or patrolling rather than teaching. The military is not permitted to win a war because the weapons or tactics necessary for victory would create "Bad press".

Another factor contributing to the frustration of goal achievement is the excess of information available to anyone who wants to be confused. Understanding is rendered nearly impossible when a person is inundated by conflicting data. A common ploy under such circumstances is to make, in effect, no decision at all but to stick with existing policy regardless of complaints or reports indicating its shortcomings and failings. Repetition of what was once acceptable then provides government by inertia.[25]

A further impediment to goal achievement is that those effecting policy would rather perpetuate errors than admit to making them. Of course, this strategy has the advantage of saving those in charge the bother of correcting or eliminating such mistakes as do exist. Unfortunately, the Veteran's Administration provides a rather sad example of what this can mean to victims of government bureaucracy. In its own hospitals, the VA often failed to enforce its own safety standards and failed to follow its own lax rules for investigating patient death rates. Further, VA consultants were quite content to push paper around instead of demanding an end to dangerous conditions that were causing needless deaths early in the

1980's. This indifference allowed the perpetuation of a venerable tradition of surgical errors. Worse yet, all this was made probable by the 1980 Congressional Invitation to Ineptitude Act which made reports dealing with the quality of VA medical care confidential.[26] And who is served by this law? Certainly not the patients! The beneficiaries are the bungling doctors and their incompetent staffs.

This is the abject lesson of American politics—the government serves those who prey on the public. Those on the inside, from the clearly criminal to the merely contemptuous, protect themselves. Although officials must occasionally reward public service, they also strive to cover up mistakes and encourage conformity to mediocre standards for the sake of the esprit de corps. Just so they all feel they belong, the dull are promoted and the bright discouraged from competence or from setting examples of excellence that others might resent. The ultimate danger of all such institutional stupidity is that it passes unrecognized as such and becomes a new and lower standard for judging the acceptability of incompetence.

Along with our misplaced faith that ours is a political system of, by and for the people, we entertain an unjustified belief in justice. We do this by listening to what we are told about the courts rather than watching what happens in them. As high priests of the legal religion, the Injustices of the Supreme Court set the general tone of their trade by sanctimoniously desecrating the Constitution while extolling its virtues.

The Fourteenth Amendment provided the Court with an excellent opportunity to show what it could do to a law. It was an amendment conceived and composed with the rights of people clearly in mind. Nevertheless, the term "Person" was expanded to include corporations as legal entities.[27] It was indeed a banner day in the history of civil rights when the Court interpreted "Person" to mean "A human being". The key phrases of the Constitution—"Due process", "Equal protection", etc.—are like so many legal spigots courts regulate to suit their circumstantial fancy.[28] Is the legal process getting too "Due"? Well, the courts can cut back a bit on dueness. Is protection of the law getting too equal? Then certain, favored people will be granted a bit more equality than others by a Court which has long since abandoned its efforts to create an open society and is instead committed to the establishment of a standardized, homogenized America.

Practically all popular beliefs about Constitutional government are results of political propaganda. At best, they are misleading; at worst, they are completely false. Civics books, for example, are written to inculcate in future citizens a sense of belonging beyond a sense of reason. In no civics book does the fledgling American find that law breaking is a major preoccupation at every level of government.[29] Although lawlessness in America has a long, dishonorable history, citizens are always surprised when they first encounter it. The Watergate affair was not unusual in the tawdry history of Presidential shenanigans; it was just exceptionally idiotic of officials who had pointedly alienated the media beforehand to have indulged in such misbehavior.

Without a doubt, the most shameful episode in the annals of official neglect and abuse of the Constitution was the detention of Japanese-Americans during World War II.[30] This was due to wartime paranoia, but it proved the impotency of the Constitution as a guarantor of rights.[31] The rights we enjoy are indulgences granted by government authorities for the moment. As grants, they are subject to revocation whenever it suits those in power to exercise this totally illegal and unconstitutional option. Further, when there is an abuse of authority, the courts are as likely to protect the villains as the victims.

Courts really are show places for the legal process. They are invariably pretentious, ritualized and somber. Upon entering a court, one gets the immediate impression that something important must go on in such an august setting. The impression is correct: justice is dispensed with. A killer is set free because some functionary dotted a "T" or crossed an "I". A defendant is railroaded because the judge or prosecutor is up for reelection and needs to toughen his image. The bottom line is not justice but the belief in justice, but on what is that belief based? Facts and knowledge and/or ignorance and stupidity?

The facts are that for every 1,000 **major** felonies, 17 perpetrators go to jail but for what? In pretrial maneuvering, armed robbery is watered down to simple robbery, and rape is plea-bargained down to assault and battery. Further, in 1983, while forty-two percent of those sent to state prisons were on parole for prior convictions, 55,000 criminals were set free on legal technicalities.[32] These are facts upon which our belief in the legal system is **not** based.

Along with our belief in Constitutional government, we believe in the dollar. It is curious to note that the dollar is impossible to define with accuracy and validity. At best, it is one of those green pieces of paper in your wallet or pocketbook. At worst, it is a figment of a collective imagination which makes the economy one of the newer permanent, floating con games in America's history of scams. Unlike the "Silver certificates", which at least said they were redeemable in hard metal, today's dollar bill is not worth the paper it is printed on in any literal or legal sense. It has value only because everyone believes in it and accepts it accordingly.

Our motto really should be changed from "In God we trust" to "In the dollar we believe". Of course, God seems to be doing Her best to separate Herself from the country, and who can blame Her. The Constitution is meaningless and the dollar worthless. It is only our determined unwillingness to perceive these facts that holds America together and keeps it going. Apparently, no fundamental facts of life, no basic knowledge of reality, no logical analysis of the establishment can shake America's faith in the system, and it is precisely this unfathomable faith which permits our national nonsense to continue.

The key to understanding the incomprehensible is that we believe in capitalism. Just why we do is a mystery. Perhaps it is because we do not perceive the estates of the rich in a cause/effect juxtaposition to urban slums. Perhaps it is because the ritual of buying and selling in the market place sustains the faith in the system. Most probably, however, it is because most of us cannot grasp the idea that "Capitalism" is just a word which has next to nothing to do with the workings of the economy.

The fact is that as an economically overdeveloped nation, America distributes poverty and misery via a politically regulated system of tribute and taxation.[33] Of course, the role of free enterprise in the economy of things is essentially negligible. In fact, the major contribution of the corner shoeshine man and local farm stand operator is not economic but psychological—justifying the continuation of capitalistic rhetoric in a world of collective regulation by megacorporations or governments. At municipal and state levels, public utilities which are not socialistically owned by government are fascistically regulated by it. However, regulation of private enterprise is most common in Washington, where federal officials routinely engage in back scratching interactions with the special interest groups they are supposed to be controlling.

As bad as such regulation is for the economy in general, "Deregulation" can lead to some unexpected problems in some areas, as it did in banking. For more than fifty years, banks hid in an artificially sheltered, unnaturally conservative environment with legal protection from competition while Federal Deposit Insurance guaranteed the survival of even the most poorly managed organizations. Stagnation replaced enterprise, and sheer incompetence became commonplace. With the opening up of competition among financial institutions in the 1980's, banks sank money into a number of black holes—soil, farmland, the Third World, commercial real estate and leveraged buyouts. In this case, it was the absence of a functional schema which proved disastrous: with no guiding cognitive model based on experience to help them understand what they were doing, manic bankers seemed immune to learning from each succeeding fiasco, and only a handful of CEOs were canned for mismanagement.[34]

On the labor scene, strong unions were thought to be a counterpoise to greedy business but in fact joined with mismanagement and big government to bamboozle the American worker. To the extent that unions obtained more pay for less work, they created unemployment and caused inflation. It may have been all well and good for an assembly line worker in Detroit to make an average of $23 per hour—until the Japanese flooded the market with better, cheaper cars. In 1984, the government protected and the consumer subsidized (to the tune of $600/car) management's ineptitude and labor's greed. Presumably, national interests were served by the protection of obsolete marketing and manufacturing strategies and the employment of workers who prevented the economic production of quality cars.

Another peculiar aspect of the American labor scene is the irrelevance of selective criteria use when people try to join the work force. Traditionally, America was a caste society covered over with egalitarian maxims and morals and an incongruous ideology of racial superiority which sanctioned the system[35] while it inhibited random interactions among equal people. Whites derived their social eminence from their technological control of the economy and, through that, the political system, although all these are eroding as the moral imperative of social justice is realized.

While it was stupid to repress talent and stifle ability in the past, it is inexcusable that we still continue to do so. Nevertheless, we continue our tradition of self-induced inefficiency by demanding the work force reflect not the distribution of ability in it but the racial composition of society in general. To this end, "Race norming"—rigging employment aptitude tests to favor minorities—has been used by thirty-eight states at the behest of President Reagan's Labor Department in order to enhance the chances of blacks and hispanics of landing jobs.[36]

If the legality and sagacity of that policy are at best dubious, one certainty in the American labor market is that the individual worker has become an anachronism. In the superficial and entertaining world of professional sports, performers may be rewarded for proficiency and technical expertise. However, in the general work force, non-performance criteria determine hiring (race and sex) and promotion (seniority), so mediocrity can be maintained by emphasis on factors irrelevant to job efficiency. In fact, a worker's main job is not to accomplish a task but to conform to and fit into a group of fellow employees.

Although it is a secondary consideration, to the extent that a job requires an employee to do something, workers must have some basic ability, acquired through training, to handle machinery or computers. This means that some people are going to be denied jobs for the outrageous reason that they are unqualified. If such people are unwilling to accept menial positions of employment, society will probably find a place for them on welfare. We already have third generation deadbeats who expect the country to provide not just an opportunity to earn a decent living but the decent living itself—as if a good income is an economic right.

In general, we now face the problem that any governmental program, policy or plan of action may quickly become maladaptive.[37] Traditional values may be irrelevant to the young, and old definitions may not even be challenged so much as ignored. The extended family has made way for the extended state, which is being computerized as it assumes its new role. All this is rather trying for anyone clinging to presumably fundamental, eternal values in an ever evolving culture. Belief in God has been partially displaced by a belief in people, and now this humanistic tradition is itself giving way to beliefs in secular organizations which are struggling to strangle themselves.

For example, the belief in federal welfare has led to government funding of urban ghettos, and as a contemporary case study of what a benign if not bungling bureaucracy cannot accomplish, our city slums compare favorably with the Indian reservations of the last century. The major difference is that reservations are legally defined areas, whereas ghettos are extralegal territories. The major similarity is that both may be characterized as tending toward the same omega point of economic, cultural and spiritual genocide. In both cases, emphasis on the level of funding and degree of sympathy misses the subtlety that providing people with food, shelter and trinkets falls short of helping them become self-sufficient.[38]

Traditionally, black culture in America was basically a tension-reducing strategy. Fundamental Christian rituals provided temporary and meaningless release from the oppressive white world. However, for all the singing, shouting and hand clapping, heavenly rewards were to be granted only those who accepted their downtrodden condition here on earth.[39] As debilitating as resignation was, it was the best coping technique available to people who were systematically denied opportunities to acquire and use skills for worldly advancement.

Now, blacks are granted opportunities to use skills even when someone else is better qualified. This perversion of the Constitutional mandate of equal protection of the laws undercuts the great social myth of contemporary America that poor minority groups are being helped by legitimate policies of the courts, charities and liberals who worship at the altered altar of "Civil rights". The concern of many people to help those in need is humane as well as laudable, but just how effective have the means adopted been in helping the needy escape the slovenly despair of the ghettos? Are our slums any smaller or more bearable for all the Head Starts and hot lunches that have been pointed in their direction? For all the good intentions of the establishment to beguile those in the slums to accept whatever is granted them, most children of the ghettos know that the easiest way up and out is through crime. This is the saddest indictment that can be made of our urban policy.

If it is demoralizing to look inward at our domestic idiocy, it is equally discouraging to note that our foreign policy for forty-five years was stuck like a broken record in a rut[40] of negativity. Over and over again, we were anti-communist, anti-communist, anti-communist. If this attitude was justifiable, it was partly because no American with an ounce of cognitive integrity could make positive pronouncements abroad about the corruption, drugs and crime in his country. We were once the hope of the world, but we betrayed that hope, so now we just struggle along like any other country trying to get on with those who depend on us and those who just have to tolerate us.

As for those perceived as our national enemy, the Soviets always called for an end to the Cold War because they defined it as attacks on or criticism of Communist states by the West. What they did to the Western bloc or anyone else was covered over and sanctified by the term "Peaceful coexistence".[41] They have finally comprehended that we really did not want to beat them in a war. Of course, we wanted even less to lose to them, but our general posture toward the Soviet Union was quite consistently defensive: we were very much oriented toward holding the line.

Now with the end of the Cold War, it is time to reverse the tradition of finding better ways to kill our enemies and develop better ways to live with them and ourselves.[42] Fortunately for everyone, the time has past when we had to have not only the weapons necessary but also the insane willingness to use them to produce the ultimate peace. We can now stop pouring hundreds of billions of dollars into weapons systems we will not have time to use unless it is the last thing we ever do. We can alter the traditional picture of the incomparable stupidity of the arms race, when the conditions which caused wars—cultural isolation, aggression, need for resources, etc.-were all promoted by the fervid commitment of the world's great powers to attain ever greater destructive capacities. Now we can concern ourselves with the underlying problems of famine, disease, poverty, ignorance and, yes, stupidity. At the same time, we can take some perverted satisfaction in knowing that every dollar spent on defense nets us five dollars worth of ill will and suspicion abroad.[43]

As for the domestic impact of the military, we were given a lesson on the power of defense complex during the Presidential campaign of 1984. President Reagan advocated a 7% increase in defense spending for the next fiscal year; Walter Mondale wanted to hold the line at 3%. Yet, a poll indicated the American public wanted no increase at all! This may be taken as an indication of 1.) recognition by "those in-the-know" of a real need for a strong defense and/or 2.) the power of business interests to

Gay Rights

promote profits at the expense of "Democracy". Regardless of the national debt and despite the popular desire to reduce defense spending, the military-industrialists will probably continue to do their worst to contribute to financial disaster[44] with policies from which the best relief would be a little reason and sanity.

Unfortunately, one way to spell "Relief" is S-T-U-P-I-D-I-T-Y, because it is this which provides us an escape from the incredible world we have constructed for ourselves. Fortunately, on the other hand, the situation is not so desperate that some fool cannot render it absurd to the point of amusement. In the case of defenseless spending, levity was provided by the Air Force General who described the price tag of $7,622 for a 10-cup coffee maker as "Reasonable"![45] This is the kind of reason which brings comic if not financial relief to beleaguered taxpayers who never did find out what price the good General would have considered "Unreasonable": $10,000? $100,000? Of course, anyone who actually believes $7,000 is a reasonable price for a coffeepot should not be serving in Air Force Procurement: he should be out selling coffeepots.

As occasional whistle blowers have discovered to their dismay, the prime concern of those in Waste Management seems to be to see that it continues. For a circuit breaker that John Q. Citizen could buy for $3.64, the Air Force paid $2,543. An hexagonal nut which cost 13 cents at the local hardware store was purchased by pentagonal nuts for $2,043—a markup of only about 1,500,000%! After repeated warnings of serious, potentially widespread criminality and accumulating evidence of misconduct,[46] Secretary of Expense Caspar Weinberger initiated disciplinary actions against the naval officer who approved an eleven part $659 ashtray. Presumably, relieving the officer of command had a sobering effect on the 400,000 bureaucrats entrenched in the Pentagon's procurement offices —especially those with career commitments to absurdity. Many of these have devoted themselves to expanding the Defense department's definition of "Procurer" to cover someone who overcharges an anonymous party (i.e., the taxpayer) for something more than just a simple screw.

Updating this theme of waste and changing the image of mismanagement to the field of human software, a memo from commander of the Navy's surface Atlantic fleet Vice Admiral Joseph S. Donnell characterized lesbian sailors as "Hard-working, career-oriented, willing to put in long hours on the job and among the command's top performers". One might think that characterization would serve as a reason for recruiting lesbians into the Navy, but whoever said the Navy was reasonable? The document concluded that lesbians should be rooted out of the service, and if there is something counter-productive in this, it is at least consistent with the prevailing rather square Pentagon policy, which maintains that homosex-

159

uality is incompatible with military service. This attitude remains despite the fact that two studies commissioned by the Pentagon found no evidence that homosexuals disrupted the armed forces but rather praised their performance and urged their retention. The Department of Defense initially suppressed these reports and then dismissed them as unresponsive to the original research request, which was to confirm the reigning schema— the demonstrably fallacious notion that the presence of homosexuals was detrimental to military efficiency.[47]

If the defense establishment policy toward efficient and productive gays is decidedly hostile and costly,[48] the relationship of America to its natural environment is basically parasitic if not suicidal. However, we have surprisingly few illusions about ourselves being anything but exploiters, as we simultaneously rape and poison our life support system. Eventually, such behavior will limit our development, and we are actually hastening that day, in that we have made exploitation something of a cultural virtue.

There are two factors which are crucial to the systematic desecration of the environment: 1.) the organization and mobilization of people for the task, and 2.) the development of machinery to facilitate the process. Our population is well suited in both quantity and quality to wrecking the environment in that there are too many of us committed to a standard of living beyond the carrying capacity of nature—that is, to a standard which is attainable for only a limited period of time.[49] In addition, there is specialization and division of labor in our attack on the environment: those not actively engaged in ravaging the land usually devote their energies to polluting the air and water. All this is done in the name of profit and for the sake of more bigger and costlier possessions for as many people as possible. It is rather sad to realize that the ultimate limits for population growth will be determined not by reasoned planning but by the efficiency with which we poison ourselves and convert our urban centers into behavioral sewers.

To accelerate this process of social suicide, we have turned to machines and computers. The guiding maxim is that the world must be made safe for technology. The worst part of this trend is not that we are evermore efficient at wrecking the environment but that we are bent on creating a world in which machines rather than people can thrive. To the extent that we become robots, we too may fit into the world we are creating. However, our success in adapting will be directly related to our willingness to renounce the differences between humanity and computers. Civilization has developed to the point that we will have to become less human as we adapt to the technology which creates us.

The message of contemporary America to itself is perfectly clear: people are out. They are obsolete, except to the extent they can serve computers. The age-old tradition of humans adapting to their tools has reached the pointless point that all phenomena (like feelings) which cannot be quantified for computers have been rendered irrelevant by them. In this sense, technology and modern art lack the same essential element—they are both devoid of human emotion.

People and feelings were distorted and abstracted out of art early in this century. As artists sought novelty of expression for its own sake, emotional impoverishment came to reign in a world of any and all contrived means devoted to no particular end.[50] Just as modern composers labor to eliminate the distinction between music and noise, modern artists express the extreme of total irrelevance that civilization has achieved. As exercises in cognitive and spiritual futility, contemporary art reflects the moral bankruptcy of Western institutions and life.

This bankruptcy is further demonstrated by the way many serious social problems develop unexpectedly, often resulting from neglect, ignorance and wishful thinking. For example, when the government insisted on busing school children in and out of cities, about 30% of the white suburban school population simply dropped out of the public school system and went to private schools. It is certainly to be hoped that the equalization of academic training achieved by busing between urbs and suburbs compensates for the effects of discrimination on the students, and to the extent that the goal of integration was achieved, liberals must have been gratified.[51] However, the discriminatory method applied was counter-productive in that it drove off many of the students counted on to serve as "Racial units" in the bus-drive to substitute one bunch of equal kids for another. Of course, this has been a lesson largely wasted on departments of human services.

The contemporary mania for social equality might be laudable were not egalitarians so passionately committed to leveling downward.[52] Formal educational systems cannot be expected to improve society because schools are now primarily social institutions designed to bring young people together in an integrated setting. The commitment to academics is not dead, but it is distinctly second to our efforts to create equal citizens. Naturally, this makes any gesture toward excellence awkwardly out of place.

In addition to our egalitarian bent, a commitment to illusion rather than achievement contributed to the deterioration of academic standards over the past few decades. At the same time that we were inflating our currency to create the illusion that we were getting more than we earned, we were inflating our diplomas[53] to create the illusion that students were accomplishing more than they learned. Of course, cheapening grades does nothing for the learning process, but it makes a lot of students feel good about themselves. The long-term result is that bloated grades and diplomas cease to be of value to anyone, but that is irrelevant to those who live in a world of symbols.

Sad to say, not everyone loses equally. Those who are the real losers are the students who need to develop skills for coping in the job market because those who need extra help are the ones most likely to get inflated grades rather than more training. Worse yet, those who aspire to escape the inner cities may have to attend schools which are physically the oldest and in which teacher turnover is the highest.

Further, in developing analytical stupidity and frustrating artistic ability, American educational institutions are highly one-sided in that they concentrate intensely on the verbal left hemisphere of the brain.[54] As befitting a highly industrialized society, the abilities to focus on fantasies, ignore facts, misapply rules and massage data to confirm preconceived illusions are all cultivated in our classrooms and labs. Rather than being wellsprings of creativity, our schools and colleges are devoted to propagating acceptable answers to established questions. In the sterility of academics, everything is reduced to reason while being renders irrelevant.

In the world at large, leaders are often the worst students and quite reluctant to learn about and understand what they are doing. Mental stagnation at upper levels of government is as common as is supposed, since rulers usually strive to maintain intact the schemas with which they started. No less of a pundit than Henry Kissinger noted that leaders of state do not learn beyond their convictions.[55] Experience may confirm beliefs or lead to minor adjustments of policy, but the mighty are ill disposed to learn they are wrong about anything. In contrast to our victory over Iraq, our government backed losers in China, Cuba, Vietnam and Iran[56] in its commitment to demonstrate America's inability to profit from its losses for the sake of being itself.

Maintaining "Identity" can really be most stupefying, as demonstrated in Louisiana in the 1960's when local officials were proceeding with all deliberate sloth to integrate the schools. A proposal that integration be started in kindergarten and then proceed one grade per year for twelve years was rejected because it would work. The good ol' boys in power did not want a plan that would work; they wanted to be themselves. The only problem with "Being yourself" is that it can create so much difficulty for everyone.

Frank Serpico was just such a problem. He wanted to be a good policeman, which to him meant upholding the law. This made him something of an anomaly in New York City during the mid-1960's. Officer Serpico found that bribery, graft and extortion were such common forms of police behavior that cop after cop was encouraged by the prevailing norms to go on the take. In a department awash in its own arrogance, he

Integrity

made a career of making enemies among his colleagues by the unheard of practice of policing the police. Naturally, by standing on principle, he became known as a trouble maker because he insisted on pointing out trouble where it existed. His career was ended by a serious wound received when his colleagues left him out on a limb during a drug raid.[57]

Even so, in terms of cleaning up the police department, Serpico's efforts were not totally in vain. Although the department ignored him as best it could for as long as possible, he finally went to the newspapers and generated enough publicity to bring about some temporary reforms. However, the point here is that he had to fight against the system just to get it to live up to its own stated standards. He was peculiarly obsessed with the notion that the government should obey the law. He discovered the hard way that the Nixonian doctrine that officials are above the law is rather common in American life, and this wisdom and his integrity was lost to the nation when he went into self-assumed exile in Europe.

In this vein, a person who insists on asserting his integrity in a world of cons and scams really can be annoying. An Hispanic, with the unlikely name of Henry Harrison, proved this point when he became a fly in the ointment of integration by insisting on doing what he felt was right. In 1984, Mr. Harrison was a fireman in Miami when he asked his superiors to remove his name from a promotion list so that he would not advance over colleagues he considered more deserving. Chief Ken McCullogh expressed shock and confusion over Harrison's reluctance to take advantage of Affirmative Action guidelines to move ahead of fellow workers who had scored higher in the qualification process.[58] From Harrison's standpoint, his decision might be considered stupid, in that he was sacrificing his own advancement for the sake of creating a more efficient fire department. The ironic point is that he had to do this in the face of regulations and expectations of the system, which was set up to promote people according to qualities irrelevant to job performance. How nice it might be if advancement of individuals within a group and improvement of group efficiency went together rather than being at odds with one another.

As vexing as officer Serpico's acts of conscience were for the establishment, Mr. Harrison's was even more so because he showed that simply obeying or abiding by the laws and rules is not enough if those regulations themselves are unconscionable. Beyond commandments inscribed in stone, Constitutions written on parchment and laws compiled in books, there is a spirit which animates a culture. It is this which provides an ethical and moral basis for judging the stupidity of official schemas. The irony inherent in culture is that our religious beliefs are so often at odds with our behavioral norms.

Progress

This problem is particularly confusing for Americans, because, more than any other nation on earth, we are a hodgepodge descended from Europeans, Africans, Asians and native Americans. We are Christians, Jews and atheists. We are capitalists, fascists and socialists. We are a dynamic conflict of many competing interests all bent on getting more than their share of the national pie. No student of society, government or economics can look upon us without a sense of bewildered amazement. If life is a temporary state of dynamically imbalanced conditions, and it is, America is certainly very much alive, but that such a chaos of conflicting schemas can flourish is due in large part to the stupidity of Americans who resolutely refuse to perceive inconsistencies where they exist. Only those who are stupid enough to try to understand what is going on find that it could not possibly "Make sense". Oddly, there is both security and danger in the incomprehensibility of the American experience: we are too complex to be wrecked by deliberate planning, but we have lost control of our own fate.

The basic problem of America is one of breadth without depth. With so much to draw on in terms of both human and natural resources, national character was shaped by pragmatic, short-term policies geared to specific and often isolated situations. So often, as both the New Dealers and Watergate Gang found, solutions became problems: the reaction to bad business and bad politics was bad government. The only thing we do not have is an American way of wrecking the country. American stupidity is creative in that there seems to be no limit on the ways we can find to take a bad situation and make it worse.

Ironically, the national commitment to our own well-being has become a fatal break preventing us from achieving the progress politicians are always proclaiming or promising. Progress is a matter of passing beyond an existing state of affairs.[59] In a material sense, this means developing a higher standard of living, and this we have achieved. However, attaining the physical comforts of material prosperity has made us both proud and uneasy, as there has been no progress toward peace of mind. Behind our pride exists the gnawing realization that immediate compassion and concern for the downtrodden and dispossessed cannot be converted into legislative programs of any significant long-term success. Slums, apathy, ignorance and stupidity remain as real and potent as ever before. In human terms, America represents little in terms of progress or even promise for the future.

164

Notes

1. **The Spotlight**. Oct. 8, 1984. Cordite Fidelity; Washington, D.C. 11.
2. Milward, A. 1976. Fascism and the Economy. In **Fascism: A Readers' Guide** edited by W. Laqueur. University of California Press; Berkeley, CA. 381.
3. Shaw, G. In a letter to Mr. Moses Harman quoted in **The Rise of Industrial America** by P. Smith. 1984. McGraw-Hill; New York. 281.
4. Lord, W. 1960. **The Good Years**. Harper & Brothers; New York. 86.
5. Arnold. T. 1937. **The Folklore of Capitalism**. Yale University Press; New Haven, CT. 107.
6. Kolko, G. 1963. **The Triumph of Conservatism**. Free Press; New York.
7. Weidenbaum, M. Jan. 2, 1992. New federal regulations threaten to bury business. **Gazette Telegraph**; Colorado Springs, CO.
8. Arnold. **op. cit. 78**.
9. Boorstin, D. 1987. **Hidden History**. Vintage; New York. 84.
10. Whyte, W. 1956. **The Organization Man**. Doubleday; Garden City, NY. 145.
11. Barnhart, R., Steinmetz, S. and Barnhart, C. 1990. **Third Barnhart Dictionary of New English**. Wilson; New York.
12. **Sun-Sentinel**. Nov. 20, 1984. Fort Lauderdale, FL. 10A.
13. **The New York Times**. Mar. 4, 1977. B2.
14. Smith, R., Sarason, I. and Sarason, B. 1982. **Psychology: The Frontiers of Behavior**. Harper & Row; New York. 51.
15. Halberstam, D. 1979. **The Powers That Be**. Knopf; New York. 113.
16. Siegel, M. Quoted in **Newsweek**. May 6, 1991. Vol. 117, No. 18, 25.
17. Tuchman, B. 1984. **The March of Folly**. Knopf; New York. 386.
18. Weisberger, B. Aug. 1964. How to Get Elected. **American Heritage**; XV, #5, 64.
19. Arnold. **op. cit. 41**.
20. Wham, W. Mar. 10, 1984. Sound the Foghorn. **The New Zealand Herald**. Aukland. 6.
21. Arnold. **op. cit. 44**.
22. Goldman, E. 1960. **The Crucial Decade and After: America, 1945-1960**. Vintage; New York. 297.
23. Treaster, J. June 14, 1992. 20 Year of War on Drugs, and No Victory. **The New York Times**. E7.
24. Flew, A. 1979. Intended conduct and unintended consequences. In **The Encyclopedia of Delusions** edited by R. Duncan and M. Weston-Smith. Wallaby; New York. 23.
25. Tuchman. **op. cit. 386**.
26. **Sun-Sentinel**. Dec. 2, 1984. Fort Lauderdale, FL. 49.
27. Lundberg, F. 1980. **Cracks in the Constitution**. Lyle Stuart; Secaucus, NJ. 236.
28. **Ibid**. 237.
29. Lieberman, J. 1973. **How the Government Breaks the Law**. Stein & Day; New York.
30. Phillips, C. 1975. **The 1940s: Decade of Triumph and Trouble**. Macmillan; New York. 110.
31. Schlesinger, Jr., A. 1973. **The Imperial Presidency**. Houghton Mifflin; Boston, MA. 116.
32. Bidinotto, R. 1989. **Crime and Consequences**. Foundation for Economic Education; Irvington-on-Hudson, NY.
33. Hammond, P. 1978. **An Introduction to Cultural and Social Anthropology**. 2nd ed. Macmillan; New York. 170.

34. Meehan, J. Mar. 2, 1992. America's Bumbling Bankers: Ripe for a New Fiasco. **Business Week**; 86-87.

35. Hammond. **op. cit.** 247.

36. Kilborn, P. May 19, 1991. "Race Norming" tests become a fiery issue. **The New York Times**; The Week in Review. 5.

37. Hammond. **op. cit.** 193.

38. Raspberry, W. Nov. 20, 1984. **The Washington Post.**

39. Hammond. **op. cit.** 342.

40. Schlesinger, Jr., A. 1978. **Robert Kennedy and His Times.** Houghton Mifflin; Boston, MA. 451.

41. Hayter, W. 1964. In **The Cold War** edited by E. Luard. London.

42. Tuchman. **op. cit.** 8.

43. Pitkin, W. 1932. **A Short Introduction to the History of Human Stupidity.** Simon and Schuster; New York. 426.

44. Humphrey, G. Quoted in **The Devil and John Foster Dulles** by T. Hoopes. 1973. Boston, MA. 196. And Thompson, M. Jan. 12, 1990. Berlin Wall may be crumbling, but Pentagon plans rising budget. **The Miami Herald.** 19A.

45. **The New York Times** (Large Type Weekly). Sept. 24, 1984. 13.

46. Johnson, H. 1991. **Sleepwalking Through History.** Anchor; New York. 177-178.

47. Gross, J. Sept. 2, 1990. Navy Is Urged to Root Out Lesbians Despite Abilities. **The New York Times.** 24.

48. Schmitt, E. June 20, 1992. Military's Anti-Gay Rule Is Costly, a Report Says. **The New York Times.** 6.

49. Erlich, P. 1968. **The Population Bomb.** Ballantine; New York. Chap. 1. Pimental, D. May, 1994. Natural Resources and an Optimum Human Population. **Population and Environment.**

50. Tomlin, E. 1979. Novelty is the chief aim in art. In Duncan and M. Weston-Smith. **op. cit.** 236.

51. Taylor, J. 1992. **Paved With Good Intentions.** Carroll & Graf; New York.

52. Purcell, H. 1979. The fallacy of environmentalism. In Duncan and Weston-Smith. **op. cit.** 95.

53. Gitlin, T. 1987. **The Sixties: Years of Hope, Days of Rage.** Bantam; New York. 431.

54. Ornstein, R. 1978. The split and the whole brain. **Human Nature,** 1, 76-83.

55. Kissinger, H. 1979. **The White House Years.** Little, Brown; Boston, MA.

56. Tuchman. **op. cit.** 383.

57. Maas, P. 1973. **Serpico.** Viking Press; New York.

58. Robertson, L. Sept. 27, 1984. **The Miami Herald.** 1D.

59. Pitkin. **op. cit.** 272.

166

VIII. The Future of Stupidity and Vice Versa

America and the Western world in general comprise only the most recent example of a civilization failing to live up to its own expectations. In this respect, we are but typical of the civilized tendency of failing to fulfill a presumed destiny. In fact, with or without expectations or destinies, one of the most consistent characteristics of civilizations is failure. Archaeologists have built a profession on studying failures. Historians build careers by explaining failures. Every day, we are immersed in ignorable warnings that we too may fail as have those who have gone before.

This basic, fundamental human constant is due to the fact that we are all pretty stupid, and no amount of information, learning or technological expertise seems to alter this subtlety one iota. The problem is that we have ready-made, socially condoned, psychologically acceptable explanations for crucial events. Unexplained is the curiosity that things routinely go wrong without evident cause and despite everyone's best efforts.

The trouble really is, of course, with the explanations, which contribute to failure by explaining away not only the inexplicable but the explicable as well. We need the assurance of having answers, so if necessary, we make them up. These myths, in turn, can prevent us from discovering valid answers to our questions. Particularly elusive is the answer to the perpetual human riddle—why are our best efforts not good enough?

Well, first of all, our efforts may not be our best because we are biased toward the particular schema which defines our ability to cope. Not only does this bias inhibit cultural improvement by limiting competence, but the majority of people, with marginal abilities, support those who goof up, feeling that they will then get similar support when their turn comes. Thus, the weak support the corrupt, because just as efficiency is regarded as a threat by the inept, accuracy of perception and analysis is regarded as a threat by the powerful.

If we want to escape this self-constructed impasse, we would do well to make fresh inquiries into our shortcomings and imperfections. Our cultural liabilities are so decisive in the way they undermine our institutions that we are compelled to understand them if we intend to be exceptions to the rule of civilized failures. Thus far, the balance sheet on Western

Reason

Civilization is more extensive but no more favorable than that of any society that has passed before us. As fast as wealth piles up here, poverty springs up there. Increases in material abundance are matched by increases in bitter resentment as production and success beget scarcity and jealousy. Scientific advances are matched by human failings, construction by decay and happiness by misery.[1] These harmonious equations are maintained by the characteristic errors, ignorance, ill will and general stupidity of civilized people.

Western Civilization owes its technological predominance to the application of reason to the study and control of nature, but a major stumbling block to the study and control of ourselves has been the assumption that, since we can use reason, we are reasonable. We have had 100 years since Freud to acknowledge that we are basically irrational, but the models for human behavior proposed by the methodical scientific community[2] are invariably idealized constructs which are much more self-consistent and orderly than people would ever want to be. The problem for behavioral scientists is that logic must be used to explain irrationality.

Although reason is useful for extending a line of thought to the next point, it is of limited value in untangling complexity. Logic is certainly a useful analytical tool, but the overall physiological condition of an organism, for example, is not particularly rational and cannot be comprehended by anyone limiting his thinking to linear logic. (E.g., there is no logic in balancing hunger and thirst, sleep or sex. These are drives or states by which competing physiological systems cooperate to maintain the dynamic imbalance we recognize as life.) The best that can be done in analyzing such phenomena is to use polygraphs to provide data for statistical models which allow us to predict the probability of normal behavior. In fact, approximation is the best way to represent matters of such complexity.

This basic principle is even more important when one attempts to understand human behavior. Behavior is very much a compromise phenomenon. It may be analyzed logically, but as a functional whole, it is comprehensible only in terms of relationships among interacting systems. Only by accepting a compromise model of the human being in all its inconsistent ineptitude based on misperceptions of the environment can one begin to understand what being human means. Although we gather a lot of information, we also ignore a lot and may even be pointedly ignorant in matters of great importance to us simply because our schema directs us to be ourselves. Likewise, the information people possess may be used inappropriately because certain behavioral patterns are preprogrammed into or excluded from the response repertoire. This is both human and stupid.

As all indications are that there was and now is more than enough stupidity to go around, to the extent that the past is a guide to the future, we should expect stupidity to continue to be our constant companion as history unfolds. Certainly, it has been an integral component of Western Civilization since the beginning. The ancient Greeks indicated their first-hand familiarity with it when they formulated Cassandra's Curse[3]—that those who prophesy the truth will not be believed. There have been numerous examples throughout history of accurate warnings wasted because recipients were not disposed to alter their beliefs simply to accommodate new and better information.

In his last plays, Euripides paired moral evil with folly and asserted that people would have to confront both as part of their being,[4] but we have been very reluctant to do so. The problem seems to be that however brilliant the human mind may be in other ways, it is not geared to compensate for its own deficiencies. The reason for this is that cognitive deficiencies (which take the form of opposition to integrity) are expressions of the social dimension of life. It is this which shapes the schema as an individual becomes a member of a reference group.

The condemnation of idealism is a constant theme coursing through the history of Western stupidity. Socrates was a case study in the stupidity of civil obedience. Christ was crucified for living up to ideals. John Huss was a religious reformer burned at the stake as a heretic in 1415.[5] Giordano Bruno was perhaps a little too philosophical a philosopher to have profited from Huss's experience and so followed his fate in 1600. Not long thereafter, Galileo was forced, under threat of physical torture, to disavow the truth about motion in the solar system. As shameful as all this was, it is embarrassing to note that for all our sophistication and technological expertise, contemporary civilization is as morally retarded and ethically handicapped as any that ever existed. In this sense, there has been no progress throughout history. Worse yet, there is no prospect for any because apparently no one in the research oriented educational establishment is even aware of the problem much less addressing the issue.

Thus, we are still imprisoned in our belief systems. For millennia, Western Civilization was enslaved by its belief in God. After She died[a] in the eighteenth century, there was a period of enlightened rationalism[6] when Europeans sank by their own bootstraps into revolutions and intercontinental wars. During the nineteenth century, Darwin seemed to suggest that, although people could modify their environment, that which was innate would remain beyond human control.[7] The only thing people could do about their stupidity was ignore it or label it something else

---

a Our born-again God has died and been resurrected a number of times and to varying degrees throughout history.

Sacrifice

and make light of it. (Of course, the saving grace was that most people were not concerned in the least about stupidity, intelligence, happiness or any other great issue; they were simply busy working at their jobs and raising families.)

Around the turn of the twentieth century, Dr. Freud reinforced Darwin and brought us back full circle to Euripides by burying the controlling forces of human motivation deep within the mind/soul (psyche), far beyond the good intentions of rational will.[8] Now the suggestion is that the controlling power of humanity is not within us but around us—not in our natural environment but in our culture. Human nature is not coded into DNA: it is structured by the way people use language to explain their lives to themselves.

Sometimes not only truth is sacrificed but the general supporting culture as well. This willingness to write off one's extended human environment for the benefit of the self-aggrandizing in-group is most obvious in the mighty. In contemporary America, the Johnson administration made this point clear in a backhanded way with its occasional lapses into realism about the grave political and moral ramifications that escalating the Vietnam war would have on the country. These moments of temporary lucidity served to underline the sad fact that the Johnson clique was quite willing to sacrifice national and party interests for the sake of Presidential image. The exceptional moments of brilliant insight contrasted starkly with the prevailing mood of gloomy fantasy and served to demonstrate only that every silver lining has a cloud.

This catchy image expresses little more than that two contrasting trends have coexisted throughout history. One is the tendency of people to accept their fate; the other is the tendency to rebel against it, and the history of Italy in this century provides examples of both trends. On Sicily, the Mafia (certainly one of the most successful organizations ever) flourishes among people pretty much resigned to accept it as a fact of life and death. On the mainland, the glory of a mad egocentric was doomed by his magnificent stupidity. Mussolini personified a fool rebelling against the limitations of his world. For example, his population policy—Brats for Glory—made the Catholic Church look like the Institute for Planned Parenthood. No leader could survive such reckless disregard for the realities of resources, no matter how charismatic he might be.[9]

Whatever its superficial appeal, the missionary complex is often darkened by a deliberate effort to create fate. Those determined to remake the world in their own image cannot accept the stupidity of the world as it is: they feel compelled to add to it. In 1961, the Kennedy administration suffered a crusading compulsion to guide the Vietnamese away from their own objectives and toward those of American policy.[10] This mission was

170

doomed because we could not perceive the native anti-colonial sentiments as anything but Communist threats to democracy.

In the case of Vietnam, no amount of information would serve to reform American reformers. The efforts of the American Intelligence community to gather data were generally quite successful. The problem was that policy makers had closed their minds to the evidence and its implications.[11] American stupidity in Vietnam was not founded on agnosticism or ignorance but misinterpretation—a determined refusal by those in power to acknowledge as valid any views conflicting with the prevailing official misperceptions which confused nationalism with communism.

When events fail to confirm beliefs, the mental condition of cognitive dissonance exists until some adjustment of or to the incoming data can be made. Usually in the face of challenge, the schema becomes rigid,[12] and data conflicting with it are sacrificed for the sake of emotional and ideological stability. During the Johnson years, the administration was frozen in a dream world completely at odds with clear evidence that official policies were not just ineffective but counter-productive. As would happen again five years later, it remained for the media and the people to save the country from the government, since those loyal to the President had become incapable of making realistic assessments of the effects of their actions on the real world.[13]

It is noteworthy that the Kennedy team liked to refer to themselves as "Crisis managers".[14] In a similar vein, before becoming President, Richard Nixon wrote a book which covered his six favorite crises up to that time. One must wonder to what extent our leaders may be disposed to create crises to test themselves, to discover how much control they have, what their limits are and who they are. Too often, rulers give themselves the choice of the disastrous or the incorrigible and then choose both.

Since many of the major, specific problems confronting contemporary civilizations are not cultural universals, they should be (theoretically, at least) solvable. Poverty, racism, sexism, family disorganization, political exploitation, ideological oppression and war are not defining characteristics of the human condition. They are all products of certain circumstances which could be altered.[15] Whether they will be altered or not is the solemn matter we address here. The great human tragedy is that we know which conditions to alter and how to alter them in order to eliminate most of the problems mentioned above. Nevertheless, we usually fail to do so because our leaders keep us from adapting to new conditions while our schemas keep us from compensating for our cultural limitations.

Indeed, it is the mark of a truly wise person to be able to put himself in his own place—to view the world accurately from his own perspective. Making due allowances for one's own values permits accuracy in perception so that behavior may be based on relevant considerations. However, it is most difficult for people to penetrate their religious myths, comprehend their plight and then apply their cognitive skills objectively so as to deal successfully with their problems. In fact, what we really need to overcome ourselves is as little humanity as possible in the scientific process of gathering and analyzing data and as much as possible in the technological process of applying knowledge and understanding. Generally, however, there is no clear distinction between the two processes of gathering and using information. As we interact with our environment, we monitor the results of our behavior; we apply what we know toward the solution of problems and then learn how effective we have been.

Unfortunately, society is better set up to learn what it believes than how ineffective it is. If lessons of life cannot be massaged into conformity with ideology, they will be rejected for the good of the directing schema. It was this very human commitment of cultural priests to cognitive consistency which led such stubborn visionaries as Huss and Bruno to the stake and Galileo to humiliation.[16]

There is nothing so unnerving for established powers as having their assumptions challenged, but challenging assumptions has been the stock in trade of great scientific revolutionaries throughout the ages. Copernicus was the first. In fact, the term "Revolutionary" is derived from his notion that the earth revolves around the sun. A major step in the development of this insight was his realization that the prevailing astronomical assumption of his day—that the earth was a fixed point around which everything else rotated—was just a subjective view which everyone took for granted.[17] Although this view was fundamentally incorrect, it was part of an ideology which was considered a consistent whole by the religious establishment. An attack on any part was construed as an attack on Christianity in general and was met with determined resistance in the form of extraneous criticisms. Basically, the gist of the counterargument was that the earth had to be the center of the universe because that was where God obviously would have placed the home of important creatures like ourselves.

Although objective observations and rational theories count for little when one attempts to refute the absurdities which sustain the power structure, science can help us understand our universe and our place in it. As a heuristic device, it has been remarkably successful, but as both a schema breaker and maker, its potential was and is invariably affected by the human need for a positive self-image. This may very much affect the selection of research projects and evaluation of gathered data. The ubiquitous and eternal human reluctance to know who we really are is, nevertheless, yielding to those committed to finding out. Naturally, the success of science has often been at the expense of those wishful fantasies which stifled our cognitive development for centuries.

Science dealt human narcissism three devastating blows courtesy of Copernicus, Darwin and Freud.[18] In all three cases, the scientific explanations (of cosmology, biology and psychology) were resented and resisted by all those who favored the more flattering established notions that we were rational beings created especially by God and placed in the center of Her universe. The scientific theories survived despite the fact that they lacked any intrinsic appeal to people in love with themselves.

Scientific theories are appealing only in an icy, intellectual way. Science is really a system of established rules for gathering and analyzing data and is supposedly accepting of conclusions derived by the process regardless of their emotional appeal. In fact, the success of science is due to the institutional establishment of the means of schema formation so that the popularity of a particular interpretation will have minimal impact on the evaluation of experimental results. As the end of science is understanding—not the establishment or perpetuation of any particular idea, it is something of a contradictory institution, being set up to both confirm and refute prevailing theory. In their ideal moments, scientists are totally objective, and they replace bias and prejudice with accuracy and integrity.

Unfortunately, real scientists are all too human, so the institutionalized enterprise of science is too encrusted with stupidity for it to save people from themselves. A classic and tragic example of scientific stupidity was the vacuum of indifference which greeted Gregor Mendel's work on the genetics of pea plants. Scientists of the day simply were not able to appreciate his findings. He would have had greater impact had he ben able to generate some controversy. As it was, he simply presented his results, which were roundly ignored by everyone else as irrelevant to what they were doing and thinking[19]—until, thirty-five years later, biologists were doing things and thinking about problems which led them to comprehend the value of his contribution.[20]

Although it may take a generation or two, the scientific community will eventually catch up with its unnatural selection of ideas and correct the markedly unscientific tendency of laboratory priests to adhere to familiar theories. Their typically human reaction to a new revelation is to compare it to the prevailing schema (i.e., theory). However, this is usually a one-way process, with the entrenched explanation being accepted as the defining standard of reference to which data and new hypotheses are expected to conform. Scientists are quite human[21] in their propensity to ignore or reject, for as long as possible, findings inconsistent with the popular theory of the day.

Dogma

The bottom line is that science is really a religion, with the devoted believers sticking to dogma whether it makes good sense or not. Every difficulty is placed in the path of the heretic who dares challenge a sacred tenet of the faith.[22] Research which might disprove an established theory may not be funded because it would prove to be at best a waste of money and at worst rather disturbing. Experimental results which are at odds with holy expectation are scrutinized very carefully if they cannot be rejected outright. If valid, disquieting results still may not be published by journal editors indoctrinated in revered theory and likely to perceive novel findings only as threats deserving of suppression. If published, original interpretations and hypotheses can always be ignored by practitioners of ye olde-tyme religion.

It is rather tragic to note some of the works which were not even ignored. A case in point was John J. Waterston's paper on the kinetic theory of gases. This was rejected by the Royal Society of London in 1845 as being "Nothing but nonsense". It was finally published in 1892 when it no longer posed a threat to the re-establishment.[23] One can but wonder how many possible advances in scientific thought have been thwarted by professionals oppressing their conventional expectations onto new, inventive ideas. For all their training and sanctimonious pronouncements about objectivity, scientists are no more tolerant than people when their self-evident, hallowed, unassailably correct and righteous views are challenged.

In fact, a Young Turk starting out in science (or any other field for that matter) should keep to himself any good ideas of importance which might threaten to advance his profession or improve his reference group. Specifically, the young scientist is well advised to begin his career by contributing some bricks of knowledge to the wall of ignorance. Initial research proposals should not challenge the major theories of the day. Revolutionary ideas should be put on "Hold" for a few years until the initiate is clearly a member of the club. Then he will have the prestige needed to get any offbeat ideas he might still entertain accepted for publication. Of course, this is all good advice well wasted on anyone cursed with an ounce of integrity or a passion for understanding.[24]

It will come as no surprise to cynics that the payoff in science is not fallible knowledge[25] but money, with most going to those who publish most. These tend to be ideological conservatives who concoct little research projects which support established theory.[26] Coupled with this tendency toward financial support for the orthodox is an organizational trend toward teamwork in research groups at the expense of the individual gogetter. The scientist is becoming decreasingly an independent thinker and increasingly a fellow worker who fits in and gets along with the team.[27]

174

Adjustments

Outside the lab, the relationship of science to the community is supposed to be one of mutual support. Scientists are really specialists at converting money into socially acceptable knowledge, so from the standpoint of the scientist, the need for financial support can be a restriction on the questions which may be asked and the answers which are permitted. In the Third Reich, anthropologists produced research which supported policies of racial supremacy. On the other hand, Arthur R. Jensen found that contemporary American culture is generally hostile to his suggestion that there is a genetic basis for the difficulties black children have in academics.[28] Fortunately, our interest here is not in the validity of this or any other study but in the social attitudes which cause controversial findings to be embraced or rejected by a given culture. It is simply irrelevant to evaluate the scientific validity of a theory or research results in terms of the effects they might have on a particular social cause. Still, that is usually how societies judge which research programs will be supported and what results will be accepted.

In a similar way, a basic concept like "Mental health" has been shaped by two stupid cultural factors. The first of these is confusion as to just what kind of world it is to which the mentally ill are supposed to adjust. The second is the tendency of those who use and define labels to take them and themselves a bit too seriously.

In terms of mental health and illness, the problem confronting all of us is that we are expected to adjust to an idiotic society. This is what makes the goal of most psychotherapy so tautologically self-defeating. As therapy proceeds, the individual is to become more self-accepting and more realistic,[29] which is just fine, if the "Self" is realistic. However, what is to be done when realism leads one to the overwhelming conclusion that the self is a bundle of contradictory needs and emotions, maniacal and depressing drives, brilliant and stupid ideas? The problem then becomes a matter of accepting this while trying to adjust to a wacky world of contradictory organizations and institutions.

When the problem of adapting to ourselves boils down to the prayer of Alcoholics Anonymous to have the serenity to accept what cannot be changed, the courage to change what can be changed and the wisdom to know the difference, one is practically driven to drink. Even professional staff members in mental hospitals do not know the difference when they attempt to distinguishing sane from normal people, or sick from healthy patients or whatever it is they are so subjectively doing. David Rosenhan demonstrated this with a study in which seven "Normal" people managed to get themselves admitted to mental hospitals by complaining that they were hearing voices. After being diagnosed as schizophrenics, they behaved as normally as possible and never were detected as impostors by

Definitions

anyone on the staffs of the institutions, although some of the patients became suspicious.[30] The disturbing lesson of this study is that mental patients are better at diagnosis of mental illness than those trained to believe the labels they stick on people.

Labels can be used not only to make people look sick to doctors but to cure them as well. This was accomplished by the trustees of the American Psychiatric Association on Dec. 5, 1973, when they voted to remove homosexuality from the psychiatric classification system.[31] In one deft stroke, millions of people formerly labeled as mentally ill were redefined as healthy. It is sad to note that the general medical community has not picked up on this method of legislating health. Cancer is so common that it could be voted a "Normal condition" so that cancer victims would no longer be considered sick. Likewise, heart attacks are common enough to be voted "Routine events", so anyone suffering one would not have to be treated as ill. Perhaps the trustees of the Psychiatric Association should be examined by some of their patients.

1973 was a good year for cosmetics, as that was also the year in which "Mental retardation" in America was redefined from an IQ of 85 and under to one of 70 and under. This automatically cured 14% of the population of retardation. Just think how normal homosexuals with IQ's between 70 and 85 must have felt. It certainly must have been nice for such people to have been officially accepted within the bounds of general society. It is even more comforting to know that by this simple, idiotic expedient of inflating standards, we could produce any number of geniuses desired. All we would have to do is drop the defining IQ level of genius the necessary number of points, and we would have that many more eggheads to create problems for us.

Physicists must envy social scientists who can cure the ill by voting and convert the abnormal to acceptability by redefining terms, but physical scientists are actually busy playing their own subjective games with nature. In fact, they have gone overboard to the point of giving up on "Reality" as a limiting condition in research. Modern physics is built on the principle that anyone's version of reality is so structured by his schema that there are as many realities as there are observers.

In the good old days of Newtonian mechanics, physicists worked in a precise, objective, determined universe which ran along like some grand celestial clock. Quantum mechanics has changed the clock into something even Dali could not have recognized. The universe is now perceived as a grand expression of undetermined microevents from which humans can garner only generalized statistical conclusions.[32]

If anything, modern physicists seem a bit too willing to dismiss reality as simply a field for subjective impressions. There is reason to believe

176

Myths

that physicists find what they seek because they create conditions which will produce results supporting their assumptions. If they expect to observe particles, they find particles; if waves, they get waves. Electrons spin as expected, and the axis of spin conforms to the investigator's prediction. Such findings prove little except that the subatomic world is as determinate as it is accommodating to experimenters. There is, thus, an alternative explanation for what physicists assert are undetermined micro-events: it may be they are determined by methods of investigation which are too crude to permit objective studies of subatomic phenomena.

It is one of the great ironies of science that the assumption of cause/effect cannot be proven. Events may be correlated, but all a true scientist can assert is that under certain conditions, particular, specified couplings are more or less probable. For example, there is a good correlation between mangled bodies and car wrecks, but which causes which cannot be proven. An unfortunate result of this philosophical limitation is a tendency to disregard the obvious fact and basic tenet of science that events are caused, much to the benefit of many of our stupider myths.

The classic case was, of course, the former controversy over the effects of tobacco on smokers. It is now generally conceded that smoking causes cancer, heart disease, strokes, etc., but even when industry insiders knew better, spokespeople for tobacco made careers of pointing out the possibility that both smoking and ill health might be due to a common cause. For example, it was suggested that hypertension might make one prone to disease (by lowering general, systemic resistance) and given to smoking for the release of tension provided by oral gratification.

Of all the myths which thrive in the face of scientific limitations, however, "Free will" is the most fundamental. Although study after study confirms that human behavior is conditioned by the interactions of the environment and people on each other, the Western belief in freedom cannot be laid to rest. Although every successful experiment in the behavioral sciences theoretically undercuts the notion of freedom, there is no great soul searching confrontation developing on this issue. Just as God adapted to Charles Darwin, freedom is adapting to B. F. Skinner and his behaviorist colleagues so that our traditional schema may be retained. In this great unacknowledged battle between science and our favorite secular religion, our cultural priests play "Mindguards", ignoring and interpreting accumulating evidence so as to minimize our awareness and anxiety as to just who and what we are. In this sense, the concept of human freedom is to the contemporary Western world what the Ptolemaic planetary system was to medieval culture—an idea that makes us feel important.

This myth is sustained not only by those who revel in the limitations of statistical analysis but also by the Existential-Humanists. These are behavioral philosophers who sort of play the sad clowns in the circus of psychology. They are very much in love with the illusion of human freedom and feel the behaviorists' assertion that humans respond predictably to combinations of internal and environmental factors robs people of their dignity. They prefer to view people as creative and inherently good beings who are striving to fulfill their potential.[33] According to them, Adolf and Attila the Huns were essentially good people just trying to realize themselves. Collectively, they constitute the "Aw, shucks..." school of psychology, and if there ever was a religious myth masquerading as philosophical idiocy, this is it.

By way of sympathy, it should be noted that the Existential movement developed as an attempt to understand how people, during the horrors of World War II, could "Rise above themselves" and find meaning in their lives. Sartre, who made a career of telling people what they wanted to hear and already believed, emphasized self-determination, choice and responsibility for rising above immediate circumstances.[34] The maxim was "We are our choices", as existence and meaning were considered to be in our own hands. We alone are supposed to decide freely what our attitudes and behavior will be.

Of course, this is nonsense! Specifically, it is nonscientific nonsense. It may make good religion, but it is lousy philosophy and no kind of psychology at all. The phrase "Rise above themselves" may sound better in French, but it is meaningless in any language. Self-control, choice and responsibility are elements of a conceptual schema people can learn, and it may be awesome but not totally surprising that some people clung to them during their desperate experiences during the war. A pat on their collective heads by self-serving Humanists might make people feel good about themselves, but it will not help anyone understand anything.

The one thing we do not want to understand is that our vaunted self-control is so patently superficial. Self-control is the ability to change behavior by consciously directing actions to achieve specific goals. However, this whole notion is rendered irrelevant by the realization that the selection of the specific goals is predetermined by a person's cultural background and individual experience. Further, people usually are and wish to remain unaware of themselves and thus may unwittingly create more problems than they solve while trying deliberately to achieve their subconsciously determined goals.[35]

Although self-control may be illusionary if not impossible, belief in it and in personal freedom have been, are and probably will continue to be major contributing factors to the normal malfunctioning of Western society. This belief—as opposed to a belief in determinism—is easy for us to accept because the English language is so implicitly moral in connotation:

Responsibility

e.g., "Innocence", "Guilt", "Courage", "Pride" and countless other words imply a sense of "Free responsibility".

However, what we please ourselves to perceive as our choices have been conditioned by our personal history, immediate environment and future expectations. This means, among other things, that the concept of "Guilt" is totally inappropriate in our legal system, as there is no possible justification for punishing those who chose "Wrong". More important, our final criterion for determining stupidity is invalidated. We found earlier that the criteria of "Knowing" and "Maladaptiveness" are much too subjective to be reliable guides to stupidity. Now we find that people cannot even choose to be stupid: they just are or are not stupid, depending on circumstances with which they interact but cannot control.

Nevertheless, and as nonsensical as it seems, there remains a moral dimension to Western stupidity simply because of our ability—imperfect though it may be—to anticipate the results of our actions. By virtue of our intentions, we must accept responsibility for our actions. Regardless of external and subconscious factors, the fact that people consciously direct their behavior toward certain ends places a moral burden on them to be accountable for the future.

This Western ethic based on individual responsibility is simply our specific form of the universal human requisite for a moral code. Although the particular code will differ from group to group, within the microcosm of a given society, its system of ethics has significance and meaning. Every group has behavioral guidelines—usually both formal laws and informal morals. All of these systems reflect the cultural imperative of people to pass judgment upon themselves.

The odd thing is that we are so often "Wrong"—that is, we are stupid according to our own standards of judgment. Often, we are wrong because we really cannot perceive what is right or wrong when we are actively and emotionally involved in a situation. The cause of this perceptual difficulty obviously is that we have schemas which guide the misapplication of misinformation by misconstruing our behavioral context.

It is all too human to know better but still do something wrong. The drug addict knows what his habit costs him day to day and may cost him in the future, just as we all know the price of deficit spending in terms of both personal credit cards and the national debt. Nevertheless, to the extent that personal and official stupidity of the future will be the result of conscious, unethical efforts on our part to permit our schemas to keep us unaware of the dangers of our behavior, we will be stupid for the worst of all possible reasons—because we want to be.

One of the reasons people so often seem to want to be stupid is that they are trying to achieve subconscious goals rather than those formally defined by society. For example, a public official may indulge in graft for his own short-term aggrandizement and counter to his role of public trustee. Likewise, your archetypical "Pig" policeman may eschew law and order for the immediate satisfaction of pushing around some hapless soul. On the other hand and a grander scale, the Watergate and Vietnam debacles might not have occurred had the irresponsible megalomaniacs involved restricted themselves to acts which were both legal and conscionable.

More to the point, the Presidents and their advisors would have fared better had they limited their behavior to what the average American considered conscionable. The real problem with the insiders of both the Johnson and Nixon administrations (as well as those involved in the Irangate scandal under Reagan) was that they considered their actions conscionable. According to their standards of evaluation (covered by such catchwords as "National security" and "Executive privilege"), their behavior was at least acceptable if not correct. Even more telling, in the case of the Watergate cover-up, acts known to be illegal were not considered illegal. Instead, they were simply considered political tricks or public relations ploys.[36] Somehow, the country managed to survive those leaders who considered their acts to be both legal and moral and were sure no one would catch them anyway.

In their sordid way, Nixon's advisors were simply striking examples of people who let loyalty to a person or reference group replace intellectual honesty as a higher form of morality. In such cases, personal integrity is not so much sacrificed as it is redefined by group values, which become the standards for judging everyone and everything. Members may come to believe in their leader or reference group with religious devotion to the point that even attempts to improve him or it may be construed as attacks. Followers and members may prove their loyalty and gain the immediate social reward of group support by lying and falsifying and distorting information. Of course, anyone who questions group assumptions or subscribes to the explicit values of the general culture is regarded as a heretic and treated as an outsider. Still, occasionally, a whistle blower will arise and assert that any leader or organization that suppresses truth and punishes virtue is not worthy of loyalty.

It is sad enough that stupidity is built into the human condition by language and social reinforcement. Much of this is effected subconsciously and must be accepted as a given of human life. However, if we have contributed anything to the cosmic design of stupidity, it is that we have converted innocent animal stupidity into conscious immorality. In the zoological kingdom, neural systems (i.e., brains) have always blocked relevancies and some have paired irrelevancies. We have compounded subjective stupidity with rational, arbitrary stupidity as we engage in calculated

Immorality

efforts to be unfair and dishonest.[b] When lying and distorting information became a conscious, rational effort, stupidity became a problem with a moral dimension. We became the first and only species to take pride in and credit for deliberately blundering into disaster after disaster. If we can but survive ourselves, stupidity is all but assured of a bright future by leaders who insult our intelligence in order to gain support by making themselves appear sanctified and righteous.

In a grander sense, thanks to modern technology, righteous leaders can find themselves suffering the throes of mental anguish for knowing more than they might have wished. Such was the ordeal of Winston Churchill when experts decoded a German message indicating an imminent attack on Coventry in November, 1940. A warning to the city would have saved hundreds of lives but would have given away the crucial secret that the British were reading top secret German communications. After much soul searching, Churchill finally decided it was to the greater good to keep mum and protect the intelligence coup, but having knowledge of the impending attack had forced him to play God.[37]

It is sad enough that our leaders must play God, but it is then all the more disturbing that our culture has coupled the most awesome technology with a general indifference toward the human problems that technology creates. In the simple world of the !Kung tribes, the technology of bows and arrows and spears is complemented by knowledge of the total environment.[38] In the sophisticated world of modern, computerized stupidity, technology is the environment. We have created an artificial culture which we believe floats above and independent of nature. Our telephones call each other up; our machines talk to each other; our computers amuse themselves with chess matches, and the robots are delighted.

While we glory in our hardware, what has become of people? They starve by the millions in Africa, while we marvel[c] at the quality of the pictures of their misery on newscasts. Our slums are accepted as givens; our prisons are filled beyond capacity, and our children are on drugs.

These are but some examples of a general and disturbing trend in the world today. Clearly, our cultural compromise between technology and humanology is out of balance. Not only the individual but humanity itself

b There is, of course, always an element of ambiguity in judging behavior, so to the extent that cheats and frauds are successful, they may be considered shrewd, canny and intelligent. Only when their successes lead them to excesses and failure rather than adaptation can they be considered stupid.

c Although the relief efforts engendered by awareness of the victims' plight is very much to the credit of everyone concerned, how much better it might have been had the disaster been foreseen and prevented by birth control.

is obsolete. In the American political tradition, there is an amusing myth that the government exists for the people. In our technological tradition, we do not even have such a myth. We exist for our machines. We do not have computers; they have us.

As a cultural force, technology is narrowing and dehumanizing in its methodology. It is very effective in its limited range, but computers tend to limit the range of those devoted to them. Although the scientific method in the form of the social sciences has been successfully applied to human affairs, this success has been confined to what we can learn about ourselves—which is all science can and should do anyway. What we do with the knowledge we gain from science is another matter entirely, and it is on this point that we are floundering. The problem is that all our scientific and technological know-how and knowledge, all our machines and computers cannot tell us what we **should** do. Scientific methods may project what results we can expect if we select a particular course of action, but that is not the same as indicating that we should or should not do it.

Thus, our faith in and commitment to scientific research are misplaced because no amount of information is going to make us better people. No amount of data would have made Hitler or Nixon better leaders: more knowledge might have made them more efficient but not better. Hence, at the most basic and general level, the crisis in Western Civilization is due not to a need for more knowledge and research data but to a failure of our ethics of action and shortcomings of our informational morality.

As for our ethics of action, there is good news and bad news. Currently, we are in a phase of consolidating, organizing and institutionalizing stupidity—concentrating it in a technoelitist computer/communication complex whose effects are broadly distributed democratically. In the future, we should expect more and more planned stupidity, as centralized, standardized bureaucrats base blunders and design disasters upon our ever deepening foundation of amorality and for an ever expanding base of dependent victims. If this is not to be, if this prognosis proves false, it will be because we finally recognize that science and technology are ethically barren and morally neutral. That is the good news.

The bad news is that our used and abused moral values have provided the ethical guidelines, rationalizations and justifications for all the political corruption, social ills and idiotic wars we have forced ourselves to endure.[39] If the past is any guide, it will not be much of a guide for the future. If our past (im)morality brought us to the brink of nuclear war, created slums, fostered crime, starvation and misery, how will those values help us cope with the new challenges technology imposes upon us? Now that we can transplant organs, someone has to decide when the donor is dead. Euthanasia will become more common as an alternative release from

182

Ethics

the lingering suffering of those afflicted with incurable but non-fatal conditions which modern medicine can prolong indefinitely. If we are to maintain our historic tradition of stupidity, we are going to have to devote more time and energy to planning our immorality. Further, we will have to develop new forms of stupidity to prevent us from coping with the problems we are creating. Futurists should take note that stupidity will be one of the more dynamic fields in our coming cultural development.

Genetic engineering and eugenics are but two fields which will pose increasing problems for society. For years, people have selectively bred birds, dogs, horses and cattle and peas, beans and melons. Is it or is it not stupid to improve our own species by similar methods? Whatever the answer, it is based on morality, if not intelligence. Historically, the answer has been "No" to the suggestion of selective human breeding. It is considered immoral to use the knowledge we possess in this field to improve ourselves by deliberate planning. The basic problem is that of finding broad agreement as to just what would constitute "Improvement". While this is a difficult matter, it should be possible to find some general principles to which everyone would agree, if we were to but try.

Such principles will themselves be determined by the values used when we judge the application of knowledge in the cause of humanity. Unfortunately, "Sci-tech" will not be much help in this regard and, as suggested earlier, may even be limiting the ethical development of Western culture by its very success with "Quantitative reductionism".[40] Science helps us learn about nature by breaking down complex phenomena into measurable units. However, all the essential complexities of biological and social systems do not lend themselves to being reduced to quantifiable bits of information. Nor do these complexities of life readily lend themselves to the stepwise logic of linear analysis. Computers which can help analyze simultaneous interactions of phenomena help overcome this limitation of dealing with one thing at a time, but they are limited to handling information which can be reduced to Computerese. Hackers just do not seem to be able to appreciate the vital importance of the human element which cannot be translated into their language.

A tragic example of this was the failure of the modern American Army to calculate morale as a factor in the Vietnam war. Secretary of Defense Robert McNamara was the consummate computer man, and everything that could be was quantified and analyzed—number of troops, amount of equipment, tons of supplies, etc. Not only on print-outs but in reality as well, the government forces enjoyed a ten to one ratio in everything calculable over the Vietcong. However, all this was outweighed by the fact that the Vietcong troops were at least ten times more willing to fight and die than the soldiers of the South Vietnamese Army. The inability of the

Analysis

Pentagon to appreciate the crucial element of motivation and incorporate it into their intensely statistical schema was a major contributing cause of American stupidity during the conflict.[41]

Looking forward in more general terms, it is with discouraged resignation that we must accept our fate of a future shaped by all kinds of stupidity, with the specific dominant form depending primarily on the evolving relationship of technology to the society it creates. As life becomes reduced to a silicon chip, knowledge will become an end in itself to the point that society is dehumanized. The best that we might hope for is that scientists will honor their own ethics for gathering information and, secondarily, promote a humane technology when applying knowledge to the creation of problems. In any event, stupidity will be an integral part of the compromise condition of social life in the future, with its precise role and style being shaped by what we expect of ourselves.

If we want to make our expectations a bit more realistic, there are a number of questions we can ask when analyzing our stupid behavior. Was it an individual or group effort? Who made the crucial decision? Did he know what he was doing? Was he trying to find out? What made it a defective decision? Did external conditions contribute to making it stupid?

For such clear-cut questions, there are ambiguous answers. To the extent that stupidity is behavioral irrelevance, one source may be found in the subjectivity of decision makers. They may be excessively concerned with their own status (maintaining or advancing it), or they may be preoccupied with the social cohesion of their reference group. On the other hand, one can be stupid by pushing objectivity to the point of social disruption, as when pointing out the silliness of someone else's religion. Normally, stupidity tailored to enhance a leader's status or a group's cohesion tends to be conservative, with relief provided when some crackpot devises a new way to be idiotic.

To the extent that future stupidity will be caused by individuals making defective decisions, an understanding of individual stupidity will help us appreciate the irrationality of the years ahead. Unlike corporations and institutions, which are incapable of feelings, a person may be emotional. That certainly can reduce one's objectivity and mental efficiency. Further, an individual invariably has developed blind spots due to the specifics of his particular life experiences. Finally, shortcomings of information processing by any single mind prevent an individual from comprehending all the complexities of any but the simplest decisions.[42]

Unfortunately, the growing trend toward institutionalized stupidity will not change the essential fact that it will still be stupidity. Only the type will change somewhat as the past predominance of individual idiocy created by enthusiastic bursts of brilliant lunacy will be overshadowed

Computers

by plodding, methodical committees which can draw upon the collective and compounded drawbacks and limitations of their members. While being unemotional may encourage institutional logic, the resultant rationality may run over people's feelings and moral sensibilities. Finally, perceiving the complexities of a situation could lead to no decision at all. After all, very few polices are totally pleasing to everyone. At some point some kind of action must be taken, and it is stupefying to analyze and debate each and every possible ramification of each and every possible act under all possible contingencies.

Nor will computers really help us avoid stupidity in the future. First, much of the human experience cannot be programmed. Feelings, hopes and emotions are not reducible to quantified bits of Computerese. Neither can any program work out all possible costs and benefits of contemplated actions. Worse yet, although computers can help us deal accurately with the data we deem relevant to the major issues relating to a given problem, these suffer deification once they are entered. Computers have become our sacred cows, and their contents and pronouncements are now holy beyond critique. Disputes are considered settled when the computer speaks, and to many priests in the field, the "Garbage in—garbage out" problem is secondary to the systematic processing of garbage. One seldom finds computer operators enthusiastically rushing to make corrections of either input or programs so that they can improve the quality of their garbage.

Garbagewise, normal human language will also make its contribution to stupidity in the future. As long as we communicate by language and use it to construct our cognitive schemas, we will misperceive events, misinterpret data and misapply principles. After all, that is what being human is all about.

If computers and language need an ally in frustrating informational morality, the basic commitment of people to adhere to their reference groups all but guarantees stupidity a rosy future. While there is no iron law of stupidity which dictates that people have to wreck their own civilizations, it just always turns out that way, and nothing in the contemporary world indicates that we are going to be exceptions to this rule. It might help were we to establish an "Information ethic" (i.e., let the facts speak), but society probably could not stand the strain of cognitive honesty and cultural consistency. A demand for intellectual integrity might reduce the establishment's abusive application of information possessed, but no one—in or out of power—can claim to be objective: everyone's schema is a composite synthesis of the obliquely interrelated worlds of factual data, social cohesion and political power, so any information ethic must be somewhat compromised by our inherent subjectivity.

185

Individual Stupidity

While there is sure to be stupid behavior in the future, there are some strategies which can be adopted so as to minimize its role and impact. At the personal level, idiocy often results from misguided efforts of people trying to avoid the psychic discomfort of cognitive dissonance. It is unfortunate that the methods adopted usually result in a maladaptive schema being preserved at the expense of crucial information about the environment. Warnings go unheeded; facts are ignored; and behavior becomes less and less relevant to reality. Although education should and could be a way to develop in people effective coping strategies for dealing with such challenges to their schemas, the history of modern science indicates that academic training as practiced up until now is no guarantee against stupidity. In fact, most educational institutions seem to inculcate specific belief systems rather than training people to find their own when traditional schemas bring themselves into disrepute.

Within institutions, stupidity can be inhibited by breaking down the isolation and compensating for the bias which contribute so much to the collective idiocy of groupthink.[d] Those indulging in it could correct their resultant errors if they are willing to reverse an earlier decision.[43] Unfortunately, egos often trip on themselves as people become so committed to a course of action that even its obviously negative consequences cannot induce a reconsideration of the matter.

The well known Peter Principle, whereby people are promoted one grade above their ability to function effectively,[44] is another example of institutional stupidity which can be corrected if options remain open. If promotions were made provisional for a short period of time so that performance could be evaluated, there might be fewer people put permanently into positions beyond their abilities to cope. (The military's "Brevet" promotional system is a step in this direction, but it is usually used to save money by paying a person the salary of his lower rank while he assumes greater responsibilities.) There would be, of course, some loss of face for any workers who were returned to their earlier positions after provisional trials, but their short-term disappointment would be the price they would pay for finding the level at which they could function effectively. In the long run, this probably would be best for everyone—the institution as well as the individuals.

The likelihood of institutional stupidity can also be reduced if decision makers acknowledge the dangers or negative consequences which may re-

---

d A listing of specific measures is presented in the last chapter of Janis's book **Groupthink**, Houghton Mifflin, 1982, and a "Balance Sheet" approach is presented in Chap. 6 of **Decision Making**, I. Janis and L. Mann, The Free Press, 1977.

sult from their actions.[45] There often is a tendency to minimize risks inherent in a given policy. This penchant to ignore risks can be an open invitation to disaster. Risks should not be minimized nor maximized—just recognized. They should be given probability and severity ratings which then should be multiplied by each other, with the product granted due consideration in deliberations.

An explicit discussion of the morality of a contemplated act might also prevent stupid behavior. Along with the legal, political, economic and social consequences of an act, its morality should be considered as well.[46] Morality is an underlying, defining factor in any controversial endeavor, and anyone who ignores it may well wish he had not.

In fact, many people might have profited from the advice a former country lawyer gave a young man starting out in the legal profession. "Strive to be an honest lawyer," he said. "If you can't be an honest lawyer, be honest." The former country lawyer was, of course, Abraham Lincoln, who made something of a career out of embodying the mores of society beyond petty role playing.

At the institutional level, the best way to promote honesty is publicity. As awkward as it would be for major political and corporate figures to conduct their business in goldfish bowls, steps in that direction would induce them to behave responsibly when considering the data at hand and attendant options. Certainly, we would not have had the Bay of Pigs and Vietnam fiascos or the Watergate and the Iran-Contra scandals had our politicos been required to plan their policies under public scrutiny.[e] As idealistic as it sounds to suggest our leaders abide by God's very first words "Let there be light",[47] it is reasonable to contend there exists an inverse correlation between public knowledge and their immorality if not stupidity. The less known about what they are doing, the more likely they are to indulge in corruption. Conversely, the more known, the less likely they will do something they should not. Thus, although an information ethic may not be a cure all for stupidity, it could be a first line of defence against public malfeasance. It should start with the people's right to know what their governments are doing and end by promoting official responsibility through accountability.

Finally, although we must use language, jargon should be avoided or at least minimized. The use of loaded terms can distort judgment by inducing a sense of self-righteous overconfidence. Especially when referring to an enemy, use of respectful labels may prevent an underestimation of the opponents' capacities and abilities.

e Or at least that of the appropriate Senate subcommittee!

Subjectivity

While it is nice to have a list of strategies for reducing the role of stupidity in the future, it is appropriate to ask whether it is really possible for any organization to protect itself from something so characteristically human. Is it possible, for example, to have an intelligent, enlightened government? The answer is, apparently, "Not really"! Plato's ideal of breeding and nurturing an elite of rational and wise leaders for government service was never tried in its purest form, although the medieval Catholic Church came pretty close to the order he envisaged.[48] In another case, China's Mandarins were noted primarily for the plutonic stability and sterility of their system, although they were also known for the corruption and inefficiency which contributed eventually to their deterioration and demise in decadent incompetence.[49]

If we are justly concerned with how to reduce stupidity, we must also consider by how much it should be reduced. After all, stupidity lets us live together while making it difficult for us to live with each other. The stupidest thing of all would be to eliminate stupidity completely, as we would soon be at each others' throats in a rage of realism and rationality.

Thus, future reformers who aspire to get people to live up to or (in the idiotic terms of the Existentialists) transcend their potential would do well to bear in mind the plight of Nietzsche's Superman as well as that of Nietzsche himself. In order to be happy, his Superman had to overcome his Will to Power—that obsession with dominance and control which usually nets disdain and resentment. In short, he had to overcome himself.[50] As the mighty rarely care to exercise this option, idealists may have to accept that, for better and worse, people are going to be themselves.

As for Nietzsche, he was happiest when he was clearly insane. The Will to Truth was for him and still is something of a terrifying, hostile, destructive principle[51] because we really do not want to know our own nature. Like the physicists who create the phenomena they want to observe, we create the perceptions we want to hold. Whether it is to our advantage or not, we can create anything out of human nature because it is and **we are so subjective**.

It is this subjectivity which makes operational definitions of stupidity (and so many other behavioral attributes—aggression, intelligence, etc.) so elusive. While there is a temptation to throw up our hands in dismay at the confusion inherent in the ambiguity of subjective phenomena, we must realize that this is not an end point for us but a beginning. It is our subjectivity which makes it not only possible but probable that we can and will be stupid, since it permits us to rationalize our behavior with unlikely explanations which are psychologically gratifying and socially acceptable. In our relativistic culture, both our abstract art and absurd theater indicate that the answer to the human riddle is not that there is no answer but that there is any answer we want. The bottom line is that there is no bottom line—just a number of fuzzy borders, each of which provides a suitable perspective for a given reference group. Subjectivity has triumphed, and all things being considered equal (whether they are or not), humanity will both flourish and fail.

As for stupidity, we may as well accept it as a limitation language and society place on our intellect. Like death, which clears away the old for the new, stupidity is an incongruity inherent in life. Humans have certainly developed, expanded and promoted it. We do so each time we endeavor to construct yet another flimsy utopia while doing our worst to keep the power structure evermore entrenched within itself. What we cannot acknowledge is that ideals are the rainbows of life—only the pursuit of illusion is real. It is an ultimate of human stupidity that we must seek what we cannot attain in a manner which prevents us from attaining it.

What we need in order to survive are systems which are not too systematic. They must be both functional and credible. This is the great human trade off. A realistic, functional system is unacceptable to super-ego standards which require inspiring beliefs. On the other hand, trying to live according to a static moral system leads to insurmountable, pragmatic problems. Fortunately, stupidity permits us a compromise blending so that we can entertain beliefs in all kinds of self-contradictory, conflicting systems while coping with some problems and creating others.

While we are capable of all kinds of compromise blendings, that needed for survival is fortunately not one of trading off the conflicting opposites of nihilists and realists. Nihilists aver there exists no eternal standard by which to judge and live, while traditional realists have argued society must be based on some universal, absolute truth—which invariably turns out to be a subjective viewpoint at best. What we all need is an eternal moral compounded from a respect for intellectual ethics and a commitment to human rights.[52] Such a moral would be compatible with academic integrity, consistent with individual dignity and based on the compelling need for people to find meaning in their lives.[53]

Equally compelling is the need to find meaning for the deaths squandered in all the bloody crusades of the past and the lives wasted in the quiet despair of our ghettos. If experience gives us the opportunity and wisdom the ability to recognize mistakes when we repeat them, we must be very stupid indeed to have been party to so much carnage and indifference so that we can create more. In honor of all those who have been sacrificed so pointlessly at the altar of stupidity, we can resurrect meaning by reflecting on our behavior and reexamining ourselves. There is no shame in admitting that our basic flaw is our need to belong—that our greatest fault is our need to be loved.

Notes

1. Chambers, W. 1952. **Witness**. Regency Gateway; Washington, D.C. 506.
2. Fishbein, M. and Ajzen, I. 1975. **Belief, Attitude, Intention, and Behavior**. Addison-Wesley; Reading; MA.
3. Virgil, P. 19 B.C. **Aeneid**, Bk. II.
4. Tuchman, B. 1984. **The March of Folly**. Knopf; New York. 381.
5. Durant, W. 1957. **The Reformation**. Simon and Schuster; New York. 167.
6. Tuchman. **op. cit.** 381.
7. Mosley, N. 1979. Humans being desire happiness. In **The Encyclopedia of Delusions** edited by R. Duncan and M. Weston-Smith. Wallaby; New York. 216.
8. Tuchman. **op. cit.** 381.
9. Pitkin, W. 1932. **A Short Introduction to the History of Human Stupidity**. Simon and Schuster; New York. 258-263.
10. Lansdale, E. 1960. In **The Pentagon Papers: History of United States Decision Making on Vietnam**. Senator Gravel edition. 4 Vols. and Index Vol. Boston, MA. 1971-1972. Vol. II, 440-441.
11. Tuchman. **op. cit.** 234.
12. **Ibid.** 347.
13. Kennan, G. Quoted in **The Limits of Intervention** by T. Hoopes. 1969. McKay; New York. 178.
14. Tuchman. **op. cit.** 286.
15. Hammond, P. 1978. **An Introduction of Social and Cultural Anthropology**. 2nd ed. Macmillan; New York. 27-28.
16. Cottrell, A. 1979. Science is objective. In Duncan and Weston-Smith. **op. cit.** 162.
17. **Ibid.** 163.
18. Skinner, B. 1971. **Beyond Freedom and Dignity**. Bantam Books; New York. 202.
19. Sturtevant, A. 1965. **A History of Genetics**. Harper & Row; New York. Chap. 2.
20. Gillispie, C. 1960. **The Edge of Objectivity**. Princeton U. Press; Princeton, NJ. 336.
21. Degler, C. 1991. **In Search of Human Nature**. Oxford U. Press; New York. viii.
22. Lyttleton, R. 1979. The Gold Effect. In Duncan and Weston-Smith. **op. cit.** 189.
23. **Ibid.** 194.
24. Strutt, J. (Lord Rayleigh) Quoted by Lyttleton. **op. cit.** 194.
25. Campbell, D. 1966. Pattern Matching as an Essential in Distal Knowing. In **The Psychology of Ebon Brunswik** edited by K. Hammond. Holt, Rinehart & Winston; New York. 103.
26. Jaroff, L. Aug. 26, 1991. Crisis in the Labs. **Time**; 138, #8, 46 and 48-49.
27. Wiener, N. Quoted by Lyttleton. **op. cit.** 196.
28. Jensen, A. 1969. How much can we boost IQ and scholastic achievement? **Harvard Educational Review**, 39, 1-122.
29. Smith, R., Sarason, I. and Sarason, B. 1982. **Psychology: The Frontiers of Behavior**. Harper & Row; New York. 426.
30. Rosenhan, D. 1973. On being sane in insane places. **Science**, 179, 250-258. (As an aside, Joseph Heller deals with this theme in his novel **Catch-22**.)
31. Smith, **et al. op. cit.** 305.
32. Cottrell. **op. cit.** 167.
33. Rogers, C. 1981. **A Way of Being**. Houghton Mifflin; Boston, MA.

34. Sartre, J-P. 1956. **Being and Nothingness.** Philosophical Library; New York.

35. Smith, et al. **op. cit.** 437.

36. Janis, I. 1982. **Groupthink.** Houghton Mifflin; Boston, MA. 227.

37. Stevenson, W. 1976. **A Man Called Intrepid.** Ballantine; New York. 165-166.

38. Hammond. **op. cit.** 37.

39. Howe, F. ca. 1920. Quoted in **America Enters the World** by Page Smith. 1985. Mc-Graw-Hill; New York. 744.

40. Koestler, A. 1979. Nothing but...? In Duncan and Weston-Smith. **op. cit.** 200.

41. Halberstam, D. 1969. **The Best and the Brightest.** Random House; New York. 464. (See also: Sheehan, N. 1988. **A Bright Shining Lie.** Random House; New York. 90-91.)

42. Janis. **op. cit.** 2.

43. **Ibid.** 151.

44. Peter, L. and Hull, R. 1969. **The Peter Principle.** William Morrow & Co.; New York.

45. Janis. **op. cit.** 148.

46. **Ibid.** 150.

47. Genesis I, 3.

48. Durant, W. 1926/1961. **The Story of Philosophy.** Simon & Schuster; New York. 34.

49. Tuchman. **op. cit.** 384.

50. Mosley. **op. cit.** 215.

51. Kaufmann, W. 1968. **Nietzsche: Philosopher, Psychologist, Antichrist.** 3rd ed. Vintage; New York. 358. Original source: Nietzsche, F. 1882, 1887. **Die Frölicher Wissenschaft.** (**The Gay Science.** Trans. W. Kaufmann. 1974. Random House; New York. 449.)

52. Thoreau, H. 1849. **Resistance to Civil Government.** (Later called **Civil Disobedience.**)

53. Rue, L. 1994. **By the Grace of Guile: The Role of Deception in Natural History and Human Affairs.** Oxford University Press; New York. 284-302.

Epilogue

In the grand, cosmic order of a deterministic universe, there can be no such thing as stupidity to a behaviorist. Behavior is simply (or complexly) caused, and the corruption of the learning process and limitations on a living system's ability to adapt are inherent in the process of life. Organic systems may be maladaptive and do fail, but because of the self-imposed restrictions of science, it is considered improper to interpret such debilitating conditions and events in terms of free choice.

On the other hand, within the microcosm of each particular cultural group, the self-deceptive language/perception complex, a social commitment to norms and pressure toward groupthink all can contribute via the neurotic paradox to setting up a positive feedback system which carries a given learning pattern to self-defeating excess. **Contrary to prevailing Darwinian dogma, this normal learning mechanism can render human behavior maladaptive**, with different groups of people and individuals commonly vying and dying to display their own particular form of the general phenomenon we call stupidity. Resultant behavior is properly termed stupid when it is justly construed as failing according to and because of the ends (purposes) and/or means (methods and morality) of the reference group.

Thus, not all failures are stupid—just those which betray a compromise commitment to perceptual accuracy and social integrity by going to an unnecessary extreme. As a general principle of cultural life, stupidity is an expression of our inherent disposition to judge—specifically, stupidity indicates a subjectively shaped negative evaluation of predetermined behavior. Stupidity is so common because people characteristically interpret their behavior favorably even if it leads eventually and inevitably to failure. This is the overwhelming lesson of past human failures—that short-term, self-deceptive misinterpretations of events can induce long-term demise.

We are indebted to those who failed so stupidly in the past, because their mistakes permit us to understand what we are presently doing. More important, we are obliged to acknowledge that our actions will shape the future. An understanding of how stupidity affects human behavior might make us better people or at least more successful at being who and what we are. This understanding places a moral burden on us to be responsible not only for ourselves but also to those poor souls who will pay the price for our next stupid failure and the next...and the next.....

192

Bibliography

Abel, R. 1989. **American Lawyers**. Oxford University Press; Oxford.

Adams, S. 1961. **Firsthand Report**. Popular Library; New York.

Alexander, R. 1975. The search for a general theory of behavior. **Behavioral Science**, 20, 97.

Arnold, T. 1937. **The Folklore of Capitalism**. Yale University Press; New Haven, CT.

Bandura, A. 1979. The self-system in reciprocal determinism. **American Psychologist**, 33, 344-358.

Barnhart, R., Steinmetz, S. and Barnhart, C. 1990. **Third Barnhart Dictionary of New English**. Wilson; New York.

Becker, E. 1973. **The Denial of Death**. Free Press; New York.

Bidinotto, R. 1989. **Crime and Consequences**. Foundation for Economic Education; Irvington-on-Hudson, NY.

Bolles, R. 1980. Ethological learning theory. In **Theories of Learning: A Comparative Approach** edited by G. Gazda and R. Corsini. Peacock; Itaska, IL.

Bondi, H. 1979. Religion is a good thing. In **The Encyclopedia of Delusions** edited by R. Duncan and M. Weston-Smith. Wallaby; New York.

Boorstin, D. 1987. **Hidden History**. Vintage; New York.

Bradley, Jus. J. Oct. 15, 1883. **United States v. Singleton**. 109 U.S. 3.

Braudel, F. 1981. **The Structures of Everyday Life**. Harper & Row; New York.

Brown, R. and Lenneberg, E. 1958. Studies in linguistic relativity. In **Readings in Social Psychology** edited by E. Maccoby, T. Newcomb and E. Hartley. 3rd ed. Holt, Rinehart and Winston; New York.

Buchler, I. and Selby, H. 1968. **A Formal Study of Myth**. Monograph Series #1, Center for Intercultural Studies in Folklore and Oral History. University of Texas; Austin, TX.

Burke, E. Apr. 4, 1774. A speech in **Parliamentary History of England** edited by T. Hansard. XVII.

Campbell, D. 1966. Pattern Matching as an Essential in Distal Knowing. In **The Psychology of Ebon Brunswik** edited by K. Hammond. Holt, Rinehart & Winston; New York.

193

Carey, A. Feb. 25, 1990. The United States of Incompetence. **Philadelphia Inquirer**. 16.

Caro, R. 1975. **The Power Broker**. Vintage; New York.

Cartwright, D. 1969. The nature of group cohesiveness. In **Group Dynamics: Research and Theory** edited by D. Cartwright and A. Zander. 3rd ed. Harper & Row; New York.

Céline, L. In **The American Heritage History of the 1920's and 1930's**. 1970. New York.

Chamberlain, N. 1970. **Beyond Malthus**. Basic Books; New York.

Chambers, W. 1952. **Witness**. Regency Gateway; Washington, D.C.

Chase, S. 1966. **The Tyranny of Words**. Harcourt, Brace, Jovanovich; New York.

Chesterfield, P. 1766. In **Letters** edited by Bonamy Dobrée. 1932. London. VI, #2410.

Churchill, W. 1957. **The Age of Revolution**. Bantam; New York.

Coleman, J., Morris, C. and Glaros, A. 1987. **Contemporary Psychology and Effective Behavior**. 6th ed. Scott, Foresman & Co.; Glenview, IL.

Colet, J. 1513. In **Renaissance Europe: 1480-1520** by J. Hale. 1971. Berkeley, CA. 232.

Converse, P. 1965. The shifting role of class in political attitudes and behavior. In **Basic Studies in Social Psychology** edited by H. Proshansky and B. Seidenberg. Holt, Rinehart and Winston; New York.

Coolidge, C. Quoted in **The Glory and the Dream** by William Manchester. 1973. Little, Brown; Boston, MA. 28.

-----. Quoted in **American Heritage**. 1965: XVI, #5, 70.

Coopersmith, S. 1967. **The Antecedents of Self-esteem**. Freeman; San Francisco, CA.

Corning, P. 1983. **The Synergism Hypothesis**. McGraw-Hill; New York.

Cottrell, A. 1979. Science is objective. In **The Encyclopedia of Delusions** edited by R. Duncan and M. Weston-Smith. Wallaby; New York.

Custance, J. 1952. **Wisdom, Madness and Folly**. Pelligrini and Cudahy; New York.

Dantzig, T. 1930. **Number, The Language of Science**. New York.

Darlington, C. 1970. The Evolution of Man and Society. **Science**, 68, 1332.

Degler, C. 1991. **In Search of Human Nature**. Oxford U. Press; New York.

Dickens, A. 1966. **Reformation and Society in Sixteenth Century Europe**. New York.

Duncan, R. and Weston-Smith, M. (Eds.) 1979. **The Encyclopedia of Delusions**. Wallaby; New York.

Durant, W. 1926/1961. **The Story of Philosophy**. Simon & Schuster; New York.

-----. 1953. **The Renaissance**. Simon and Schuster; New York.

-----. 1957. **The Reformation**. Simon and Schuster; New York.

----- and A. 1967. **Rousseau and Revolution**. Simon and Schuster; New York.

Durbin, M. 1973. Cognitive anthropology. In **The Handbook of Social and Cultural Anthropology** edited by J. Honigmann. Rand McNally; Chicago, IL.

Earle, J. 1946. **Hearing before the Joint Committee on the Investigation of the Pearl Harbor Attack**. 79th Congress. U.S. Government Printing Office; Washington, D.C. Part 26, 412.

Elliott, R. 1987. **Litigating Intelligence: IQ Tests, Special Education, and Social Science in the Courtroom**. Auburn House; Dover, MA.

Ellsberg, D. 1971. The quagmire myth and the stalemate machine. In the spring issue of **Public Policy**.

Encyclopedia Britannica, The. 1930. 14th ed. London.

Erasmus, D. 1511. **In Praise of Folly**. (Translated by L. Dean and republished by Hendricks House Farrar Straus. 1946.)

-----. 1516. **Colloquies**. (University of Chicago Press; Chicago, IL. 1965.)

Erdelyi, M. 1974. A new look at the new look: perceptual defense and vigilance. **Psychological Review**, 32, 109-118.

Erikson, E. 1974. **Dimensions of a New Identity: The 1973 Jefferson Lectures in the Humanities**. Norton; New York.

Erlich, P. 1968. **The Population Bomb**. Ballantine; New York.

Evans, H. and Eberhard, M. 1970. **The Wasps**. University of Michigan Press; Ann Arbor, MI.

Fest, J. 1970. **The Face of the Third Reich**. Pantheon; New York.

Festinger, L. 1954. A theory of social comparison processes. **Human Relations**, 7, 117-140.

-----. 1957. **A Theory of Cognitive Dissonance**. Stanford University Press; Stanford, CA.

Fischer, J. 1964. **The Stupidity Problem, and Other Harassments**. Harper & Row; New York.

Fishbein, M. and Ajzen, I. 1975. **Belief, Attitude, Intention, and Behavior**. Addison-Wesley; Reading, MA.

Fleming, T. Feb. 1964. The Enigma of General Howe. **American Heritage**; XV, #2, 11ff.

-----. 1975. **1776: Year of Illusions**. Norton; New York.

Flew, A. 1979. Intended conduct and unintended consequences. In **The Encyclopedia of Delusions** edited by R. Duncan and M. Weston-Smith. Wallaby; New York.

Freud, A. 1966. **The Ego and the Mechanisms of Defense**. International Universities Press; New York.

Freud, S. 1920. **Beyond the Pleasure Principle**. Hogarth Press; London.

-----. 1921. **Group Psychology and the Analysis of the Ego**. (Bantam; New York. 1965.)

-----. 1927. **The Ego and the Id**. Hogarth Press; London.

-----. In **The Standard Edition of the Complete Psychological Works of Sigmund Freud** edited by J. Strachey. 1950. Hogarth Press; London. Vol. 3.

Fried, M. (Ed.) 1969. **Readings in Anthropology**. Crowell; New York. Vol. 2.

Fronde, J. 1892. **Spanish Story of the Armada**. New York.

Galbraith, J. 1981. **A Life in Our Times**. Houghton Mifflin; Boston, MA.

-----. June 20, 1994. Quoted in **USA Today** by Mark Memmott. 3B.

Garcia, J., McGowan, B., Ervin, F. and Koelling, R. 1968. Cues: their relative effectiveness as a function of the reinforcer. **Science**, 160, 794-795.

Genesis I, 3.

Gillispie, C. 1960. **The Edge of Objectivity**. Princeton University Press; Princeton, NJ.

Gitlin, T. 1987. **The Sixties: Years of Hope, Days of Rage**. Bantam; New York.

Goldman, E. 1960. **The Crucial Decade and After: America, 1945-1960**. Vintage; New York.

Goleman, D. 1985. **Vital Lies, Simple Truths**. Simon and Schuster; New York.

Goodall, J. 1971. **In the Shadow of Man**. Houghton Mifflin; Boston, MA.

Gross, J. Sept. 2, 1990. Navy Is Urged to Root Out Lesbians Despite Abilities. **The New York Times**. 24.

Gur, R. and Sackheim, H. 1979. Self-deception: a concept in search of a phenomenon. **J. Personality and Social Psychology**, 37, #2, 147-170.

196

Haas, H., Fink, H. and Hartfelder, G. 1959. Das Placeboproblem (translation). **Psychopharmacology Service Center Bull.**, 2, 1-65. (U.S. Pub. Health Service).

Halberstam, D. 1969. **The Best and the Brightest.** Random House; New York.

-----. 1979. **The Powers That Be.** Knopf; New York.

Haldeman, H. (with J. DiMona) 1978. **The Ends of Power.** Dell; New York.

Halle, K. 1967. **The Irrepressible Churchill: A Treasury of Winston Churchill's Wit.** World Publishing; New York.

Hamilton, D. 1979. A cognitive-attributional analysis of stereotyping. In **Advances in Experimental Social Psychology** edited by L. Berkowitz. Academic Press; New York. Vol. 12.

Hammond, P. 1978. **An Introduction to Cultural and Social Anthropology.** 2nd ed. Macmillan; New York.

Hargreaves, R. 1973. **Superpower: A Portrait of America in the 1970's.** St. Martin's; New York.

Hart, J. 1982. **When the Going Was Good.** Crown; New York.

Hayter, W. 1964. In **The Cold War** edited by E. Luard. London.

Heller, J. 1961. **Catch-22.** Simon and Schuster; New York.

Herskovits, M. 1950. **Man and His Works.** Knopf; New York.

Hilgard, E., Atkinson, R. and Atkinson, R. 1975. **Introduction to Psychology.** 6th ed. Harcourt, Brace, Jovanovich; New York.

Hilsman, R. 1967. **To Move a Nation.** Doubleday; Garden City, NY.

Hoebel, E. 1954. **The Law of Primitive Man: A Study in Legal Dynamics.** Harvard University Press; Cambridge, MA.

Hofstadter, R. 1963. **Anti-intellectualism in American Life.** Knopf; New York.

Holmes, E. 1878. **The Life of Mozart, Including His Correspondence.** Chapman & Hall; London.

Holton, G. Jan. 1953. On the duality and growth of physical science. **American Scientist**, 41, 91.

Horney, K. 1950. **Neurosis and Human Growth.** Norton; New York.

Horowitz, M. 1992. **Person Schemas and Maladaptive Interpersonal Patterns.** University of Chicago Press; Chicago, IL.

Howe, F. ca. 1920. Quoted in **America Enters the World** by Page Smith. 1985. McGraw-Hill; New York. 744.

Hughes, P. 1947. **A History of the Church.** New York. Vol. III.

Humphrey, G. Quoted in **The Devil and John Foster Dulles** by T. Hoopes. 1973. Boston, MA. 196.

Jacobs, R. and Campbell, D. 1961. The perpetuation of an arbitrary tradition through several generations of a laboratory microculture. **J. Abnormal Social Psychology**, 62, 649-658.

Janis, I. 1982. **Groupthink**. Houghton Mifflin; Boston, MA.

----- and Mann, L. 1977. **Decision Making**. The Free Press; New York.

Jaroff, L. Aug. 26, 1991. Crisis in the Labs. **Time**; 138, #8, 45-51.

Jedin, H. 1957. **A History of the Council of Trent**. London. Vol. I.

Jensen, A. 1969. How much can we boost IQ and scholastic achievement? **Harvard Educational Review**, 39, 1-122.

Johnson, H. 1991. **Sleepwalking Through History**. Anchor; New York.

Johnson, L. and Ley, R. 1990. **Origins of Modern Economics: A Paradigmatic Approach**. Ginn Press; Needham Heights, MA.

Jones, A. 1964. **The Latter Roman Empire**. University of Oklahoma Press; Norman, OK.

Kahneman, D. 1973. **Attention and Effort**. Prentice-Hall; Englewood Cliffs, NJ.

Kant, I. 1781. **Kritik der reinen Vernunft**. (**Critique of Pure Reason**. Translated and published many times: e.g., J. M. Dent & Sons; London.)

Karon, B. and VandenBos, G. 1981. **Psychotherapy of Schizophrenia**. Jason Aronson; Northvale, NJ. 42.

Kaufmann, W. 1968. **Nietzsche: Philosopher, Psychologist, Antichrist**. 3rd ed. Vintage; New York.

Kelley, H. 1952. Two functions of reference groups. In **Readings in Social Psychology** edited by G. Swanson, T. Newcomb and E. Hartley. 2nd ed. Holt, Rinehart and Winston; New York.

Kelman, H. 1965. Compliance, identification, and internalization: three processes of attitude change. In **Basic Studies in Social Psychology** edited by Proshansky, H. and Seidenberg, B. Holt, Rinehart and Winston; New York.

Kennan, G. Quoted in **The Limits of Intervention** by T. Hoopes. 1969. McKay; New York.

Kennedy, R. June 1, 1961. A memorandum quoted in **Robert Kennedy and His Times** by A. Schlesinger, Jr. 1978. Ballantine Books; New York. 477.

Kennedy, T. Quoted in **Ted Kennedy: In Over His Head** by Gary Allen. 1980. '76 Press; Atlanta, GA.

Kierkegaard, S. 1849. **The Sickness Unto Death**. (Translated by W. Lowrie. Anchor; Garden City, NY. 1954.)

Kilborn, P. May 19, 1991. "Race Norming" tests become a fiery issue. **The New York Times**; The Week in Review. 5.

Killian, L. 1952. The significance of multiple-group membership in disaster. **American J. Sociology**, 57, 309-314.

Kissinger, H. 1979. **The White House Years**. Little, Brown; Boston, MA.

Koestler, A. 1979. Nothing but...? In **The Encyclopedia of Delusions** edited by R. Duncan and M. Weston-Smith. Wallaby; New York.

Kolcum, E. Mar. 3, 1986. Morton Thiokol Engineers Testify NASA Rejected Warnings on Launch. **Aviat. Week and Space Tech.** 18.

Kolko, G. 1963. **The Triumph of Conservatism**. Free Press; New York.

Krutch, J. W. 1953. **The Measure of Man**. Grosset & Dunlap; New York.

Kuhn, T. 1970. **The Structure of Scientific Revolutions**. 2nd ed. University of Chicago Press; Chicago, IL.

Lau, R. and Russel, D. 1980. Attribution in the sports pages. **J. Personality and Social Psychology**, 39, 29-38.

Lewicki, P. June 23, 1992. Quoted in "Your Unconscious Mind May Be Smarter Than You" by D. Goleman. **The New York Times**. C11.

Lewinsohn, P., Mischel, W., Chaplin, W. and Barton, R. 1980. Social competence and depression: the role of illusory self-perceptions. **J. Abnormal Psychology**, 89, 203-212.

Lieberman, J. 1973. **How the Government Breaks the Law**. Stein & Day; New York.

Lippmann, W. 1922. **Public Opinion**. Harcourt, Brace; New York.

Lockard, J. and Paulhus, P. (Eds.) 1988. **Self-deception: An Adaptive Mechanism?** Prentice Hall; Englewood Cliffs, NJ.

Locke, J. 1690. **An Essay Concerning Human Understanding**. (Clarendon Press; Oxford. 1894.)

Lord, W. 1960. **The Good Years**. Harper & Brothers; New York.

Luborsky, L. 1990. **Understanding Transference**. Basic Books; New York.

Lundberg, F. 1980. **Cracks in the Constitution**. Lyle Stuart; Secaucus, NJ.

Lyttleton, R. 1979. The Gold Effect. In **The Encyclopedia of Delusions** edited by R. Duncan and M. Weston-Smith. Wallaby; New York.

Maas, P. 1973. **Serpico**. Viking Press; New York.

Machiavelli, N. 1513. **The Prince.** (Penguin Books; Baltimore, MD. 1961)

Mackay, C. 1852. **Extraordinary Popular Delusions and the Madness of Crowds.** 2nd ed. [Harmony Books; New York. 1980.]

MacKinnon, D. 1967. Assessing creative persons. **J. Creat. Behav.**, 1, 291-304.

Magruder, J. July 26, 1973. In an interview with Charles Wheeler in **Listener.** BBC; London.

Malthus, T. 1798. **An Essay on the Principle of Population.** (The University of Michigan Press; Ann Arbor, MI. 1959.)

Maslow, A. 1963. The need to know and the fear of knowing. **J. General Psychology,** 68, 118-119.

Matthew V, 22.

McCullough, D. 1977. **The Path Between the Seas.** Simon and Schuster; New York.

McMillen, S. 1968. **None of These Diseases.** Fleming H. Revell Co.; Old Tappan, NJ.

McNaughton, J. 1967. A memorandum for the President in **The Pentagon Papers: History of United States Decision Making on Vietnam.** Senator Gravel edition. 4 Vols. and Index Vol. Boston, MA. 1971-1972. Vol. IV, 478.

Meehan, J. Mar. 2, 1992. America's Bumbling Bankers: Ripe for a New Fiasco. **Business Week;** 86-87.

Meredith, W. 1770. In **Parliamentary History of England** edited by T. Hansard. XVI, 872-873.

Meyerriecks, A. 1972. **Man and Birds: Evolution and Behavior.** Pegasus, Bobbs-Merrill Co.; Indianapolis, IN.

Milward, A. 1976. Fascism and the Economy. In **Fascism: A Readers' Guide** edited by W. Laqueur. University of California Press; Berkeley, CA.

Morgan, E. 1935. In a review of **Trial Techniques** by Irving Goldstein. **Harvard Law Review,** 49, 1387-1389.

Morison, S. 1950. The rising sun in the Pacific: 1931-April, 1942. **History of United States Naval Operations in World War II.** Vol. 3. Little, Brown; Boston, MA.

Morris, R. 1967. **Fair Trial.** Harper & Row; New York.

Mosley, N. 1979. Humans being desire happiness. In **The Encyclopedia of Delusions** edited by R. Duncan and M. Weston-Smith. Wallaby; New York.

Mowrer, O. 1950. **Learning Theory and Personality Dynamics.** Ronald Press; New York.

Muller, H. 1966. **The Loom of History**. Oxford University Press; New York.

Neisser, U. 1976. **Cognition and Reality: Principles and Implications of Cognitive Psychology**. Freeman; San Francisco, CA.

Nevins, A. and Hill, F. Dec. 1962. Power is the Prize. **American Heritage**; XIV, #1, 50.

New York Times, The. Mar. 4, 1977. B2.

New York Times, The. (Large Type Weekly). Sept. 24, 1984. 4 and 13.

Nietzsche, F. 1882, 1887. **Die Frölicher Wissenschaft. (The Gay Science.** Translated by W. Kaufmann. 1974. Random House; New York.)

Nixon, R. 1978. **R.N.: The Memoirs of Richard Nixon**. Grosset & Dunlap; New York.

Ornstein, R. 1978. The split and the whole brain. **Human Nature**, 1, 76-83.

Ortega y Gasset, J. 1957. **The Revolt of the Masses**. Norton; New York.

O'Toole, G. 1991. **Honorable Treachery**. Atlantic Monthly Press; New York.

Payne, R. 1973. **The Life and Death of Adolf Hitler**. Praeger; New York.

Peter, L. and Hull, R. 1969. **The Peter Principle**. William Morrow & Co.; New York.

Phillips, C. 1975. **The 1940s: Decade of Triumph and Trouble**. Macmillan; New York.

Piaget, J. 1932. **The Moral Judgement of the Child**. Macmillan; New York.

-----. 1954. **The Construction of Reality in the Child**. Translated by M. Cook. Basic Books; New York.

Pimental, D. May, 1994. Natural Resources and an Optimum Human Population. **Population and Environment**.

Pitkin, W. 1932. **A Short Introduction to the History of Human Stupidity**. Simon and Schuster; New York.

Pitt-Rivers, J. 1961. **The People of the Sierra**. University of Chicago Press; Chicago, IL.

Plato. ca. 355 B.C. **Laws**. (Harvard University Press; Cambridge, MA. 1967).

Plumb, J. June, 1960. Our Last King. **American Heritage**; XI, #4, 95-96.

Pope, K. and Singer, J. 1978. The waking stream of consciousness. In **Human Consciousness and Its Transformations: A Psychological Perspective** edited by J. Davidson, E. Davidson and G. Schwartz. Plenum; New York.

Prange, G. 1981. **At Dawn We Slept**. Penguin; New York.

201

Proshansky, H. and Seidenberg, B. (Eds.) 1965. **Basic Studies in Social Psychology.** Holt, Rinehart and Winston; New York.

Purcell, H. 1979. The fallacy of environmentalism. In **The Encyclopedia of Delusions** edited by R. Duncan and M. Weston-Smith. Wallaby; New York.

Raspberry, W. Nov. 20, 1984. **The Washington Post.**

Ráth-Végh, Dr. I. 1938. **Az emberi butaság kulturtörténete.** Cserepfalvi; Budapest. **(From the History of Human Folly.** 1963. Corvina Press; Hungary.)

-----. 1939. **Uj butasdgok az emberiség kulturtörténetéböl.** Cserepfalvi; Budapest. **(New Stupidities from the Cultural History of Mankind.)**

-----. 1940. **Vége az emberi butaságnak.** Cserepfalvi; Budapest. **(End to Human Stupidity.)**

Redl, F. 1942. Group emotion and leadership. **Psychiatry.** 573-596.

Reedy, G. 1966. From a mimeographed paper prepared for a conference at the Center for the Study of Democratic Institutions. Cited in **The Imperial Presidency** by A. Schlesinger, Jr. 1973. Houghton Mifflin; Boston, MA. 214.

-----. 1970. **The Twilight of the Presidency.** New Amsterdam Library; New York.

Reinsch, P. 1905. The negro race and European civilization. **American J. Sociology,** 11, 148.

Richet, C. 1919. **L'homme stupide.** E. Flammarion; Paris. **(The Follies of Mankind.** 1925. Brantanos; New York.)

Ridgway, General M. July, 1971. Indochina: disengaging. **Foreign Affairs.**

Ripley, G. 1839. **Letters on the Latest Form of Infidelity.** Boston, MA.

Robertson, L. Sept. 27, 1984. **The Miami Herald.** 1D.

Robertson, W. 1976. **The Dispossessed Majority.** Howard Allen; Cape Canaveral, FL.

Rogers, C. 1970. **Carl Rogers on Encounter Groups.** Harper & Row; New York.

-----. 1981. **A Way of Being.** Houghton Mifflin; Boston, MA.

Rosenhan, D. 1973. On being sane in insane places. **Science,** 179, 250-258.

Roszak, T. Mar/Apr 1993. **Sierra,** 78, #2, 59.

Rowe, J. 1947. In a memorandum entitled **The Politics of 1948** allegedly prepared by Clark Clifford for President Truman. Cited in **The Best Years: 1945-1950** by J. Goulden. 1976. Atheneum; New York. 366-367.

Rue, L. 1994. **By the Grace of Guile: The Role of Deception in Natural History and Human Affairs.** Oxford University Press; New York.

Russell, B. 1945. **A History of Western Philosophy**. Simon and Schuster; New York.

Ryan, C. 1974. **A Bridge Too Far**. Simon and Schuster; New York.

Sagan, C. 1980. **Cosmos**. Random House; New York.

Sambursky, S. 1956. **The Physical World of the Greeks**. Routledge & Kegan Paul; London.

Sapir, E. 1964. Cited in **Language in Culture and Society: A Reader in Linguistics and Anthropology** edited by D. Hymes. Harper; New York.

Sartre, J-P. 1956. **Being and Nothingness**. Philosophical Library; New York.

Schachter, S. 1966. The interaction of cognitive and physiological determinants of emotional state. In **Anxiety and Behavior** edited by C. Spielberger. Academic Press; New York.

Schiller, F. 1802. **The Maid of Orleans**. (Die Jungfrau von Orleans)

Schlesinger, Jr., A. 1965. **A Thousand Days**. Houghton Mifflin; Boston, MA.

-----. 1973. **The Imperial Presidency**. Houghton Mifflin; Boston, MA.

-----. 1978. **Robert Kennedy and His Times**. Houghton Mifflin; Boston, MA.

Schmitt, E. June 20, 1992. Military's Anti-Gay Rule Is Costly, a Report Says. **The New York Times**. 6.

Sears, R. 1936. Experimental studies of projection: I. Attribution of traits. **J. Social Psychology**, 7, 151-163.

Seligman, M. 1970. On the generality of the laws of learning. **Psychological Review**, 77, 406-418.

Shaff, D. 1910. **History of the Christian Church**. Grand Rapids, MI. Vol. 6.

Shaver, K. 1981. **Principles of Social Psychology**. 2nd ed. Winthrop; Cambridge, MA.

Shaw, G. In a letter to Mr. Moses Harman quoted in **The Rise of Industrial America** by P. Smith. 1984. McGraw-Hill; New York. 281.

Sheehan, N. 1988. **A Bright Shining Lie**. Random House; New York.

Sherif, M. 1958. Superordinate goals in the reduction of intergroup conflict. **American J. Sociology**, 63, 349-356.

-----. 1965. Formation of social norms: the experimental paradigm. In **Basic Studies in Social Psychology** edited by H. Proshansky and B. Seidenberg. Holt, Rinehart and Winston; New York.

Shirer, W. 1959. **The Rise and Fall of the Third Reich**. Simon and Schuster; New York.

Siegel, M. Quoted in **Newsweek**. May 6, 1991. Vol. 117, No. 18, 25.

Singer, J. (Ed.) 1990. **Repression and Dissociation: Implication for Personality Theory, Psychopathology, and Health**. U. of Chicago Press; Chicago, IL.

Skinner, B. 1948. "Superstition" in the pigeon. **J. Experimental Psychology**, 38, 168-172.

-----. 1971. **Beyond Freedom and Dignity**. Bantam Books; New York.

Sloan, H. May 18, 1973. From an interview in **The New York Times**.

Smith, R., Sarason, I. and Sarason, B. 1982. **Psychology: The Frontiers of Behavior**. Harper & Row; New York.

Spengler, O. 1918. **The Decline of the West**. Edited by H. Werner. 1962. Modern Library; New York.

Spiro, M. 1952. Ghosts, Ifaluk, and teleological functionalism. **American Anthropologist**, 54, 497-503.

Spotlight, The. Oct. 8, 1984. Cordite Fidelity; Washington, D.C. 11.

Stevenson, C. 1938. Paraphrased in **Means of Ascent** by R. Caro. 1990. Vintage; New York. 165.

Stevenson, W. 1976. **A Man Called Intrepid**. Ballantine; New York.

Stockman, D. 1986. **The Triumph of Politics**. Harper & Row; New York.

Strutt, J. (Lord Rayleigh) Quoted in The Gold Effect by R. Lyttleton in **The Encyclopedia of Delusions**, 1979, edited by R. Duncan and M. Weston-Smith. Wallaby; New York. 194.

Sturtevant, A. 1965. **A History of Genetics**. Harper & Row; New York.

Sulin, R. and Dooling, D. 1974. Intrusions of a thematic idea in retention of prose. **J. Experimental Psychology**, 103, 255-262.

Sun-Sentinel. Nov. 20, 1984. Fort Lauderdale, FL. 10A.

Sun-Sentinel. Dec. 2, 1984. Fort Lauderdale, FL. 49.

Swinton, J. Quoted in **The Rise of Industrial America** by P. Smith. 1984. Mc-Graw-Hill; New York. 379.

Szasz, T. 1979. The lying truths of psychiatry. In **The Encyclopedia of Delusions** edited by R. Duncan and M. Weston-Smith. Wallaby; New York.

Tabori, P. 1993. **The Natural History of Stupidity**. Barnes & Noble; New York. (Originally published as **The Natural Science of Stupidity**. 1959. Chilton; Philadelphia, PA.)

Taine, H. 1876. **L'Ancine Régime**. Paris.

Talleyrand-Perigord, C. 1796. In a letter of Mallet du Pan from **Chevalliar de Panat.**

Taylor, A. 1963. **The First World War.** Putnam; New York.

Taylor, J. 1992. **Paved With Good Intentions.** Carroll & Graf; New York.

Terman, L. 1906. **Genius and Stupidity.** Thesis; Clark University, Worcester, MA. [Reprint of a 1906 edition in 1975 by Arno Press; New York.]

Terrace, H. 1966. Stimulus control. In **Operant Behavior** edited by W. Honing. Appleton-Century-Crofts; New York.

Thibaut, J. and Kelley, H. 1959. **The Social Psychology of Groups.** Wiley; New York.

Thompson, M. Jan. 12, 1990. Berlin Wall may be crumbling, but Pentagon plans rising budget. **The Miami Herald.** 19A.

Thomson, D. 1962. **Europe Since Napoleon.** Longmans; London.

Thomson, J. Apr. 1968. How could Vietnam happen? An autopsy. **The Atlantic Monthly.**

Thoreau, H. 1849. **Resistance to Civil Government.** (Later called **Civil Disobedience.**)

Toland, J. 1976. **Adolf Hitler.** Doubleday; Garden City, NY.

Tomlin, E. 1979. Novelty is the chief aim in art. In **The Encyclopedia of Delusions** edited by R. Duncan and M. Weston-Smith. Wallaby; New York.

Treaster, J. June 14, 1992. 20 Year of War on Drugs, and No Victory. **The New York Times.** E7.

Treasure, G. 1966. **Seventeenth Century France.** New York.

Tuchman, B. 1962. **The Guns of August.** Bantam; New York.

-----. 1984. **The March of Folly.** Knopf; New York.

Valentine, A. 1962. **Lord George Germain.** Oxford.

Van Doren, C. 1991. **A History of Knowledge.** Ballantine; New York.

Virgil, P. 19 B.C. **Aeneid.**

Vonnegut, M. 1975. **The Eden Express.** Bantam Books; New York.

Wagner, R. 1971. **Environment and Man.** Norton; New York.

Waite, R. 1971. Adolf Hitler's guilt feelings: a problem in history and psychology. **J. Interdisciplinary History,** 1, #2, 229-249.

Waldegrave, J. Quoted in **King George III** by J. Brooke. 1972. New York.

Wallace, R. 1981. **The Italian Campaign.** Time-Life Books; Alexandria, VA.

Washburn, S. and Hamburg, D. 1965. The implications of primate research. In **Primate Behavior: Field Studies of Monkeys and Apes** edited by I. DeVore. Holt, Rinehart and Winston; New York.

Washburn, S. and Moore, R. 1973. **Ape into Man.** Little, Brown; Boston, MA.

Webster's New World Dictionary. 1970. 2nd ed. World; New York.

Weidenbaum, M. Jan. 2, 1992. New federal regulations threaten to bury business. **Gazette Telegraph;** Colorado Springs, CO.

Weisberger, B. Aug. 1964. How to Get Elected. **American Heritage;** XV, #5, 64.

Weisz, P. and Keogh, R. 1982. **The Science of Biology.** 5th ed. McGraw-Hill; New York.

Welch, C. 1979. Broken eggs, but no omelette: Russia before the revolution. In **The Encyclopedia of Delusions** edited by R. Duncan and M. Weston Smith. Wallaby; New York.

Welles, J. Feb. 1981. The sociobiology of self-deception. **Human Ethology Newsletter,** III, #1, 14-19.

Wham, W. Mar. 10, 1984. Sound the Foghorn. **The New Zealand Herald.** Aukland, New Zealand. 6.

White, T. 1969. **The Making of the President 1968.** Atheneum; New York.

Whorf, B. 1956. Science and linguistics. In **Language, Thought, and Reality: Selected Writing of Benjamin Lee Whorf** edited by J. Carroll. MIT Press; Cambridge, MA.

Whyte, W. 1956. **The Organization Man.** Doubleday; Garden City, NY.

Wiener, N. Quoted in The Gold Effect by R. Lyttleton in **The Encyclopedia of Delusions,** 1979, edited by R. Duncan and M. Weston-Smith. Wallaby; New York. 196.

Wilson, E. 1975. **Sociobiology.** Harvard University Press; Cambridge, MA.

Wohlstetter, R. 1962. **Pearl Harbor: Warning and Decision.** Stanford University Press; Stanford, CA.

Wolfe, B. Feb. 1960. The Harvard Man in the Kremlin Wall. **American Heritage;** XI, #2, 102.

Wylie, R. 1978. **The Self Concept. Vol. 2. Theory and Research on Selected Topics.** University of Nebraska Press; Lincoln, NB.

Zimbardo, P. 1970. The human choice: individuation, reason, and order versus deindividuation, impulse, and chaos. In the 1969 **Nebraska Symposium of Motivation** edited by J. Arnold and D. Levine. University of Nebraska Press; Lincoln, NB. 237-307.

ADDENDUM

Although in the preface I made a specific point of saying I would not use a personal example of stupidity in this book, I have had the misfortune to run into a classic example of it as a result of the book. It illustrates the regrettable, corrupting impact on learning when intellectual ethics are sacrificed to protect a colleague who is wrong.JFW

This book was reviewed by Dr. Thomas O. Blank of the School of Family Studies and Center on Aging at the U. of Connecticut, Storrs. The review appeared in the Sept., 1993 issue of **Contemporary Psychology**, a journal of reviews sponsored by the American Psychological Association (APA). It was very harsh, in some ways unprofessional and demonstrated Dr. Blank's inability to understand what he had read.

I availed myself of the opportunity to respond in the "Point/Counterpoint" format made available to aggrieved authors by the journal. This consisted of an exchange of statements between myself and Dr. Blank and appeared in the May, 1994 issue. In his last comment, to which I had no opportunity to reply in print, he alleged that my stated view "Normal human behavior is not necessarily adaptive" could be accessed elsewhere.

I received an advanced copy of this statement and twice challenged him in writing to document his claim but received not even the courtesy of a reply. In April, I wrote Dr. John Harvey, the editor of the journal, asking him to see to it that Dr. Blank document his claim or that an appropriate correction be published in a forthcoming issue. He was explicit in his refusal to do anything to resolve the matter.

I then turned to the APA and had a number of phone conversations and exchanged letters with Leslie Cameron, Director, APA Journals, in May and June regarding this matter, all to no effect. Dr. Gary Vanden-Bos, Executive Director, Publications, called me in early June and we spoke for about an hour. He assured me Dr. Blank was correct in saying my ideas could be found elsewhere, but when challenged to document the claim, like everyone else, he failed to do so.

In late June, I wrote, Dr. Raymond Fowler, Chief Executive Officer, again to no effect. He claimed the APA was out of options at this point, because they could not force Dr. Blank to document his claim. I pointed out they could request him to do so or publish a correction on their own but received no reply to this suggestions. (A year later, in the summer of 1995, Deputy CEO L. Michael Honker went psychotic in claiming a source meant the exact opposite of what the author wrote. This was indeed a marvel of mental gymnastics performed in the guise of "Interpretation".)

In Aug., 1994, I commenced a likewise fruitless effort to get the University of Connecticut to hold Dr. Blank accountable. After a brief phone conversation with me, Dr. Steven Anderson, Dean of the School of Family Studies, prevailed upon him to send me a list of books (with no page numbers) in which he did not even try to document the claim he had made in print. He tried instead to document a substitute claim—that maladaptation was a central theme in the books listed. Maladaptation is in fact a common behavioral process, but that was not the issue in dispute, so I asked him once again to document his claim that my idea that **normal** behavior can be maladaptive could be accessed elsewhere. I received no reply.

Dr. Fred Marianski, Associate Provost for Academic Affairs, deftly avoided involvement by claiming the issue was not in his field of expertise so he would "Leave it to the professionals". His superior, Dr. Thomas Tye, Vice President and Provost for Academic Affairs, failed to return several phone calls. President Dr. Harry Hartley was properly insulated by staffer Carol Flynn, who thwarted my efforts to inform him of his dysfunctional faculty and administrators on the grounds that he has no control over academic affairs presumably in the same way the President of General Motors has nothing to do with making cars. At the conclusion of my one phone conversation with Dr. Richard Besdine, Director of The Traveler's Center on Aging, he assured me either he or Dr. Blank would get back to me: I have since heard from neither.

Likewise, the American Association for the Advancement of Science failed to hold either Dr. Blank or anyone else responsible in this matter. Rather than dealing with it as an error in the scientific literature, Dr. C. K. Gunsalus's Committee on Scientific Freedom and Responsibility feigned psychosis and claimed they simply did not perceive the issue as I did. One way to advance science is by correcting errors in the literature: they just did not perceive an undocumentable claim as an error (and besides, overturning Darwinian psychology is too petty a matter to bother with). This was unprofessional in the extreme but rather common among people upset by intellectual integrity. Dr. Al Teich, Director, Directorate for Science and Policy Programs, would not return my calls.

Thus did the scientific establishment react to an error in the literature. Striking by its absence in all parties was any trace of intellectual integrity. Not one person would stand up for the truth. Not one was committed to helping people learn, know and understand. Not one insisted Dr. Blank document his erroneous claim that my ideas could be found elsewhere or publish a correction. He had made an error, so everyone circled the wagons to protect him. **I have never known a case where so many well educated people have distinguished right from wrong and chosen to be wrong.** That choice makes them a disgrace to science and humanity.

208

ADDENDUM UPDATED

How nice it would be to add that in the two years since the last printing of this book, Dr. Blank's allegation that the idea that normal is not necessarily adaptive has been documented or his error corrected. Sad to say, neither case obtained. Rather, my experience has confirmed the central idea of the book—that our social and political lives warp our intellectual life, and there is no better example of this phenomenon than the intransigence with which the academic/scientific establishment stands by its error in this particular case. This is all the more remarkable because the institutions involved have rules which call for all parties to conduct themselves properly, but a basic problem is that they prefer to break rather than abide by or enforce their own rules for proper professional conduct.

The University of Connecticut has bylaws which require accuracy on the part of all faculty members at all times, but the fact that Dr. Blank has published misinformation is of no moment to anyone at that institution. Further, all members of the university community are required to foster intellectual honesty, but no one involved with this case has done anything that could possibly be construed as so doing. For example, in January, 1997, when I asked the new president, Philip Austin, to secure a proper reference for me from Dr. Blank, he replied he had no advice for me. In turn, I pointed I had not asked him for advice and repeated my request, to which he never responded.

So also were the dean of the Graduate School, Thomas Giolas, and Provost Mark Emmert absolutely adamant in their refusal to abide by much less enforce their own bylaws. The basic dodge was that since the APA has done nothing to remedy the situation, nothing is wrong. Aside from the obvious fact that this is passing the buck and a total abnegation of academic responsibility on the part of the school's chief administrators, this tactic is based on a major fallacy: it assumes the APA is a professional scientific organization dedicated to truth. Unfortunately, it isn't.

At the very best, the APA is a public relations outfit dedicated to promoting the power, status, image, careers and incomes of its members. Just in the course of trying to get the matter at hand corrected, I have stumbled across a number of uncorrected errors published in APA journals dating back to 1970. In Robyn Dawes' published letter of resignation from the organization in 1988, he cited the lack of commitment on its part to the rational application of knowledge as a requirement and stated his view that the organization had failed miserably to assure a professional practice of psychology based on available scientific knowledge.

Such a flagrant indifference to knowledge is unfortunately common at the APA (which, in my lighter moments, I refer to as the American Psy-

209

chotics Association because of the institution's callous disregard of reality). For example, Dr. Dawes referred to the organization's efforts to convince the public its members have a special expertise not only in the absence of any evidence for such expertise but indeed in the face of evidence that it does not exist. So, in my case, the fact that no one could document Dr. Blank's allegation meant nothing to anyone at the APA.

Typical of the mishandling of this case was the action of Dr. Norman Abeles when he chaired the APA publications and communications (P&C) board. In June, 1995, the board determined no further action (i.e., documentation) was required in the matter, but it based this decision on the mistaken belief that Dr. Blank had provided a reference. When I pointed this error out to him and asked him to reconsider and base the decision on the facts, he refused to do so and thence became president of the organization. In February and March, 1997, I repeatedly asked the new chair of the P&C board, Prof. Judith Worrell, to place this matter on its agenda but all to no effect: she just would not deal with the issue.

As for the AAAS, the story is essentially the same: the constitution requires the promotion of responsibility but no one will deign to anything in this case to hold those involved accountable to basic standards of science. Current president Jane Lubchenco passed up an opportunity in August, 1996, by side stepping the issue. In this regard, she was but typical of all parties contacted: none would deal with the problem, so by default, every decision by everyone favored the person who is wrong.

The basic problem really is that no one cares about the publication of misinformation in the scientific literature. Dr. Blank published an error, but so what? Those who are supposed to be exercising control over the quality of science are frankly indifferent to such breaches of intellectual ethics. (Indeed, in February, 1997, the APA's Office of Ethics, Dr. Stanley Jones presiding, declined to investigate this case—leading one to conclude that the publication of an undocumentable statement is ethical.)

The bottom line is that science is not a self-correcting institution. Perhaps sometimes it is but not always and not necessarily. If I had to present one good example of institutional stupidity to the world, this would be as good as any. All these professors and PhD's with all their education evince not the slightest interest in much less even a minimal commitment to knowledge or truth. Not one! Not one would stand up and say, "There is something wrong here, let's fix it."

From this I conclude there is something very wrong with our educational system. Our best educated elite have absolutely no ethical qualms whatsoever in their professional field of expertise. The saddest commentary I can make on the hope that science will save us is it cannot to the degree scientists refuse to deal with the reality of unethical conduct.

210